WHERE IS HISTORY GOING?

BY THE SAME AUTHOR . . .
The Suicide of Christian Theology
The Quest for Noah's Ark
Damned Through the Church

WHERE IS HISTORY GOING?

by

JOHN WARWICK MONTGOMERY

Essays in Support of the Historical
Truth of the Christian Revelation

With a Commendatory Letter by C. S. Lewis

BETHANY FELLOWSHIP, INC.
Minneapolis, Minnesota

To the memory of
C. S. Lewis
who rightly believed that the fulfillment of history
takes place in the land of Narnia

PREFACE

Jean Guitton, the eminent lay Roman Catholic theologian and member of the French Academy, has described his conversations with a certain Dr. Couchoud, who declared: "I believe everything in the Apostle's Creed, except the phrase, 'He suffered *under Pontius Pilate*.'" This 20th century gnostic was not bothered by what he regarded as the true spiritual message of Christianity; only the historical particularity of it disturbed him. "And besides," he would say, "consider how beneficial to faith my view is. Unbelievers invariably endeavor to destroy faith by reducing Jesus to a mere historical being — they make faith vulnerable by putting Him on the plane of history. But I, by elevating Him above that level, make faith invulnerable."

"Invulnerable, perhaps," replied Guitton, "but totally evacuated of meaning. What you reject is the heart of Christianity: the mystery of a *real* incarnation."[1]

Precisely; and the entire collection of essays comprising this book could be regarded as an extended commentary on and reinforcement of Guitton's answer. Here an effort is made to show, first, that Christianity offers a concrete and satisfying answer to the perennial question, "Where is history going?" on the basis of the genuine incarnation of God in history; second, that Christ's incarnation is the center of the Christian faith and can be dispensed

---

[1] Jean Guitton, *Journal, 1952-1955* (Paris: Librairie Plon, 1959), pp. 19-21.

with only at the cost of totally destroying the faith itself; third, that the incarnation of God in Christ was an event in ordinary history and therefore (since this is what we *mean* by "event in ordinary history") is truly demonstrable on the basis of historical evidence; and, lastly, that all attempts — whether Christian or non-Christian, orthodox or heterodox — to render Christianity "invulnerable" by removing its Lord from the realm of verifiable history achieve the most tragic possible Pyrrhic victory, for they turn the Christian faith into a meaningless gnosticism which can no more compel men's allegiance than the mystery religions of old or the theosophies of the present.

The essays contained in this volume will also make clear that Dr. Couchoud is by no means an isolated oddity. He could, in fact, be taken as a veritable prototype of contemporary thought in its treatment of Jesus. Whether we look at historian McNeill, secular philosopher Stroll, Christian philosopher Clark, Neo-orthodox theologian Barth, ontological liberal Tillich, or the post-Bultmannians engaged in a "new quest for the historical Jesus," we find a common pattern: presuppositionalism is allowed to reign and the Jesus of the primary documents is subordinated to a priori commitments. To a greater or lesser degree, the central figure of the Christian faith is disassociated from the realm of historical verifiability, resulting either in His outright rejection (Stroll, McNeill), or in His transformation into a meaningless existential or ontological symbol (Tillich, the post-Bultmannians), or in His exemption from historical testability and consequent dependence on blind fideism (Barth, Clark).

The author of these essays is convinced that in a world of increasing unbelief nothing is to be gained by a posture of defensiveness in regard to the historical claims of Christianity. Our task as Christian historians and theologians is not to clothe the gospel with an alleged "invulnerability" by dehistoricizing it; we are to render ourselves and our message as historically vulnerable as did our Lord Himself when He deigned to enter fully and unreservedly into the maelstrom of human history. If we so present Him, His historical claims will assuredly prevail, for, as those who had eyewitness contact with Him declared, His manifestation in history was accompanied by "many infallible proofs."

Only when the Christian message is offered in these uncompromising terms does unbelief find itself properly faced with "the offense of the Cross": the watershed decision as to whether to accept the historical evidence of salvation in Christ and reject one's own autonomy, or to rationalize away the facts in the interests of retaining control of one's sinful existence. The presentation of the Christian message in its full historical dimension is the sole means to achieve the kind of confrontation playwright Chayefsky describes:

GIDEON: Let me go, God.

ANGEL: Let you — whatever does that mean? Gideon, there is no divorce from God. I am truth and exist. You cannot deny that I am. I stand palpably here before you, as real as rock, a very actual thing with whom you have commerced face-to-face.

GIDEON: Aye, my Lord. I see you and hear you. So I beg of you, my Lord — go from my sight. Make not your presence known to me again that I might say: "God is a dream, a name, a thought, but not a real thing."

ANGEL: But I am a real thing.

GIDEON: I would pretend that you were not.[2]

Hopefully the present work can reduce pretense in relation to the claims of Christianity, and aid both Christian and non-Christian to see that the Christ of history does indeed "stand palpably here before you, as real as rock, a very actual thing with whom you have commerced face-to-face."

JOHN WARWICK MONTGOMERY

6 January 1969
The Epiphany of our Lord

---

[2] Paddy Chayefsky, *Gideon: a Play* (New York: Random House, 1962), pp. 128-29.

ACKNOWLEDGMENTS

The articles contained in this book have appeared previously in various American, British and continental theological publications; bibliographical data on their original publication follows:

"Where is History Going?": *Religion in Life*, Spring, 1964.

"Jesus Christ and History" (Parts I and II): *His*, Magazine of the Inter-Varsity Christian Fellowship, December, 1964-March, 1965; *His* Magazine Reprints; *¿Es Confiable el Christianismo?* trans. by Ana Maria Swenson (Casa Bautista de Publicaciones, 1968) (in Spanish).

"The Christian Church in McNeill's *Rise of the West*": *The Evangelical Quarterly*, October-December, 1966.

"Karl Barth and Contemporary Philosophy of History": *The Cresset*, November, 1963; *Evangelical Theological Society Bulletin*, May, 1963.

"Tillich's Philosophy of History": *The Gordon Review*, Summer, 1967; *The Lutheran Scholar*, January, 1968; *Themelios*, Vol. 4, No. 2 (1967).

"Gordon Clark's Historical Philosophy": *The Philosophy of Gordon Clark*, ed. Ronald H. Nash (Philadelphia: Presbyterian and Reformed Publishing Co., 1968).

"Toward a Christian Philosophy of History": *Jesus of Nazareth: Saviour and Lord*, ed. Carl F. H. Henry (Grand Rapids, Mich.: Wm. B. Eerdmans, 1966); *Revue Réformée*, Vol. 18, No. 3 (1967) (in French).

"Afterword: Church History Today": *Evangelical Theological Society Bulletin*, Spring, 1966.

"God Plus Three: A Review of *History: Written and Lived* by Paul Weiss": *Christianity Today*, July 19, 1963.

The opportunity to collect these essays in a single volume has afforded the author an occasion to make slight improvements in style and content, and, in certain instances, to restore material which journal editors, solicitous of space limitations, dropped from the author's original manuscript texts.

CONTENTS

WHERE IS HISTORY GOING?

1. WHERE IS HISTORY GOING?*

H ENRY FORD is said to have defined history as "the succession
of one damned thing after another." Such a definition, if taken
seriously (and Ford would no doubt have been appalled to find it
taken seriously), is based on the assumption that history is not going anywhere — that history has no ultimate goal or purpose.

This judgment is by no means uncommon in our time. At
the American Historical Association's annual luncheon conference in Chicago, December 30, 1962, Arthur Schlesinger (formerly
of Harvard, recently of the White House), in speaking on the
general topic, "The Historian and History," stated his opposition
to all monistic philosophies of history and identified his own position with William James' pluralism. For the kind of question
we have posed in the title of this paper — "Where is history going?" — Schlesinger saw a parable in the words of the dying
Gertrude Stein; when she asked on her deathbed, "What is the
answer?" and none came, she said, "Then what is the question?"
An answer was impossible because the question had no meaning.

Schlesinger makes his historical philosophy even more explicit in his latest book, *The Politics of Hope*. A selection from
this book appeared under the title "Speaking Out: The Failure

---

*A lecture delivered on the University of British Columbia campus,
January 29, 1963, under the joint sponsorship of the University Religious
Council and the Lutheran Student Foundation.

of World Communism," in the May 19, 1962, *Saturday Evening Post*. There Schlesinger concludes:

> American liberalism stands in sharp contrast to the millennial nostalgia which still characterizes both the American right and the European left — the notion that the day will come when all conflict will pass, when Satan will be cast into the lake of fire and brimstone, and mankind will behold a new heaven and a new earth. . . . Freedom is inseparable from struggle; and freedom, as Brandeis said, is the great developer; it is both the means employed and the end attained. This, I believe, states the essence of the progressive hope — this and the understanding that the struggle itself offers not only better opportunities for others but also a measure of fulfillment for oneself.

For Schlesinger, then, the idea of history having a single purpose or goal is meaningless and deceptive; one must struggle for maximum freedom in the present, and see in this struggle itself the fulfillment that others have mistakenly attached to some ultimate historical millennium.

But in spite of the pithy quality of Henry Ford's alleged definition and in spite of the appealing elements in Schlesinger's argument, such historical nihilisms and pluralisms ring a bit hollow. Is the question, "Where is history going?" really a question that has no answer? Is it a question that has a multiplicity of equally possible answers? The problem, I believe, parallels — and is indeed a special case of — the basic philosophical problem of the one and the many. The human mind finds it exceedingly difficult to look upon diversity and plurality, in the universe in general or in history in particular, without seeking for a single explanation that can give meaning to it all. In a criticism of philosopher Paul Weiss' *Modes of Being*, which conceives the universe as having four ultimate dimensions of being, W. N. Clarke perceptively wrote in the *Yale Review* (September, 1958): "Until Professor Weiss moves a little closer to the common insight of all the great metaphysicians of the past, namely, that there can be no many without a One, I fear that his four-fold universe neither is nor can ever really be." Perhaps in history, also, "there can be no many without a One."

Let us begin with some of the representative attempts, since the rise of modern secularism in the eighteenth-century "Enlightenment," to find unity and meaning in the historical process. An analysis of the strengths and weaknesses of these attempts will, I believe, lead us to a solution of a radically different and strikingly more satisfactory kind.

Secular Historiography Since the "Enlightenment"[1]

Symbolic of the modern world view, ushered in by the eighteenth-century "Age of Reason," was the dramatic rededication on November 9, 1793, of the Cathedral of Notre Dame to the goddess Reason. From then on, human reason, rather than supposedly "revealed" religion, would provide the answers to man's ultimate problems. We shall briefly consider the answers provided by five modern secular thinkers to the question, "Where is history going?" and see how close to a satisfactory solution the goddess Reason has led them. The five thinkers will span the modern secular era, for we shall take up, in turn, Kant, Hegel, Marx, Spengler, and Toynbee.

The most profound thinker to be influenced by the eighteenth-century Enlightenment was a philosopher who is often studied in the context of the nineteenth century. However, the outlook of Immanuel Kant "was singularly unhistorical, and he remained in this as in other respects a typical product of the Enlightenment rather than a forerunner of the Romantic Age which was shortly to follow."[2] Kant asserted that "the history of the human race, viewed as a whole, may be regarded as the realization of a hidden plan of nature to bring about a political constitution, internally, and, for this purpose, also externally perfect, as the only state in which all the capacities implanted by her in mankind can be fully developed."[3] Kant, in other words, held that history is a

---

[1] For a more comprehensive presentation of the material to follow, see my recent book, *The Shape of the Past: An Introduction to Philosophical Historiography* ("History in Christian Perspective," Vol. I; Ann Arbor, Mich.: Edwards Brothers, 1962).

[2] W. H. Walsh, *Philosophy of History: An Introduction* (New York: Harper Torchbooks, 1960), p. 122.

[3] This is Kant's eighth proposition in his "Idea of a Universal History from a Cosmopolitan Point of View"; the translation by W. Hastie is reprinted in Patrick Gardiner, ed., *Theories of History* (Glencoe, Ill.: Free Press, 1959), p. 30.

rational process — that reason actually provides the plan and the goal of history. On the surface this does not appear to be the case always and everywhere, Kant admits, but in reality man's "unsociableness" — his "envious jealousy and vanity" and "unsatiable desire of possession or even of power" — turns man from "idleness and inactive contentment" to "further development of his natural capacities."[4]

Kant's view suffers from two serious objections: it does not take evil seriously, for it employs the argument that the end justifies the means (in actuality, the means employed always alters the character of the end, so that if an evil means is used, the end becomes evil); and it attempts to say something substantial about the plot of history without investigating the data of historical experience. These objections are sufficient to destroy Kant's proposed philosophy of history, but the importance of his endeavor cannot be denied; he projected what many would attempt after him: the creation of a philosophy of history on the basis of pure reason.

The great German philosopher Hegel argued that "world history is a rational process,"[5] and that it moves in dialectical fashion through four great "world-historical" epochs (Oriental, Greek, Roman, and Germanic) toward the goal of freedom. In this process, each nation's hour strikes but once, and then it serves as the vehicle of the world spirit of reason and makes its specific contribution to the history of mankind. Great men play their unique roles at crucial junctures — roles which cannot be judged as "good" or "bad" by ordinary moral standards. Hegel's philosophy of history can be (and has been) severely criticized on many counts: it errs (as did Kant's) in purporting to deduce historical substance and goal from reason itself; it suffers from Hegel's Germanic point of view; and its doctrine of the crucial hours of the nations and its metaethical evaluation of great men in history can easily be employed to justify national imperialism and unprincipled actions by individuals.

These difficulties in Hegel's system should not, however, ob-

---

[4]*Ibid.*, p. 26.

[5]On Hegel's philosophy of history, note especially Jean Hyppolite, *Introduction à la philosophie de l'historie de Hegel* (Paris: Marcel Rivière, 1948).

scure its one great merit: the notion of the dialectic and the application of it to history. By dialectic, Hegel meant the tendency both in life and in thought for a position to spawn its own opposite, and for these two extremes to be succeeded by a compromise which partakes of some elements of both of them. Numerous historical examples of dialectic movement will suggest themselves; one illustration is the history of France before, during, and after the French Revolution. The absolute, authoritarian monarchy of the Old Régime can be considered a thesis to which the near anarchy and libertarianism of the Revolutionary period arose as an antithesis; out of both extremes eventually developed a republican form of government which adopted certain elements of both extremes.

It is important to realize that the Hegelian dialectic is really a formal principle which neither discloses the goal of a process nor places any value judgment upon it. The dialectic can describe a continual refinement of evil as well as a continual refinement of good. Indeed, one of the chief errors made by Hegel himself lay in his conviction that the historical dialectic is moving toward the specific goal of freedom. In actuality, the dialectic never requires such a conclusion. Moreover, though Hegel saw reason as the motivating force of the dialectic process in history, the dialectic need not center on ideas. In point of fact, it is the very flexibility of the dialectic concept that has made it so useful to historians and philosophers whether they have held Hegel's idealistic presuppositions or not.

Marx and his co-worker Friedrich Engels derived from Hegel an understanding of the dialectic process, and also held the positivistic conviction that history follows inexorable natural laws, which, if understood, would allow the future to be predicted. However, in taking over Hegel's dialectic, Marx boasted that he "stood it on its head." For Hegel the dialectic represented the action of the world spirit of rationality in the historical process, but for Marx such a metaphysic was completely unrealistic. Marx had been greatly influenced by the German materialist philosopher Ludwig Feuerbach, who believed that *"der Mensch ist, was er isst"* (man is what he eats), and consequently he saw materialistic (or more specifically, economic) factors as the determinants of the dialectic. Instead of thought determining nature, Marx maintained that nature determines thought. He built his economic theory of surplus value on this materialistic conception of the dialectic, and became convinced that class struggle, revolutionary action, and, ultimately, a classless society are the inevitable products of the dialectic action. In applying this philosophy to history, Marx recognized four major stages of development: "In broad outline we can designate the Asiatic, the ancient, the feudal, and the modern bourgeois modes of production as progressive epochs on the economic formation of society."[6] The bourgeois-capitalist phase he regarded as the precursor of the millennial classless society.

Marx's philosophy of history, though accepted with religious veneration by large numbers of people in the world today, falls to the ground on many counts. Its dogmatic materialism is really an unrecognized metaphysic which does not bear up under scrutiny. Moreover, "even if we assume that all history is a history of class struggles, no scientific analysis could ever infer from this that class struggle is *the* essential factor that 'determines' all the rest."[7] Historical events since Marx's day have belied his prophecy that only revolution against capitalism will satisfy the proletariat. Labor unions and governmental antitrust and antimonopolistic legislation have given workers such a high standard of living in the West that good television reception is closer to their hearts than a forceful overthrow of society! Finally, Marx held a very ambiguous view of human nature, in that he saw men as evil exploiters of one another, and yet capable of an idyllic, classless existence once a suitable economic environment was provided. The present state of the U.S.S.R. is an excellent evidence that human nature requires the continuing restraint of government, and that a Marxist state, far from "winnowing away," shows great rigidity and a powerful tendency to fall under the control of a new class — not

---

[6]This statement appears in Marx's Preface to *A Contribution to the Critique of Political Economy*. Orthodox Marxist historians usually interpret historical events a priori in terms of these categories; thus the American Civil War is regarded as a victory of the bourgeois-capitalist phase (represented by the industrialized North) over the older feudal phase (represented by the agrarian, slaveholding South). For a good general presentation of the Marxist philosophy of history over against misinterpretations of it, see Georgi Plekhanov, *Essays in Historical Materialism* (New York: International Publishers, 1940).

[7]Karl Löwith, *Meaning in History* (Chicago: University of Chicago Press, Phoenix Books, 1957), p. 43.

a temporary "dictatorship of the proletariat" but a permanent dictatorship of bureaucratic totalitarians.[8]

The two most ambitious twentieth-century attempts to provide secular scientific conceptualizations of human history have been made by Oswald Spengler and Arnold Toynbee. Spengler, in his classic, *The Decline of the West*, argued that history moves in cyclical patterns, and that self-contained human cultures follow a life cycle similar to that of living organisms and nature.[9] Thus a culture develops from barbarism to a civilized classical period, and finally stagnates, decays, and dies in a new barbarism of hypercommercialism. Instead of employing the periodization of ancient, medieval, and modern history, Spengler speaks of four cycles: Indian, Arabian, Antique, and Western (beginning about A.D. 900), which go through the phases of spring, summer, autumn, and winter. "Spengler discovers no enduring progress, no guiding spirit, no ultimate goal, merely an endless repetition of approximately similar experiences."[10]

Spengler was so certain of the scientific character of his interpretation that he claimed it possible to predict the future of our civilization on the basis of its present position (thus his book title), and he made the astounding statement in his Preface to his first edition: "I am convinced that it is not merely a question of writing one out of several possible and merely logically justifiable philosophies, but of writing *the* philosophy of our time, one that is to some extent a natural philosophy and is dimly presaged by all. This may be said without presumption."[11]

Although Spengler's predictions of Western decline seem to be especially well fulfilled in the First World War, the Second World

---

[8]See Milovan D(j)ilas, *The New Class; An Analysis of the Communist System* (New York: Prager, 1957).

[9]The Spenglerean cycle patterns are well set out in diagrammatic form by Edwin Franden Dakin, *Cycles in History* ("Foundation Reprints," No. 7; Riverside, Conn.: Foundation for the Study of Cycles, 1948).

[10]G. P. Gooch, *History and Historians in the Nineteenth Century* (2d ed.; London: Longmans, Green, 1952), p. xxxv.

[11]*The Decline of the West: Form and Actuality*, trans. C. F. Atkinson (New York: Alfred A. Knopf, 1926), p. xv. Spengler frequently claimed that he was not employing the methods of the natural sciences, and that there is no such thing as absolute truth; but it is clear that in practice he operates with positivistic presuppositions.

War, the Korean War, and the current "cold war," we must not blind ourselves to the serious fallacies in his work. He assumes that systems of relations (cultures) created by organic beings must have the same life cycles as those beings; but this is by no means necessary (philosophies created by men are also systems of relations, and they obviously do not absorb life cycles — though in many cases it is perhaps unfortunate that they don't!). Spengler suffers from numerous unrecognized value judgments: for example, "Instinct is favored as opposed to understanding, the life of the soil as opposed to the life of the city, faith and reverence for tradition as opposed to rational calculation and self-interest."[12] Why should these values be accepted rather than a host of others? Finally,

> Spengler's book is loaded with a mass of historical learning, but even this is constantly deformed and perverted to fit his thesis. To take one example out of many, he maintains that as part of its fundamental character the classical or Graeco-Roman culture lacked all sense of time, cared nothing for the past or the future, and therefore (unlike the Egyptian, which had a keen time-sense) did not build tombs for its dead. He seems to have forgotten that in Rome orchestral concerts are held every week in the mausoleum of Augustus; that the tomb of Hadrian was for centuries the fortress of the Popes; and that for miles and miles outside the city the ancient roads are lined with the vastest collection of tombs in the whole world. Even the positivistic thinkers of the nineteenth century, in their misguided attempts to reduce history to a science, went no farther in the reckless and unscrupulous falsification of facts.[13]

The most influential living philosopher of history[14] is by all odds Arnold Toynbee, author of the massive work, *A Study of*

---

[12]Gardiner, *op. cit.*, p. 188. It is instructive to contrast Spengler's antipathy to the metropolis with Lewis Mumford's *The City in History* (New York: Harcourt, Brace & World, 1961).

[13]R. G. Collingwood, *The Idea of History* (New York: Oxford University Press, Galaxy Books, 1956), pp. 182-83.

[14]Walsh argues that Toynbee should not be termed a "historian," for his interests are not those of practicing historical investigators (*op. cit.*, pp. 167-68). This is a doubtful argument, for it could be maintained that practicing historians would more truly fulfill their function if they demonstrated live concern for the issues Toynbee raises.

History. The title of his book should be observed closely, for it indicates a fundamental difference between his approach and Spengler's: Toynbee is presenting, not "*the* philosophy of our time," but "*a* study" of world history; in this sense he rejects the pretentions of absolutistic positivism. In a discussion with Pieter Geyl, Toynbee stated:

> I should never dream of claiming that my particular inter-pretation is the only one possible. There are, I am sure, many different alternative ways of analyzing history, each of which is true in itself and illuminating as far as it goes, just as, in dissecting an organism, you can throw light on its nature by laying bare either the skeleton or the muscles or the nerves or the circulation of the blood. No single one of these dissections tells the whole truth, but each of them reveals a genuine facet of it. I should be well-content if it turned out that I had laid bare one genuine facet of history, and even then, I should measure my success by the speed with which my own work in my own line was put out of date by further work by other people in the same field.[15]

Toynbee, then, is not a positivist, but he is a scientific historian, in that he searches for general laws which can give meaning to and assist in the understanding of the historical process.

To what conclusions does he come? He has stated that the "two keys" to his interpretation of history are civilizations and religions.[16] By "civilizations" Toynbee means "the smallest intelligible fields of historical study," i.e., "whole societies and not arbitrarily insulated fragments of them like the nation-states of the modern West."[17] He isolates thirty-four civilizations, including thirteen "independent" civilizations, fifteen "satellite" civilizations,

---

[15]Toynbee, in Geyl, Toynbee, and Sorokin, *The Pattern of the Past: Can We Determine It?* (Boston: Beacon Press, 1949), pp. 81-82. The same debate is reprinted in Gardiner, *op. cit.*, pp. 307-19.

[16]In a National Broadcasting Company "Wisdom Series" film discussion with Christopher Wright, teaching fellow at Harvard University. The film is distributed by Encyclopaedia Britannica Films, Inc.

[17]Toynbee, *Civilization on Trial* (London: Oxford University Press, 1948), chap. 1.

and six "abortive" civilizations.[18] Each of these is distinguished by a dominant motif; the "Sinic," for example — roughly equivalent to Chinese — is characterized by deep respect for family tradition. These civilizations are analyzed in an attempt to determine their patterns of cultural genesis, growth, and breakdown; and Toynbee presents his "challenge-and-response" theory to explain why so many of them have died. In essence, this theory holds that no civilization dies because of determinist necessity, but because of inadequate response on its own part to the challenges facing it; Western civilization, for example, now faces the challenge of nuclear war, and our response to this challenge can mean the difference between life or death for our society. Here Toynbee introduces Aristotle's principle of the Golden Mean, and states that a challenge of the greatest stimulating power will be neither too severe (so as to discourage response) nor too mild (so as to present no vital issue); it must strike the mean to elicit maximum response.

Toynbee's second "key," which receives increasing emphasis in the later volumes of A Study of History, is religion.[19] Its significance lies in the fact that it provides the only creative way to transform society and move beyond a collapsing culture. Therefore Toynbee can say that "the societies of the species called civilizations will have fulfilled their function when once they have brought a mature higher religion to birth,"[20] and can express the hope that, with the higher religions acting as "chrysalises," there will arise a "future oecumenical civilization, starting in a Western framework and on a Western basis, but progressively drawing contributions from the living non-Western civilizations embraced in it."[21] He refuses to believe that any one of the four living "higher

---

[18]A Study of History, XII (Reconsiderations) (London: Oxford University Press, 1961), 546-61. This represents Toynbee's latest position. "In the course of the first ten volumes of this book I arrived at a list of twenty-three full-blown civilizations, four that were arrested at an early stage in their growth, and five that were abortive" (p. 546).

[19]So strong is this emphasis that Geyl titles his critique of Vols. VII-X of A Study of History, "Toynbee the Prophet" (Pieter Geyl, Debates With Historians [London: B. T. Batsford, 1955], pp. 158-78).

[20]Civilization on Trial, p. 236.

[21]A Study of History, XII, 559. Toynbee makes it clear in his "reconsiderations," however, that he has come to believe that "religion is an end in itself," not just a means to an end (p. 94 n).

religions" (Buddhism, Christianity, Islam, and Hinduism) has "a monopoly of truth and salvation"; he holds "a belief in the relative truth and relative saving-power of all the higher religions alike."[22] Christianity has a special role to play in the world of today because it is the dominant faith of Western civilization; but this does not mean that it is true while other religions are false, or that it will necessarily remain the most advanced human religious expression.

Toynbee's philosophy of history has been the subject of an amazing number and variety of critiques, and this is one of the best proofs of the importance of his work. However, it must be said that the great majority of evaluations of *A Study of History* have been negative. We could not possibly include here all the critics' arguments, and the following is intended as no more than a summary of several of the more damning evaluations.

1. As Toynbee himself admits, he has used Hellenic civilization (his particular historical specialty) as a model or pattern for the interpretation of other civilizations. But there is no compelling reason why Hellenic civilization should serve as the model, and, indeed, it is so inappropriate for dealing with certain other civilizations that Toynbee is led to pervert historical data by forcing them into foreign categories.[23]

2. Toynbee frequently chooses his examples to fit his a priori theories, rather than modifying his theories to accord with the facts.[24]

---

[22]*Ibid.*, p. 99. Cf. his emotively charged statement: "The writer of this Study will venture to express his personal belief that the four higher religions that were alive in the age in which he was living were four variations on a single theme, and that, if all the four components of this heavenly music of the spheres could be audible on Earth simultaneously, and with equal clarity, to one pair of human ears, the happy hearer would find himself listening, not to a discord, but to a harmony" (*A Study of History*, VII [London: Oxford University Press, 1954], 428). However, he admits that "as far into the future as we can see ahead" he does "not expect that they will agree to make a merger of their different doctrines, practices, and institutions, in which their common spiritual treasure is diversely presented" (*A Study of History*, XII, 100 *n*).

[23]This is pointed out particularly well by the experts in the history of Islam, Russia, etc., who have contributed to *The Intent of Toynbee's History*, ed. Edward T. Gargan (Chicago: Loyola University Press, 1961).

[24]See Geyl's critique, "Toynbee Once More: Empiricism or Apriorism?" in Geyl's *Debates With Historians*, pp. 144-57.

3. Because of his interest in obtaining a general, synoptic view of human history in the large, his treatment of particular historical problems is often superficial and misleading.[25]

4. Toynbee's work evidences "creeping determinism," illustrated by his "hardening of the categories," i.e., "a tendency in the later volumes to treat as established laws what were earlier stated merely summatively or, at any rate, tentatively."[26]

5. "Toynbee still believes that the idea of 'challenge and response' constitutes a magical key to the why and how of human creativity. But is it not, after all, little more than a formal principle, like Hegel's dialectic, which cannot provide us with a canon of interpretation?"[27]

6. Toynbee's view of religion is eclectic and syncretic, and as such does violence to the historical uniqueness and particularistic claims of Christianity.[28] The core of Christianity lies in its historical particularity, and Toynbee's neo-Mahayana Buddhist spirituality thus opposes the very essence of the Christian message.[29]

THE SLOUGH OF DESPOND

Our rapid overview of five of the major secular philosophies of history of modern times has brought us to a discouraging conclusion: neither Kant nor Hegel nor Marx, neither Spengler nor Toynbee has succeeded in arriving at an answer to the perennial

---

[25]To take a single, but typical example: Gilmore, in discussing European history from 1453 to 1517, shows that "Latin Christendom, far from being the least likely candidate for expansion [Toynbee's view] emerges as the candidate most likely to succeed." Myron P. Gilmore, *The World of Humanism* (New York: Harper, 1952), p. 34.

[26]William Dray, "Toynbee's Search for Historical Laws," *History and Theory*, I (1960), 49; F. H. Underhill, "The Toynbee of the 1950's," *Canadian Historical Review*, XXXVI (1955), 227.

[27]Gerhard Masur, Review of *A Study of History*, Vol. XII, in *American Historical Review*, LXVII (1961), 79.

[28]To disregard the testimonies of Jesus and of the primitive church concerning the uniqueness and finality of Christianity (e.g. John 14:6; Acts 4:12) is to do no less than abrogate one's position as a historian.

[29]See Will Herberg, "Arnold Toynbee — Historian or Religious Prophet?" *Queen's Quarterly*, LXIV (1957), 421-33. Herberg also takes Toynbee to task, as have so many others, on his negative evaluation of Judaism.

question: "Where is history going?" Schlesinger's negativistic attitude to monistic interpretations of history now appears more
understandable than it did at the outset of our discussion. Indeed,
this attitude is but one variety of a widely held contemporary
discouragement with attempts to answer ultimate questions of any
kind. The logical positivism movement in philosophy, as represented by the "Vienna Circle" and A. J. Ayer, is perhaps only the
clearest manifestation of this tendency.

A concrete example is provided by the celebrated mathemati-
cian E. T. Bell's posthumous work, *The Last Problem*, in which he
hypothesizes that our atomic age will end in disaster, and asks:
"What problems that our race has struggled for centuries to solve
will be open when the darkness comes down?" He rejects ultimate
philosophical problems, for "realists may be pardoned for suspect-
ing that some are pseudo-problems incapable of solution," and
determines to "leave them aside and look for others on an understandable level."[30] The result? His "last problem" is the still
unsolved mathematical puzzle, Prove or disprove that if n is a
number greater than 2, there are no numbers, a, b, c such that
$a^n + b^n = c^n$.

Comparable rejection of the larger questions of ultimate meaning and purpose characterizes the work of a number of prominent
historians and philosophers of history of the present century, who
have seen in the failures of the previously discussed historical
generalists an absolute prohibition against single answers in history. Thus Charles A. Beard and Carl Becker became historical
pragmatists, and Benedetto Croce and R. G. Collingwood rejected
"objective," "scientific" history and stressed the artistic nature of
the historians' work — the need for subjective, imaginative re-liv-
ing and re-enactment of the past.[31]

The inevitable consequence of this subjective reaction can be
seen in the contemporary French existentialist historian, Raymond
Aron, who argues that history, instead of having a single meaning,
is legitimately capable of a "plurality of systems of interpretation"
and that the only way for the individual to "overcome the relativity
of history" is "by the absolute of decision," which affirms "the

---

[30]New York: Simon & Schuster, 1961, pp. 9-10.
[31]On Beard, Becker, Croce, and Collingwood, see my *Shape of the Past*,
pp. 89 ff.

power of man, who creates himself by judging his environment, and by choosing himself."[32] Such individualistic, anthropocentric relativism — which, incidentally, likewise characterizes Bultmann's theology of history — is in reality an admission of philosophical lassitude and malaise in the face of repeated failures to discover an ultimate meaning for the historical process.

Coupled with this twentieth-century intellectual "slough of despond" is a desperate emotional need to find significance in man's historical enterprise. This is nowhere better illustrated than in modern man's changed conception of time itself. The great art historian Panofsky, in his *Studies in Iconology*, has shown how the figure of Father Time has radically changed from ancient to modern times. In the ancient world, time was depicted in positive terms. "In none of these ancient representations do we find the hourglass, the scythe or sickle, the crutches, or the signs of a particularly advanced age," writes Panofsky after analyzing early depictions of time; "in other words," he continues, "the ancient images of time are either characterized by symbols of fleeting speed and precarious balance, or by symbols of universal power and infinite fertility, but not by symbols of decay and destruction."[33] Panofsky shows that the humanistic Renaissance was responsible for fusing a personification of dynamic classical time with the frightening figure of Saturn — thus creating the image of Time the Destroyer. And today? Today the drawings of Father Time retain virtually none of the creative force of their ancient counterparts; for us, time is seen as a debilitating agent — a symbol of the decay to which all life is subject. Thus the figure of Father Time reminds us of the bankruptcy of our modern attempts to infuse meaning into history, and yet, by the very persistence of the personification, recalls the continuing need of mankind to think of time in personal terms — in terms of intelligent, purposeful will.

And the modern response to a supposedly incurable historical meaninglessness? Denis Baly perceptively describes the contemporary reaction as two-pronged: the creation of myths to "explain"

---

[32]Raymond Aron, *Introduction to the Philosophy of History*, trans. G. J. Irwin (London: Weidenfeld and Nicolson, 1961), pp. 86 ff., 334.

[33]Erwin Panofsky, *Studies in Iconology: Humanistic Themes in the Art of the Renaissance* (2d ed.; New York: Harper Torchbooks, 1962), p. 73.

history, and the effort to subjugate history to man's totalitarian control:

> In such a disintegrating situation man reacts in two contradictory ways. On the one hand he tries to take some aggressive action which will provoke events, and thereby demonstrate at least his partial control over them, and on the other hand he submits to events, retreating into a protective and self-effacing camouflage, thereby hoping to escape the brutal attention of the fates. Neither of these reactions in the long run, however, is effective, and both are indeed humiliating. . . . A curious custom in the villages of the Middle East may perhaps be quoted as illustrating in some sense both these reactions. There, at the time of an eclipse, the children come out into the streets banging pots and pans together to "frighten away the whale that is swallowing the sun." What has now become a childish game is, however, the last relic of one of the most ancient beliefs in the world, the belief that at the Creation the gods vanquished the dragon of chaos, and as a symbol of order set the sun and moon in the sky to perform their regular and appointed functions. But men lived ever under the fear that chaos could return, and when the chief symbols of order seemed to them to be being attacked, they took up arms against the dragon, fearing that he was not dead after all. It was not enough for them to have explained history; they must always be on the watch to control it, lest chaos and meaninglessness return.[34]

This double response to lack of meaning in history, so patently illustrated in our day by Marxist communism and by the "American way of life," brings us back with renewed concern to our original question: "Where is history going?" Can we find genuine meaning and purpose in history, and thereby avoid the consequences of unrealistic myth-making?

INVASION FROM OUTER SPACE: THE CHRISTIAN CONCEPTION OF HISTORY

In order to reach solid ground in the problems before us, we must obtain a clear picture as to why the secular philosophies of history discussed earlier fail to achieve success. The attempts of

---

[34]Denis Baly, *Academic Illusion* (Greenwich, Conn.: Seabury Press, 1961), pp. 66-67.

Kant, Hegel, Marx, Spengler, and Toynbee — and of all the great secular philosophers of history, for that matter — are, even when they fail, of inestimable value; for, by inversion, they can lead us to the conditions without which all attempts to achieve a valid interpretation of total history must likewise fail.

What are the major deficiencies in the philosophies of history which we have considered? First, the goals they set for history (e.g., Kant's reason, Hegel's freedom, Marx's classless society, Toynbee's ecumenical civilization) cannot be demonstrated to have a necessitarian character about them. Secondly, in choosing their respective goals, the secular philosophers of history continually make judgments as to what is significant and what is valuable (e.g., Hegel's idealism, Marx's materialism, Spengler's favoring of instinct, agrarian society, and reverence for tradition); but in no case are they able to justify these value judgments in absolute terms. Thirdly, the secular philosophers of history always enter upon their work with an unjustified, unprovable concept of human nature (e.g., the optimistic view of man held by Kant, Hegel, and Toynbee, the ambiguous view held by Marx, and the pessimistic view held by Spengler). Fourthly, these philosophers gratuitously presuppose ethical principles (e.g., Hegel's exempting of history's "great men" from the ordinary standards of right and wrong; Marx's willingness to let the end justify the means in bringing about the classless society through revolution).

And what do these four crucial deficiencies have in common? They all reflect what has often been called the "human predicament" — the lack of absolute historical perspective on the part of finite man. Consider: because a man stands in history at a particular place, and cannot see into the future, he cannot possibly demonstrate that his conception of total history will have permanent validity. For the same reason — lack of perspective on the human drama as a whole — he cannot in any absolute sense know what is more or less significant or valuable in the total history of mankind. Moreover, because he is able to acquaint himself personally with only a fraction of all the members of the human race, past, present, and future, his conception of human nature can have only limited value, and is certainly not an adequate basis for historical generalization. Lastly, the secularist's ethical ideals will also reflect his stance in history, and will not be capable of justification in absolute terms.

Now perhaps we see why, to take an especially clear example, Hegel's concept of four "world-historical" epochs (Oriental, Greek, Roman — and Germanic as the goal of the process) appears so ludicrous to us, but was regarded in all seriousness by him. From his early nineteenth-century position in history, the Germanic peoples did seem to be on the side of destiny. From our present historical stance, such a view retains little appeal. The basic problem thus becomes clear: Since no historian or philosopher — or anyone else for that matter — sits "in a house by the side of the road" and watches all of history pass by, no one, from a secular, humanistic viewpoint, can answer the question, "Where is history going?" All of us are — to use Jack Kerouac's phrase — "on the road." Our historical searchlights are incapable of illuminating all of the path we have traversed, and they continually meet a wall of fog ahead of us. In this human predicament, secular philosophers of history have often, unwittingly, served as blind men leading the blind.

Is there, then, no way out? Is there no answer to the question of history's meaning — a question that has cried for an answer in every epoch of human history and particularly demands an answer today? There is indeed an answer; but, as we have seen, it cannot arise from the human situation itself, because of man's limited perspective on the historical process. What is needed is, in space-age lingo, an "invasion from outer space."

Specifically, let us suppose that the historical process were known in its entirety by a God who created both the process and the people who take part in it. Now if this were the case, and if that God entered the human sphere and revealed to men the origin and goal of the historical drama, the criteria for significance and value in the process, the true nature of the human participants in the drama, and the ethical values appropriate to the process, then, obviously, the question, "Where is history going?" could be successfully and meaningfully answered. A gigantic *If*, you say. True, but this is precisely the central contention of the Christian religion: that God *did* enter human life — in the person of Jesus the Christ — and *did* reveal to men the nature and significance of history and human life, and *did* bring men into contact with eternal values. "God was in Christ," says the Christian proclamation, "reconciling the world unto himself."

What is this Christian conception of history, and how can it be validated? The conception can perhaps best be understood in terms of the threefold work of the Christian God, as manifested in His trinitarian nature. The God of the Christian faith presents Himself as Father, Son, and Holy Spirit — as Creator, Redeemer, and Sanctifier of man's historical life. The Christian understanding of history can be visualized as a line which begins with creation, centers on the redemptive act of God in Jesus Christ, and finds its termination in a sanctifying final judgment:

| CREATION:
God's Sovereignty | REDEMPTION:
God's Love | LAST JUDGMENT:
God's Restoration
of all things |

Karl Löwith has well characterized the Christian view of history as "linear but centered"[35] in contrast with the ancient Greek belief in the hopeless cyclical repetition of the ages.

Because God is the creator and preserver of history, every act of the historical drama is meaningful. Jesus assured men that though five sparrows are sold for two farthings, "not one of them is forgotten before God. . . . ye are of more value than many sparrows." No historical act is too insignificant to be outside the Father's care. Indeed, as the Reformer Calvin asserted on the basis of clear biblical teaching, God is the sovereign Lord of history. He is "not such as is imagined by sophists, vain, idle, and almost asleep, but vigilant, efficacious, operative, and engaged in continual action."[36] The Christian doctrine of creation is thus a remedy for all forms of historical nihilism.

The Christian God is also a God of redemption. The Christian revelation teaches that the entire human race is subject to self-centeredness, and that this basic selfishness cannot be cured by human beings themselves. As Luther well put it, man is *incurvatus in se*, "curved in upon himself," and therefore views his own interests — whether personal or national — as more important than anyone else's. It was on the basis of this Christian realism that the great Cambridge historian Lord Acton formulated his axiom:

---

[35]*Op. cit.*, p. 182.
[36]*Institutes*, I, xvi, 3.

"Power tends to corrupt; absolute power corrupts absolutely." But the God of the Christian faith saw man in his desperate need, and entered the human situation in the person of Jesus Christ expressly to solve man's egocentric dilemma. By living a life of complete selflessness, Jesus was able to do what no mere human being could ever do: take other men's wrongs upon Himself, along with the death penalty that these sins deserved. By His death and subsequent resurrection He conquered the powers of sin and death, and freed all members of the human race who recognize their need and accept what He has done for them. This great act of self-giving love becomes the center of history and the criterion of significance for interpreting all other acts. It creates an absolute ethic of love, and binds all men together in the bonds of love, since Christ died for all without exception.

G. Kitson Clark comments as follows on Jesus' words from the Cross, "Father, forgive them; for they know not what they do":

> That last sentence ought probably to be printed at the beginning of all history books, both as a prayer and as a statement of fact. It is not a denial of the existence and power of evil: at that moment such a denial would have been impossible. Nor is it a denial of the pain, mental and physical, which evil causes. To deny that would also at that moment have been impossible. But that pain was not carried over to the account of those who had caused the evil: it was accepted, absorbed and cancelled by the Judge. By such an action the cords of sin which bound the world were cut away.
>
> I cannot tell you what that means, but I can say this. This is not only an event of eternal importance: it is also plainly an example which must be followed. . . . It is necessary to connect oneself with the common lot of humanity till the mind, like Pope's spider, "feels at each thread, and lives along the line." Yet the effort and the pain are, with divine assistance, the way to freedom.[37]

The Christian Scriptures also speak of God's judgmental work: His Holy Spirit reproves the world "of sin, and of righteousness, and of judgment" (John 16:8). Throughout human history God has judged the actions of men. As Calvin said:

---

[37]Clark, *The Kingdom of Free Men* (Cambridge: Cambridge University Press, 1957), pp. 204-5.

He subdued the pride of Tyre by the Egyptians; the insolence of the Egyptians by the Assyrians; the haughtiness of the
Assyrians by the Chaldeans; the confidence of Babylon by the
Medes and Persians, after Cyrus had subjugated the Medes. The
ingratitude of the kings of Israel and Judah, and their impious
rebellion, not withstanding His numerous favours, He repressed
and punished, sometimes by the Assyrians, sometimes by the
Babylonians. . . . Whatever opinion be formed of the acts of men,
yet the Lord equally executed His work by them, when He
broke the sanguinary sceptres of insolent kings.[38]

Of course this immanent judgment is seldom as transparent as
it was in the events to which Calvin refers. Yet Augustine saw it
clearly in the fall of decadent Rome, and we today can hardly
avoid seeing it in the annihilation of the demonic fascism of the
Third Reich. The Christian faith affirms that such immanent judgment prevails throughout history, for "as a man sows, so shall he
also reap." Even though the Christian sees only "through a glass,
darkly," he remembers the question of one of Thornton Wilder's
characters in his novel *The Cabala*: "Do they think, the [skeptical]
fools, that their powers of observation are clearer than the devices
of a god?"

Moreover, history is moving toward a final Judgment, a climax
in which "the heavens shall be rolled together as a scroll," and in
which the evils of human egotism throughout history will finally
be put right. On that day, we are told, "there is nothing covered,
that shall not be revealed; neither hid, that shall not be known"
and, "whatsoever ye have spoken in darkness shall be heard in the
light; and that which ye have spoken in the ear in closets shall be
proclaimed upon the housetops" (Luke 12:2-3). This promise of
final, perfectly just judgment at the end of time gives the Christian
conception of history a direction and an ultimate meaning. Every
moment of the Christian's life must then be lived existentially in
the light of John Donne's question, "What if this present were
the world's last night?"[39] The time of the end cannot be calculated, but the fact of the end is certain. For the Christian, that
day holds not terror but anticipation, for not only will all things

---

[38]*Institutes*, IV, xx, 30-31.
[39]Cf. C. S. Lewis, *The World's Last Night, and Other Essays* (New
York: Harcourt, Brace & World, 1960).

be made right, but he will see, face to face, his God and Savior, who once died to redeem him from the hell of self and restore him to perfect freedom in Christ.

And the validation for the Christian conception of history — the evidence of its truth? Can we know that it is not just a myth, like the banging of pans to "frighten away the whale that is swallowing the sun"? We can indeed. In the next two chapters I give the objective, historical evidence, which I shall do no more than summarize here:[40]

1. On the basis of accepted principles of textual and historical analysis, the Gospel records are found to be trustworthy historical documents — primary source evidence for the life of Christ.

2. In these records Jesus exercises divine prerogatives and claims to be God in human flesh. He rests His claims on His forthcoming resurrection.

3. In all four Gospels, Christ's bodily resurrection is described in minute detail; Christ's resurrection evidences His deity.

4. The fact of the resurrection cannot be discounted on a priori, philosophical grounds; miracles are impossible only if one so defines them — but such definition rules out proper historical investigation.

5. If Christ is God, then He speaks the truth concerning the absolute divine authority of the Old Testament and of the soon-to-be-written, apostolic New Testament; concerning His death for the sins of the world; and concerning the nature of man and of history.

6. It follows from the preceding that all biblical assertions bearing on philosophy of history are to be regarded as revealed truth, and that all human attempts at historical interpretation are to be judged for truth value on the basis of harmony with scriptural revelation.

There is, however, another way to attest Christ's claims, and I shall conclude with it. He promised, "If any man's will is to do his [God's] will, he shall know whether the teaching is from God" (John 7:17, RSV). And the Apostle Paul, writing under divine guidance, tells us that "faith cometh by hearing, and hearing by the

---

[40]See also Montgomery, *The Shape of the Past*, especially Pt. I, chap. V.

word of God" (Romans 10:17). This means that if any person honestly wishes to discover the truth of Christ's claims, he need only put himself in contact with God's word in Scripture and Church, and God's word will attest itself in his personal experience. Only a suspension of disbelief is necessary: "Lord, I believe; help thou mine unbelief." I can say that I have never known anyone (including myself) who has prayed this doubter's prayer without having it answered in the affirmative.

As the Roman world fell apart, and all of Western civilization collapsed with it, men's hearts failed them for fear. It was then that Cyprian spoke for himself and for others of the Christian persuasion: "We want to stand upright amid the ruins of the world, and not lie on the ground with those who have no hope."[41] Today we look out on a world which has uncomfortable parallels with Cyprian's time. Secular philosophies of history, because they are themselves conditioned by the flux of passing time, are incapable of standing upright. But the One who stood upright on a cross two thousand years ago — and who can transform our lives today — and who will assuredly come again with glory to judge the quick and the dead, He is able to lift us from the ground, and give us the gift of a historical hope that will never be disappointed.

---

[41]Cf. Ethelbert Stauffer, *Christ and the Caesars: Historical Sketches*, trans. K. and R. Gregor Smith (Philadelphia: Westminster Press, 1955).

2. JESUS CHRIST AND HISTORY*

Part I
What Does a Historian Know About Jesus Christ?

*The immediate occasion for this and the following chapter was a Philosophy Club lecture delivered at the University of British Columbia on November 26, 1962 by Professor Avrum Stroll, who alleged, according to a Canadian Press dispatch widely publicized, that "a Jesus probably did exist but so many legends have grown about him that it is impossible for scholars to find out anything about the real man," that "the Gospels of St. Matthew, St. Mark, St. Luke and St. John were written long after Jesus was crucified and provide no reliable historical information about him," and that "it is almost impossible to derive historical facts from the legends and descriptions of miracles performed by Jesus." (The text of Professor Stroll's lecture is given in full in Appendix A.) In response to Professor Stroll's lecture, I was invited by the Lutheran Student Movement — U.B.C. Chapter to deliver on that campus the essays comprising this and the following chapter; these lectures were presented to capacity audiences of students and faculty on January 29 and 30, 1963, and were subsequently read with appreciation by C. S. Lewis shortly before his death (see Appendix B). Professor Stroll now teaches in the Department of Philosophy at the University of California (San Diego campus) — Herbert Marcuse's bailiwick — where the University Bookstore publishes his C.B.C. lectures, *Reason and Religious Belief*, a series which, while negatively evaluating the traditional theistic proofs for God's existence, Anselm's ontological proof, and pragmatic religious claims, makes no attempt whatever to face the historical challenge that "God was in Christ, reconciling the world unto Himself."

THE EARLIEST RECORDS we have of the life and ministry of Jesus give the overwhelming impression that this man went around not so much "doing good" as making a decided nuisance of himself.

The parallel with Socrates in this regard is very strong: both men infuriated their contemporaries to such an extent that they were eventually put to death. But whereas Socrates played the gadfly on the collective Athenian rump by demanding that his hearers "know themselves" — examine their unexamined lives — Jesus alienated His contemporaries by continually forcing them to think through their attitude to Him personally. "Who do men say that I the Son of man am?"; "Who do you say that I am?"; "What do you think of Christ? whose son is He?": these were the questions Jesus asked. And it seems patently clear that the questioner was not asking because He really didn't know who He was and needed help in finding out! Unlike the "sick" characters in Jules Feiffer's Greenwich Village cartoons, when Jesus asked, "Who am I?" He was evidently fully aware of His own character. What He sought to achieve by His questions was a similar awareness of His nature on the part of others.

In these chapters I shall again pose Jesus' irritating questions concerning Himself: Who was He? Who did He claim to be? Is there compelling evidence in support of His claims? The first part will discuss the documentary basis of Jesus' life and claims, and thereby provide the necessary background for the second part, titled, "The Divinity of Jesus Christ," in which the claims themselves will be explicitly set forth, together with the attestation for them by way of the Resurrection.

In spite of the tension which these issues will engender (they have always done so, since they inevitably require a rethinking of one's personal *Weltanschauung* — one's philosophy of life), I raise the questions with pleasure, since once upon a time, when I was an undergraduate honors philosophy student at Cornell University, I myself encountered this crucial problem area, and as a result became a Christian believer. Like Cambridge professor C. S. Lewis, I was brought "kicking and struggling"[1] into the kingdom of God by the historical evidence in behalf of Jesus' claims; and resultant

---

[1]*Surprised by Joy* (New York: Harcourt, Brace & World, 1955), p. 229.

experiential (existential, if you will) satisfaction with the Christian world-view makes me more than willing to present the case for your consideration.

The immediate occasion for these chapters has already been alluded to. On November 26, 1962, Dr. Avrum Stroll of the University of British Columbia Philosophy Department delivered a lecture titled, "Did Jesus Really Exist?" Professor Stroll's remarks were widely publicized, and I replied to them in the public press. His position — which I regard as historically untenable — is summed up in the closing sentence of his address: "An accretion of legends grew up about this figure [Jesus], was incorporated into the Gospels by various devotees of the movement, was rapidly spread throughout the Mediterranean world by the ministry of St. Paul; and that because this is so, it is impossible to separate these legendary elements in the purported descriptions of Jesus from those which in fact were true of him."

In my judgment, Professor Stroll arrives at this conclusion as a result of committing four serious historical-philosophical errors, and we shall take these up forthwith. But first I wish to indicate that in one very important respect at least, Dr. Stroll and I are in full agreement. Over against President Briggs of the University Philosophy Club, who declared in a Canadian Press news dispatch following the Stroll lecture, "As a matter of fact we consider these topics, atheism and Jesus Christ, as not very important" — as compared, for example, with the question of "whether the earth's fuel is running out" — I regard the issues raised by Dr. Stroll as of the most paramount significance. If even a fraction of the claims which Jesus made for Himself, and which His followers made for Him, are true, then the uncommitted will find themselves faced with what Paul Tillich has well termed a "shaking of the foundations" — the necessity for a complete realignment of personal philosophy. On the other hand, if Jesus' claims are unfounded, then the Apostle Paul was absolutely correct when he wrote that if Christ is not risen from the dead, then we Christians are of all men most miserable (I Corinthians 15:14-19).

Astute observers of our neurotic epoch seem to be more concerned about the running out of the spiritual rather than the natural fuel supply of the world. And the question of the historical validity of Jesus' claims bears directly upon this twentieth-century religious bankruptcy. In spite of our radically different viewpoints on the *de facto* validity of the historical portrait of Jesus presented in the New Testament documents, I believe that Dr. Stroll would heartily second me when I express agreement with the following statement by Millar Burrows of Yale, the foremost American expert on the Dead Sea Scrolls:

> There is a type of Christian faith, . . . rather strongly represented today, [that] regards the affirmations of Christian faith as confessional statements which the individual accepts as a member of the believing community, and which are not dependent on reason or evidence. Those who hold this position will not admit that historical investigation can have anything to say about the uniqueness of Christ. They are often skeptical as to the possibility of knowing anything about the historical Jesus, and seem content to dispense with such knowledge. I cannot share this point of view. I am profoundly convinced that the historic revelation of God in Jesus of Nazareth must be the cornerstone of any faith that is really Christian. Any historical question about the real Jesus who lived in Palestine nineteen centuries ago is therefore fundamentally important.[2]

Four Historical-Philosophical Errors

Granted the "fundamental importance" of the question Professor Stroll raises, how correct is he in arguing concerning Jesus that "the information we have about Him is a composite of fact and legend which cannot reliably be untangled"? Professor Stroll's argument involves four major fallacies, and these vitiate his entire presentation. Two of these fallacies are of a historical character, and two are of a philosophical-logical nature. Taken together, they destroy his argument not only in historical and philosophical respects, but also in the theological sphere, since Christian theology cannot be divorced from logic and history. Let it be noted that I am not criticizing Dr. Stroll as a theologian (he himself expressly stated in his lecture that he was "not a theologian"); but I am claiming that he overstepped scholarly bounds in making his historical judgments, and that he commits philosophical blunders incongruous with his academic specialization.

What are Dr. Stroll's four errors? We shall mention them

---

[2]*More Light on the Dead Sea Scrolls* (New York: Viking Press, 1958), p. 55.

briefly now and come back to each in turn as our discussions proceed.

First, he relies almost exclusively upon the judgments of modern "authorities" in dealing with the question of the reliability of the New Testament documents. The proper scholarly procedure is, of course, to face the documentary problems directly, by way of the accepted canons of historical and literary method. Professor Stroll himself points up this type of logical fallacy when he writes in his popular manual, *Philosophy Made Simple*:[3] "*It is not the prestige of an authority which makes a statement true or false but rather the citing of evidence either to confirm or* [*sic*] *disconfirm the statement*" (Stroll's italics). Moreover, the modern "authorities" cited by Professor Stroll are consistently of a particular kind. They represent a radical tradition of New Testament criticism which reflects nineteenth-century rationalistic presuppositions (e.g., Albert Schweitzer), and which issues in the form-critical school (*formgeschichtliche Methode*) of Dibelius and Bultmann — an approach regarded as misleading and outmoded by much of recent biblical scholarship. For example — and the instance is typical — A. H. McNeile of Trinity College, Dublin, and C. S. C. Williams of Merton College, Oxford, in their *Introduction to the Study of the New Testament*,[4] present seven thoroughly damning criticisms of the *Formgeschichte* approach. We shall take up some of these criticisms at the end of this chapter. What we wish to stress at this point is Professor Stroll's apparent lack of awareness of such criticisms.

Secondly, Dr. Stroll commits the unpardonable historical sin of neglecting primary documents. The earliest records of Christianity we possess are not the Gospel accounts but the letters of Paul. These Dr. Stroll dispenses in one paragraph of nine lines in his 20-page paper, on the remarkable grounds that "all of them have at one time or other been challenged as genuine" and "Paul never met Jesus." In point of fact, except for the so-called Pastoral Epistles and Ephesians, it would be next to impossible to find any competent present-day scholarship that denies the Pauline

---

[3]Avrum Stroll and Richard H. Popkin, *Philosophy Made Simple* ("Made Simple Books"; Garden City, N.Y.: Doubleday, 1956), p. 165.

[4]*Introduction to the Study of the New Testament* (2d. ed.; Oxford: Clarendon Press, 1955).

authorship of the corpus of letters purporting to have been written by him. And the fact that Paul had not himself been one of Jesus' original disciples is of minor significance when we remember that the author of one of the four Gospels (Luke) also wrote the Book of Acts, in which every effort is made to show that Paul's teachings about Jesus were accepted by the original Apostles as fully consistent with their own remembrance of Jesus' message.

In the third place, Professor Stroll again violates his own philosophical canons by committing the logical error of *petitio principii*: "begging the question." In Stroll's *Philosophy Made Simple* (*loc. cit.*), we read (author's italics): "*The Fallacy of Begging the Question . . . occurs when either the same statement is used both as a premise and [sic] a conclusion in an argument, or when one of the premises could not be known to be true unless the conclusion were first assumed to be true.*"

How does this circular argumentation operate in Professor's Stroll's own discussion of Jesus' existence? He writes: "Even if there were reason to believe some of the material [in the Gospels] to express eye witness [sic] accounts of Jesus' [sic] life, the accretion of legend, the description of miracles performed by Jesus, which exist in these writings make it difficult, if not impossible, to extract from them any reliable historical testimony about the events described." Here Dr. Stroll says that *regardless* of the question of eyewitness testimony, he rejects the authenticity of the Gospel accounts on the ground that they attribute miracles to Jesus. But how does one know whether miracles occurred in connection with Jesus' life unless he investigates the primary documents? Obviously Dr. Stroll is arguing in a circle, and presupposing that miracles did not in fact occur in Jesus' life. As C. S. Lewis effectively points out in his classic work, *Miracles*,[5] in the course of analyzing Hume's classic argument against miracles:

> Now of course we must agree with Hume that if there is absolutely "uniform experience" against miracles, if in other words they have never happened, why then they never have. Unfortunately, we know the experience against them to be uniform only if we know that all the reports of them are false. And we can know all the reports to be false only if we know al-

---

[5]*Miracles* (New York: The Macmillan Company, 1947), pp. 121-24.

ready that miracles have never occurred. In fact, we are arguing in a circle.

As we shall see in the next chapter, no historian can legitimately rule out documentary evidence simply on the ground that it records remarkable events. If the documents are sufficiently reliable, the remarkable events must be accepted even if thy cannot be successfully explained by analogy with other events or by an a priori scheme of natural causation. L. J. McGinley's criticism of Bultmann — upon whom Dr. Stroll heavily relies — can as well be applied to him: "Whenever Bultmann denies the historic worth of a passage because of the supernatural content, he has ceased to be . . . an historian evaluating sources . . . and his criticisms have no value in the study of the Gospel text."[6]

Lastly, Professor Stroll erroneously "explains" the "unhistorical" picture of Jesus in the New Testament documents as the product of a "messianic fever" characteristic of the Palestinian Jews living under the yoke of Roman oppression in the first century of our era. He parallels the Essene "messiahs" of the Dead Sea scrolls with Jesus, and argues that the "psychological instability" of the time produced a divine Christ out of an eschatologically orientated Nazarene teacher by the name of Jesus. As we shall see, this entire argument demonstrates a baleful and inexcusable ignorance of the nature of Jewish messianic expectation at the time of Christ. Historically it can be proven beyond question that on every important point Jesus' conception of Himself as Messiah differed radically from the conceptions held by all parties among the Jews, and particularly that it cannot be harmonized with the Essene "Teacher of Righteousness" described in the scrolls from the Dead Sea. Moreover, as we shall also see, the transformation of a human Jesus to a divine Christ was a task of which neither the Apostolic company nor Paul was psychologically or ethically capable — even if Jesus had met their stereotyped messianic expectations, which He did not. Here Professor Stroll has stepped onto quicksand where his unhistorical allegations are totally incapable of bearing philosophical weight.

---

[6]*Form-criticism of the Synoptic Healing Narratives* (Woodstock, Md.: Woodstock College Press, 1944), p. 71.

ARE THE NEW TESTAMENT DOCUMENTS
HISTORICALLY TRUSTWORTHY?

So much for our rapid overview of the principal fallacies in Dr. Stroll's paper. Now we shall take the first of the major questions to be dealt with, namely, are the New Testament documents of sufficient historical worth that we can gain from them a reliable picture of Jesus' claims concerning Himself and of the claims made for Him by others? Here, let it be noted, we do not naively assume the "inspiration" or "infallibility" of the New Testament records, and then by circular reasoning attempt to prove what we have previously assumed. We regard the documents (even though today they are usually printed on fine India paper with verse numbers) only as documents, and we treat them as we would any other historical materials. Our procedure in determining documentary reliability will avoid Professor Stroll's first error — that of deferring to modern, rationalistic "authorities" — for we shall go directly to the documents themselves and subject them to the tests of reliability employed in general historiography and literary criticism. These tests are well set out by C. Sanders, in his *Introduction to Research in English Literary History*[7] as "bibliographical," "internal," and "external." (Incidentally, since Sanders is a Professor of Military History, it seems unlikely that I can be criticized for theological bias in referring to him!)

By *the bibliographical test*, we mean the analysis of the textual tradition by which a document reaches us. In the case of the New Testament documents, the question is: Can we arrive at a stable, reliable textual foundation for the claims of Jesus as set out in these records? The answer to this question is an unqualified Yes. Sir Frederic G. Kenyon, formerly Director and Principal Librarian of the British Museum, thus summarizes the textual advantage which the New Testament documents have over all the other manuscripts of ancient classical authors:

> In no other case is the interval of time between the composition of the book and the date of the earliest extant manuscripts so short as in that of the New Testament. The books of the New Testament were written in the latter part of the first century;

---

[7]*Introduction to Research in English Literary History* (New York: The Macmillan Company, 1952), pp. 143 ff.

the earliest extant manuscripts (trifling scraps excepted) are of the fourth century — say, from 250 to 300 years later. This may sound a considerable interval, but it is nothing to that which parts most of the great classical authors from their earliest manuscripts. We believe that we have in all essentials an accurate text of the seven extant plays of Sophocles; yet the earliest substantial manuscript upon which it is based was written more than 1400 years after the poet's death. Aeschylus, Aristophanes, and Thucydides are in the same state; while with Euripides the interval is increased to 1600 years. For Plato it may be put at 1300 years, for Demosthenes as low as 1200.[8]

But even this is not the whole story. Since the time when Kenyon wrote the above words, numerous papyri of portions of the New Testament documents have been discovered, and these, going back to end of the first century, bridge the 250- to 300-year gap of which Kenyon spoke. In evaluating these recent papyri discoveries, Kenyon concluded, shortly before his death: "The interval then between the dates of original composition and the earliest extant evidence becomes so small as to be in fact negligible, and the last foundation for any doubt that the Scriptures have come down to us substantially as they were written has now been removed. Both the *authenticity* and the *general integrity* of the books of the New Testament may be regarded as finally established."[9]

Moreover, as A. T. Robertson, the author of the most comprehensive grammar of New Testament Greek, wrote in his *Introduction to the Textual Criticism of the New Testament*:[10] "There are some 8,000 manuscripts of the Latin Vulgate and at

---

[8]*Handbook to the Textual Criticism of the New Testament* (2d ed.; London: The Macmillan Company, 1912), p. 5. See below, Appendix C, for Professor Edwin M. Yamauchi's evaluation of Kenyon's evidence.

For confirmation of these intervals between date of composition and date of earliest substantial text, together with numerous other examples, see F. W. Hall's list of "MS. Authorities for the Text of the Chief Classical Writers," in his *Companion to Classical Texts* (Oxford: Clarendon Press, 1913), pp. 199 ff.

[9]*The Bible and Archaeology* (New York and London: Harper & Row, 1940), pp. 288-89; Kenyon's italics.

[10]*Introduction to the Textual Criticism of the New Testament* (Nashville, Tenn.: Broadman Press, 1925), p. 70.

least 1,000 for the other early versions. Add over 4,000 Greek manuscripts and we have 13,000 manuscript copies of portions of the New Testament. Besides all this, much of the New Testament can be reproduced from the quotations of early Christian writers." To express skepticism concerning the resultant text of the New Testament books (as represented, for example, by Nestle's *Novum Testamentum Graece*) is to allow all of classical antiquity to slip into obscurity, for no documents of the ancient period are as well attested bibliographically as is the New Testament.

The second test of documentary attribution and authenticity is that of *internal evidence*. Here historical and literary scholarship continues to follow Aristotle's eminently just dictum that the benefit of the doubt is to be given to the document itself, not arrogated by the critic to himself.[11] This means that one must listen to the claims of the document under analysis, and not assume fraud or error unless the author disqualifies himself by contradictions or known factual inaccuracies. Thus, in the case of the Pauline letters, we must give considerable weight to their explicit claim to have been written by the Apostle. In the case of the whole gamut of New Testament documents we must regard in all seriousness their repeated asseverations that they are recording eyewitness testimony or testimony derived from equally reliable sources.

Examples could be multiplied; here are but a few: Luke's Gospel begins with words "Inasmuch as many have undertaken to compile a narrative of the things which have been accomplished among us, just as they were delivered to us by those who from the beginning were eyewitnesses and ministers of the word, it seemed good to me also, having followed all things closely for some time past, to write an orderly account for you, most excellent Theophilus, that you may know the truth concerning the things of which you have been informed" (rsv). The Fourth Gospel claims to have been written by an eyewitness to the Crucifixion. In John 19:35 the author says, "He who saw it has borne witness — his testimony is true, and he knows that he tells the truth" (rsv). I John, in its opening lines, likewise affirms eyewitness contact with Jesus: "That which was from the beginning, which we have heard, which we have seen with our eyes, which we have

---

[11]See Aristotle's *Art of Poetry* (*De Arte Poetica*), 1460b—1461b.

looked upon and touched with our hands, concerning the word of life — the life was made manifest, and we saw it, and testify to it, and proclaim to you the eternal life which was with the Father and was made manifest to us — that which we have seen and heard we proclaim also to you" (RSV).

Sometimes the internal evidence of primary historical authority is not as direct as in the above instances, but is no less decisive. For example, C. H. Turner[12] pointed out that Mark's Gospel reflects an eyewitness account of many scenes, for when the third person plural passes on to a third person singular involving Peter, we have the indirect equivalent of first person direct discourse, deriving from the Apostle. Such internal considerations, both direct and indirect, provide a weighty basis for the claim that the New Testament documents are reliable historical sources.

Thirdly, historians rely upon *external evidence* in matters of documentary authenticity or attribution. Here the question is asked: Do other historical materials confirm or deny the internal testimony provided by the documents themselves? Careful comparison of the New Testament documents with inscriptional and other independent early evidence has in the modern period confirmed their primary claims. For example, Sir William M. Ramsay, after years of painstaking archeological and geographical investigation of Luke's Gospel, rejected the negatively critical attitude to Luke taken by the 19th century Tübingen school, and concluded: "Luke's history is unsurpassed in respect of its trustworthiness."[13]

Moreover, as to the authorship and primary historical value of the Gospel accounts, exceedingly valuable confirmatory evidence comes from independent written sources. Papias, bishop of Hierapolis (*ca.* 130), writes as follows on the basis of information obtained from the "Elder" (Apostle) John (I quote from Papias, as recorded in Eusebius' *Historia ecclesiastica*, III. 39):

> The Elder used to say this also: Mark, having been the interpreter of Peter, wrote down accurately all that he [Peter] mentioned, whether sayings or doings of Christ; not, however, in order. For he was neither a hearer nor a companion of the

---

[12]*A New Commentary on Holy Scripture*, Pt. III, pp. 42-124.

[13]*The Bearing of Recent Discovery on the Trustworthiness of the New Testament* (reprint ed.; Grand Rapids, Mich.: Baker Book House, 1953), p. 81.

Lord; but afterwards, as I said, he accompanied Peter, who adapted his teachings as necessity required, not as though he were making a compilation of the sayings of the Lord. So then Mark made no mistake, writing down in this way some things as he [Peter] mentioned them; for he paid attention to this one thing, not to omit anything that he had heard, nor to include any false statement among them.

Of the Gospel according to Matthew, Papias says: "Matthew recorded the oracles in the Hebrew [i.e., Aramaic] tongue" (*ibid.*), and the acceptance the book received in the primitive Church argues strongly for its early date and historical value. McNeile and Williams write: "[Matthew's] Gospel was the first favourite in the early Church although it lacked the prestige of the two chief centers of Christendom, Rome and Ephesus; and the prestige also of the two chief apostolic names, Peter and Paul. And the strongly Judaic elements in it would have discredited it if it had appeared in the second century. All of which imply its early, widely known, and apostolic credit."[14]

Another superlative external testimony to the primacy of the Gospel accounts is provided by Irenaeus, bishop of Lyons, who writes in his *Adversus haereses*, III. 1 (*ca.* 180):

Matthew published his Gospel among the Hebrews [i.e., Jews] in their own tongue, when Peter and Paul were preaching the gospel in Rome and founding the church there. After their departure [i.e., death, which strong tradition places at the time of the Neronian persecution in 64], Mark, the disciple and interpreter of Peter, himself handed down to us in writing the substance of Peter's preaching. Luke, the follower of Paul, set down in a book the gospel preached by his teacher. Then John, the disciple of the Lord, who also leaned on his breast [this is a reference to John 13:25 and 21:20], himself produced his Gospel, while he was living at Ephesus in Asia.

The value of Irenaeus' remarks is especially great because he had been a student of Polycarp, bishop of Smyrna (martyred in 156 after being a Christian for 86 years), and Polycarp in turn had been a disciple of the Apostle John himself. Irenaeus had often heard from Polycarp the eyewitness accounts of Jesus received

---

[14]*Op. cit.*, p. 33.

from John and others who had been personally acquainted with Jesus.[15]

On the basis, then, of powerful bibliographic, internal, and external evidence, competent historical scholarship must regard the New Testament documents as deriving from the first century and as reflecting primary-source testimony concerning the person and claims of Jesus. Specifically, on the basis of such considerations as have just been set forth, present-day scholarship dates the more important New Testament materials as follows: the Pauline letters, 51-62; Mark's Gospel, 64-70; the Gospels according to Matthew and Luke, 80-85; Acts, shortly after Luke, which is really "Part One" of the two-part work; John's Gospel, no later than A.D. 100. It should be emphasized that the dates here given are in general the *latest* possible ones for the books in question. There is excellent reason for earlier dating in most cases (e.g., Luke-Acts should probably be dated prior to 64, since Paul almost certainly died in the Neronian persecution, yet Acts does not record his death). As a sensitive barometer to the current archeologically based trend toward even earlier dating of these documents, we have the statement of the world's foremost biblical archeologist, W. F. Albright (whom, incidentally, Dr. Stroll cites at one point in his lecture, but not on this issue): "In my opinion, every book of the New Testament was written by a baptized Jew between the forties and the eighties of the first century A.D. (very probably sometime between about A.D. 50 and 75)."[16]

Earlier I mentioned briefly Professor Stroll's heavy reliance upon the work of a radical school of New Testament critics, the so-called *formgeschichtliche Methode* school of Dibelius and Bultmann. We are now in a position to see why this school has been steadily losing ground in scholarly circles during the last two decades. The form critics attempt, by literary analysis, to "get behind" the New Testament documents as they have come down to us. The Gospels, for example, are assumed to be the end product of a process of oral tradition that was shaped, and freely altered, by the early Church according to its own needs — according to its *Sitz im Leben*. Remarkably enough, this approach had already been flogged to death in the history of Homeric criticism,

---

[15]See Eusebius, *H.E.*, V. 20.
[16]Quoted in an interview for *Christianity Today*, January 18, 1963.

in an attempt to "get behind" the Iliad and the Odyssey as we
have them. The result was complete chaos, for, in the absence of
any objective manuscript evidence to indicate where one "pre-
literary" source left off and another began, the critics all differed
with one another. H. J. Rose, in discussing the dreary history of
the problem in his standard *Handbook of Greek Literature from
Homer to the Age of Lucian*,[17] writes: "The chief weapon of the
separatists has always been literary criticism, and of this it is not
too much to say that such niggling word-baiting, such microscopic
hunting of minute inconsistencies and flaws in logic, has hardly
been seen, outside of the Homeric field, since Rymar and John
Dennis died."

In Dibelius, Bultmann, and company, this kind of flaw-hunting
has been seen in the New Testament field since Rose's day, but
its weaknesses are now widely recognized. Not only does the
method depend upon rationalistic presuppositions against the supernatural (as we previously indicated) and leave the gates wide
open to subjectivity of interpretation, it principally falls down
because *the time interval between the writing of the New Testament documents as we have them and the events of Jesus' life
which they record is too brief to allow for communal redaction
by the Church.*

John Drinkwater, in his *English Poetry*, has rejected this approach in the study of English ballads and, as McNeile and Williams[18] correctly note, "No Gospel section passed through such
a long period of oral tradition as did any genuine ballad." This is
not to say that New Testament writers did not ever employ
sources; we have seen that Luke expressly asserts that he did so.
But it is to say that with the small time interval between Jesus'
life and the Gospel records, the Church did not create a "Christ
of faith" out of a simple, moralistic Jesus. We know, from the
Mishna[19] that it was Jewish custom to memorize a Rabbi's teaching, for a good pupil was like a "plastered cistern that loses not a
drop"; and we can be sure that the early Church, impressed as it
was by Jesus, governed itself by this ideal. Moreover — and of this

---

[17]*Handbook of Greek Literature from Homer to the Age of Lucian*
(London: Methuen, 1934), pp. 42-43.
[18]*Op. cit.*, p. 58.
[19]*Mishna Aboth*, II. 8.

Professor Stroll particularly should take note — none of the form-critical researches has ever been successful in yielding a non-supernatural picture of Jesus, for "all parts of the gospel record are shown by these various groupings to be pervaded by a consistent picture of Jesus as the Messiah, the Son of God.[20]

In conclusion, let us hear a clear statement of the implications of the evidence which has been presented. F. F. Bruce, whom we have just quoted, is one of the foremost contemporary experts on the Dead Sea scrolls, and presently serves as Rylands Professor of Biblical Criticism and Exegesis in the University of Manchester. He writes as follows of the primary-source value of the New Testament records:

> The earliest preachers of the gospel knew the value of . . . first-hand testimony, and appealed to it time and again. "We are witnesses of these things," was their constant and confident assertion. And it can have been by no means so easy as some writers seem to think to invent words and deeds of Jesus in those early years, when so many of His disciples were about, who could remember what had and had not happened. Indeed, the evidence is that the early Christians were careful to distinguish between sayings of Jesus and their own inferences or judgments. Paul, for example, when discussing the vexed questions of marriage and divorce in I Corinthians 7, is careful to make the distinction between his own advice on the subject and the Lord's decisive ruling: "I, not the Lord," and again, "Not I, but the Lord."

> And it was not only friendly eyewitnesses that the early preachers had to reckon with; there were others less well disposed who were also conversant with the main facts of the ministry and death of Jesus. The disciples could not afford to risk inaccuracies (not to speak of willful manipulation of the facts), which would at once be exposed by those who would be only too glad to do so. On the contrary, one of the strong points in the original apostolic preaching is the confident appeal to the knowledge of the hearers; they not only said, "We are witnesses of these things," but also, "As you yourselves also know" (Acts 2:22). Had there been any tendency to depart from the facts in any material respect, the possible presence of hostile wit-

---

[20]F. F. Bruce, *The New Testament Documents* (5th ed.; London: Inter-Varsity Fellowship, 1960), p. 33.

nesses in the audience would have served as a further corrective.[21]

What, then, does a historian know about Jesus Christ? He knows, first and foremost, that the New Testament document can be relied upon to give an accurate portrait of him, and that this portrait cannot be rationalized away by wishful thinking, philosophical presuppositionalism, or literary maneuvering. What exactly that portrait delineates, and the radical consequences of it will be set out in the next chapter.

[21]*Ibid.*, pp. 45-46.

3. JESUS CHRIST AND HISTORY

Part II
The Divinity of Jesus Christ

I N THE PREVIOUS CHAPTER we confronted some exceedingly important facts concerning the historicity of the founder of Christianity. We discovered that on the basis of the accepted canons of historical method — on the basis of bibliographic, internal, and external evidence — the New Testament documents must be regarded as reliable sources of historical information. Indeed we learned that the documentary attestation for these records is so strong that a denial of their reliability necessarily carries with it total skepticism with regard to the history and literature of the classical world. We found the New Testament books to contain eyewitness testimony to the life and claims of Jesus, and to have been in circulation while friends and foes who had known Jesus were still alive and able to refute exaggerated, inaccurate, or unwarranted statements about Him.

Now if you are not inclined in the direction of Christianity — as I was not when I entered university — the most irritating aspect of the line of argumentation that I have taken is probably this: it depends in no sense on theology. It rests solely and squarely upon historical method, the kind of method all of us, whether Christians, rationalists, agnostics, or Tibetan monks, have to use in analyzing historical data. Perhaps at this point we can understand why C. S. Lewis, the great Renaissance English scholar, in describing his conversion from atheism to Christianity, writes:

> Early in 1926 the hardest boiled of all the atheists I ever knew sat in my room on the other side of the fire and remarked that the evidence for the historicity of the Gospels was really surprisingly good. "Rum thing," he went on. "All that stuff of Frazer's about the Dying God. Rum thing. It almost looks as if it had really happened once." To understand the shattering impact of it, you would need to know the man (who has certainly never since shown any interest in Christianity). If he, the cynic of cynics, the toughest of the toughs, were not as I would still have put it — "safe," where could I turn? Was there then no escape?[1]

Subsequently, says Lewis, "God closed in on me." How "God closes in" when we face the implications of historically reliable New Testament documents is the subject of this chapter. We shall first examine the picture of Jesus in the primary documents that we have already validated. Then we shall consider the great evidential event, the Resurrection, which attests the claims Jesus made for Himself and the religion which He proclaimed.

The Divine Jesus of the Primary Documents

As we noted at the beginning of the previous chapter, Jesus was especially concerned to bring His contemporaries to a sound and accurate conception of Himself. We may assume that He would want us also to arrive at a conception of Him which is consistent with His real personality. No one wants to be misunderstood; and surely it is vitally important in the case of a person such as Jesus, who has had such tremendous influence on the history of the world, that misunderstanding be eliminated at all costs.

Yet in the twentieth century there has been a powerful tendency to create Jesus in the image of the time rather than to find out what the documents say about Him. A bizarre, though in many

---

[1]*Surprised by Joy* (New York: Harcourt, Brace & World, 1955), pp. 223-24.

ways typical, example is Bruce Barton's work, which attained great popularity a generation ago, titled, *The Man Nobody Knows: A Discovery of the Real Jesus.* The title was more well chosen than Barton realized, for he clearly demonstrates that the Jesus of history is a man *he* doesn't know! Listen to representative chapter titles (they of course refer to Jesus): "The Executive," "The Outdoor Man," "The Sociable Man," "The Founder of Modern Business." It is the last appellation that the author (himself, inevitably, a business man) particularly stresses; indeed, the book's title page quotation reads: "Wist ye not that I must be about my Father's business?"

But such dehistoricizings of Jesus are by no means limited to popular literature. Ironically, professional theologians have been more responsible than almost any other people in the twentieth century for producing unhistorical Jesuses. For example, we have the evaluation of Jesus given by Walter E. Bundy, in his book, *The Religion of Jesus*:[2]

> In our modern approach to Jesus we must leave him where and how and what he was, as real as he was — human. . . . In all of his life and work Jesus placed himself on the side of humanity. Speculation only separates him from us and makes him increasingly unreal. There are very definite religious dangers in deification — dangers destructive of Christianity.

As a liberal modern of the twentieth century, Bundy paints a purely human portrait of Jesus, and warns against the dangers of regarding Him as divine. But what, in fact, *was* Jesus' like? Is He pictured in the reliable documentary sources as Barton's "business executive"? As Bundy's simple moral teacher, a Western Confucius going about giving people good advice that they didn't want anyway? Or as someone far different from the ideals of twentieth-century humanism?

To answer this question we must strike behind the welter of modern "reconstructions" of Jesus' life. We must go to the primary sources themselves. Only then will we avoid what C. S. Lewis in another work describes as the demonic creation of imaginary Jesuses. Listen to Screwtape, an elder devil, instructing his nephew on the fine art of antidocumentary temptation:

---

[2]*The Religion of Jesus* (Indianapolis, Ind. Bobbs-Merrill, 1928), p. 324.

In the last generation we promoted the construction of . . . a "historical Jesus" on liberal and humanitarian lines; we are now putting forward a new "historical Jesus" on Marxian, catastrophic, and revolutionary lines. The advantages of these constructions, which we intend to change every thirty years or so, are manifold. In the first place they all tend to direct men's devotion to something which does not exist, for each "historical Jesus" is unhistorical. The documents say what they say and cannot be added to; each new "historical Jesus" therefore has to be got out of them by suppression at one point and exaggeration at another, and by that sort of guessing (*brilliant* is the adjective we teach humans to apply to it) on which no one would risk ten shillings in ordinary life, but which is enough to produce a crop of new Napoleons, new Shakespeares, and new Swifts, in every publisher's autumn list.[3]

In going to the documents to determine the *de facto* historical picture of Jesus — as distinct from Screwtapean constructions — we should keep two important caveats in mind. First, "red-letter" Bibles notwithstanding, no attempt will be made to distinguish Jesus' conception of Himself from the New Testament writers' conceptions of Him. All efforts to make such a distinction (and radical theological scholarship has frequently aimed at this kind of separation) are pointless and doomed to failure from the outset, because Jesus' words themselves have come to us by way of the New Testament writers. The inability to distinguish Jesus' claims for Himself from the New Testament writers' claims for Him, however, should cause no dismay, since (1) the situation exactly parallels that for all historical personages who have not themselves chosen to write (e.g., Alexander the Great, Augustus Caesar, Charlemagne), and we would hardly claim that in these cases we can achieve no adequate historical portraits; (2) the New Testament writers, as we saw in our last lecture, record eyewitness testimony concerning Jesus, and can therefore be trusted to convey an accurate historical picture of Him.

A second preliminary caveat has to do with the approach we take to discovering Jesus' nature. We have no right to begin with the presupposition that Jesus can be no more than a man — for

---

[3]*The Screwtape Letters* (new ed.; London: Geoffrey Bles, Ltd., 1961), pp. 103-104.

then, obviously, our conclusions will simply reflect our preconceptions instead of representing the actual contents of the documents. We must, in other words, objectively try to discover the
Jesus of the primary historical records, whether we agree with
them or not. The question for us, it appears to me, is not whether
Jesus is pictured as a man. Virtually no one today would question
this, for the records tell us that He was hungry and tired; that
He wept; that He suffered, bled, and died — in short, that He
was indeed human. The question we today face is not whether
He was a man, but whether He was depicted as *no more than
a man*. It is instructive that the early Church had to face the
heresy of docetism, which did question Jesus' humanity — the
docetists were so impressed by the evidence for Jesus' divinity
that to them He only "seemed" (Greek, *dokein*) to be a man.
But for us humanistically orientated moderns, the divinity of Jesus is the question, and only the documents can provide the answer
to it.

   And what do the documents say? They say unequivocally and
consistently that Jesus regarded Himself as no less than God in
the flesh, and that His disciples, under the pressure of His own
words and deeds, came to regard Him in this same way. Let us
consider the prime New Testament records, in chronological
order, and follow them by a significant passage from an early
non-Biblical source.

The Letters of Paul

   We begin with the letters of Paul, since, as pointed out in the
last chapter, they are the earliest materials we possess bearing on
primitive Christianity. They date, you will remember, between A.D.
51 and 62, and are firmly wedded to the Gospel records by way of
Luke-Acts, where the stamp of approval is placed upon Paul by
the original Apostles. We can thus quote Paul without hesitation.
Baur and the Tübingen school of the nineteenth century were
totally unsuccessful in driving a wedge between Jesus and Paul,
and present-day biblical scholarship has rejected their approach
and conclusions (see J. G. Machen's classic, *The Origin of Paul's
Religion*).

   In Paul's writings the divine character of Jesus is affirmed in
three unequivocal ways. (1) Paul applies to Jesus the Greek word

kyrios ("Lord"), which was used in the pre-Christian Greek translation of the Old Testament (the "Septuagint") as the equivalent of the Hebrew name of God, *Jehovah* (better, *Yahweh* or *YHVH*).[4] Note the implications of this: Paul, a monotheistic Jew, trained under the great Rabbi Gamaliel and therefore thoroughly conversant with the Old Testament, ascribes to Jesus a word employed to render into Greek the most holy name of the one God!

Consider as an example of Paul's identification of Jesus with the God of the Old Testament the following passages:

> *Isaiah* 45:22-23
>
> Look unto me, and be ye saved, all the ends of the earth: for I am God, and there is none else. I have sworn by myself, the word is gone out of my mouth in righteousness, and shall not return, That unto me every knee shall bow, every tongue shall swear.
>
> *Philippians* 2:10-11 (RSV)
>
> . . . at the name of Jesus every knee should bow, in heaven and on earth and under the earth, and every tongue confess that Jesus Christ is Lord [*kyrios*], to the glory of God the Father.

Here Paul takes an Old Testament passage expressing in the most lofty and explicit terms the majesty and oneness of God, and applies it directly to Jesus, to whom he refers as *kyrios*. Instances of this kind can be multiplied with ease; see, for instance, II Thessalonians 1:9 (quoting Isaiah 2:10, 19, 21); I Corinthians 1:31 and II Corinthians 10:17 (quoting Jeremiah 9:23 f.); I Corinthians 10:9 (quoting Numbers 21:5 f.).[5]

(2) With the phrases "Our God and Father and our Lord Jesus Christ (I Thessalonians 3:11) and "Our Lord Jesus Christ and God our Father" (II Thessalonians 2:16), Paul uses a *singular*

---

[4] The Hebrew word *YHVH* was actually not pronounced in Old Testament times, out of reverence. Instead, the vowels for the Hebrew word "Lord" — *Adonai* — were given to it, and *Adonai* was substituted in public reading. Thus it was natural for the Hellenistic Jews who prepared the Septuagint — in Alexandria, from *ca.* 300 to *ca.* 100 B.C. — to use *kyrios* in rendering into Greek the Hebrew *YHVH*. (For another view of this linguistic point, see C. S. Lewis' letter — Appendix B.)

[5] See also the composite work, *Who Say Ye That I Am?*, ed. W. C. Robinson (Grand Rapids, Mich.: Wm. B. Eerdmans, 1949), pp. 133 ff.

verb. This makes patently clear that for him, Jesus and the God of the Old Testament were conceived of as an essential unity. This conclusion is made even stronger (if that were possible!) by the fact that both phrases appear in *prayers;* thus Paul believed that prayer could be directed indiscriminately to God the Father or Jesus.

(3) Paul held that Jesus would reappear as divine judge at the end of the age (II Thessalonians 1:7-10):

> . . . the Lord Jesus shall be revealed from heaven with his mighty angels, in flaming fire taking vengeance on them that know not God, and that obey not the gospel of our Lord Jesus Christ: Who shall be punished with everlasting destruction from the presence of the Lord, and from the glory of his power; when he shall come to be glorified in his saints, and to be admired in all them that believe (because our testimony among you was believed) in that day.

The Gospels

Next let us look at the earliest of the four Gospels, Mark, which was written no later than A.D. 64-70 by a companion of the Apostle Peter. At the very outset of this book Mark makes clear beyond all shadow of doubt that Jesus should be personally identified with the God of the Old Testament. He writes:

> The beginning of the gospel of Jesus Christ, the Son of God. As it is written in the prophets, "Behold, I send my messenger before thy face, who shall prepare thy way; the voice of one crying in the wilderness: Prepare the way of the Lord, make his paths straight" (RSV, with marginal reading).

Here Mark has quoted Malachi 3:1, but with a highly significant alteration. The prophetic verse reads: "Behold, I [Jehovah] will send my messenger, and he shall prepare *the way before me.*" But Mark changes the verse so that it reads "he shall prepare *thy way,*" i.e., Jesus' way. Mark is saying, in other words, that when the God of the prophets spoke of preparing for *His own* coming, he was speaking of the preparation for *Jesus'* coming; or, putting it as simply as possible, Jesus *is* the God of the prophets.

This affirmation, which in the Greek text of Mark stands like a red flare at the beginning of the book, is confirmed again and again throughout the book. In chapter 2, Jesus forgives sin — and the scribes recognize, correctly, that He is blaspheming if He is not God, for only God can forgive sins.

> And when he returned to Capernaum after some days, it was reported that he was at home. And many were gathered together, so that there was no longer room for them, not even about the door; and he was preaching the word to them. And they came, bringing to him a paralytic carried by four men. And when they could not get near him because of the crowd, they removed the roof above him; and when they had made an opening, they let down the pallet on which the paralytic lay. And when Jesus saw their faith, he said to the paralytic, "My son, your sins are forgiven." Now some of the scribes were sitting there, questioning in their hearts, "Why does this man speak thus? It is blasphemy! Who can forgive sins but God alone?" And immediately Jesus, perceiving in his spirit that they thus questioned within themselves, said to them, "Why do you question thus in your hearts? Which is easier, to say to the paralytic, 'Your sins are forgiven,' or to say, 'Rise, take up your pallet and walk'? But that you may know that the Son of man has authority on earth to forgive sins" — he said to the paralytic — "I say to you, rise, take up your pallet and go home." And he rose, and immediately took up the pallet and went out before them all; so that they were all amazed and glorified God, saying, "We never saw anything like this!" (RSV)

But is Jesus not perhaps regarding Himself simply as the man with special privileges? Does He not use the expression "Son of man"? This expression, which humanists have often appealed to as equivalent to "representative humanity" is really one of the loftiest ascriptions given to God's Messiah in the Old Testament (see Daniel 7:13). Jesus expressly applies this imagery to Himself at His trial, and brings upon Himself condemnation for — let it be noted — blasphemy (Mark 14:61-64):

> Again the high priest asked him, "Are you the Christ, the Son of the Blessed?" And Jesus said, "I am; and you will see the Son of man sitting at the right hand of Power, and coming with the clouds of heaven." And the high priest tore his mantle, and said, "Why do we still need witnesses? You have heard his blasphemy. What is your decision?" And they all condemned him as deserving death (RSV).

Although not much good can be said about the high priest at this kangaroo court, this much is certain: he correctly recognized that Jesus was claiming to be no less than God incarnate, and if He was not what He claimed, then He was a blasphemer.

The Gospels according to Matthew (the Apostle) and Luke (a physician who accompanied Paul on his missionary journeys) were written no later than A.D. 80-85. (Albright would say probably before 75), and they present the same divine-human picture of Jesus given in Mark. The Virgin Birth account in these two Gospels is unequivocal. Even though the Hebrew word *almah* in the Isaiah prophecy can mean "young woman" as well as "virgin," the Greek *parthenos* employed in Matthew and Luke must mean "virgin." As Karl Barth has correctly noted, the Virgin Birth demonstrates that God the Father uniquely entered history in Jesus, and was the active agent in His advent. Moreover, the, Jesus of these Gospels makes absolute claims for Himself that are unthinkable apart from deity. For example, in Matthew 10:32-33, 39, Jesus says:

> So every one who acknowledges me before men, I also will acknowledge before my Father who is in heaven; but whoever denies me before men, I also will deny before my Father who is in heaven. . . . He who finds his life will lose it, and he who loses his life for my sake will find it (RSV).

Jesus states His divine life-purpose as follows: "The Son of man came . . . to give his life a ransom for many" (Matthew 20:28), and this assertion is also integral to Mark's Gospel (Mark 10:45). Jesus' last words in the Gospel according to Matthew (28:18-20) are also consonant only with deity, for they ascribe to Him the divine attributes of omnipotence and omnipresence and place Him on the same plane as the Father:

> And Jesus came and spake unto them, saying, All power is given unto me in heaven and in earth. Go ye therefore, and teach all nations, baptizing them in the name of the Father, and of the Son, and of the Holy Ghost: Teaching them to observe all things whatsoever I have commanded you: and, lo, I am with you alway, even unto the end of the world.

In the Book of Acts, written by Luke, Paul is converted to Christianity in the recognition, on the Damascus road, that Jesus

WHERE IS HISTORY GOING?

is *kyrios* (Acts 9:5). The entire Apostolic preaching (as C. H. Dodd has so effectively pointed out) centers on the Lordship of Jesus. "What must I do to be saved?" is the question. "Believe on the Lord Jesus and you shall be saved" is the consistent answer (cf. Acts 16:30-31). Indeed, "there is salvation in no one else, for there is no other name under heaven given among men by which we must be saved" (Acts 4:12, RSV).

The Fourth Gospel is thoroughly Christocentric, and identifies the eternal Father with the historic Jesus at every point. The Prologue affirms Jesus' pre-existence and eternal oneness with God. The *egō eimi* ("I am") sayings ("I am the light, bread," etc.) allude to the "I am that I am" revelations of the God of the Old Testament (see Exodus 3:14).[6] Salvation occurs only through Jesus; He says in John 14:6 (RSV), "I am the way, and the truth, and the life; no one comes to the Father, but by me." And the numerous miracle-signs (*sēmeia*) performed by Jesus in this Gospel, culminating in the Great Sign — the Resurrection, are recorded "that you may believe that Jesus is the Christ, the Son of God and that believing you may have life in his name" (John 20:31, RSV). Indeed the Gospel reaches its climax with the "doubting Thomas" incident, in which Thomas is confronted by the resurrected Jesus and confesses, "My Lord and my God!" (*ho kyrios mou kai ho theos mou*), John 20:28. This picture of Jesus in John's Gospel is especially meaningful when we remember that the apostolic authorship of the book is attested by Irenaeus, who knew Polycarp, a disciple of John himself.

Thus a consistent portrait of Jesus emerges from the earliest New Testament documents: a divine portrait of One who could say, "He who has seen me has seen the Father" (John 14:9, RSV). And this is how Christians from the earliest days have regarded Him. In the very first description of Christian worship from the pen of a non-Christian we read: "On an appointed day they [Christians] were accustomed to meet before daybreak, and to recite a hymn antiphonally to Christ, as to God." This significant passage comes from a letter written *ca.* A.D. 112 by the governor of Bithynia, Pliny the Younger, to the Emperor Trajan

---

[6]Incidentally, there is almost certainly an etymological connection between the Hebrew name of God, YHVH, and the Hebrew verb "am" — HYH; cf. with Exodus 3:14 the parallel verse, Exodus 6:3.

(Epis. X, xcvi). From that day to this all Christians — Eastern Orthodox, Roman Catholic, and Protestant — have worshiped Christ as God on the basis of the historically impeccable testimony of Jesus' own followers and of those who knew them intimately.

The Jesus of the primary documents, then, is one hundred and eighty degrees removed from the "business man" of Barton, the humanistic moralist of Bundy, the catastrophic reformer of the Marxists, and from all other twentieth-century attempts to create Him in the image of cultural idealism. We may not like the Jesus of the historical documents. But like Him or not, we meet Him there as a divine being on whom our personal destiny, both in time and in eternity, depends.

JESUS: CHARLATAN, LUNATIC, OR GOD?
THE NEW TESTAMENT WRITERS: EXAGGERATORS OR HISTORIANS?

Now we have reached the point where an interpretation of the documentary picture of Jesus becomes mandatory. Granted that the documents portray a divine Christ; was He *in fact* divine? Logically, if Jesus was *not* divine, as the records unequivocally claim He was, then we are reduced to three, and only three, interpretations of the data, namely,

1. Jesus claimed to be the Son of God but knew He was not; i.e., He was a charlatan;

2. Jesus thought He was the Son of God, but actually He was not; i.e., He was a lunatic;

3. Jesus never actually claimed to be the Son of God, though His disciples put this claim in His mouth; i.e., the disciples were charlatans, lunatics, or naive exaggerators.

I believe that a careful consideration of these three interpretations will show that no one of them is consonant with history, psychology, or reason, and that therefore, by process of elimination, we are brought to an affirmation of Jesus' deity not only as a claim, but also as a fact.

The idea of Jesus as a charlatan — as an intentional deceiver who claimed to be something He knew He was not — has never had much appeal, even among fanatical anti-religionists. Jesus' high ethical teachings and noble personal character have made such an interpretation improbable in the extreme. W. E. H. Lecky, the great nineteenth-century historian and certainly no believer in revealed religion, spoke thus of Jesus in his *History of European Morals from Augustus to Charlemagne*:[7] "The character of Jesus has not only been the highest pattern of virtue, but the strongest incentive to its practice, and has exerted so deep an influence, that it may be truly said, that the simple record of three short years of active life has done more to regenerate and to soften mankind, than all the disquisitions of philosophers and than all the exhortations of moralists."

This judgment has been echoed thousands of times through the centuries by men of all, or no, religious persuasions. Is it possible that such a Jesus would have committed one of the most basic moral errors of all — allowing the end to justify the means — and based His entire life and ethical teachings upon a colossal lie as to His real nature? He was at pains to convince the men of His time that the devil is a liar and the father of lies, and that those who lie are the devil's children (John 8:44). Would He Himself then have lied concerning the essence of His own character and purpose? To answer anything but an unqualified No is to renounce all sound ethical judgment.

But perhaps Jesus' claims to deity and messiahship had their source not in intentional deception, but in Jesus' honest misunderstanding of His nature? This is the position taken by Schweitzer in 1906 (not 1910, *contra* Dr. Stroll) in his *Quest of the Historical Jesus*, a work which was epochal because of its recognition of the eschatological character of Jesus' message, but which is almost universally regarded by New Testament scholars today as setting out a "historical Jesus" who reflects Schweitzer's own rationalistic presuppositions.

Now it is of real interest that Schweitzer felt it necessary to vindicate his Jesus (who misunderstood His own nature) from the charge of psychiatric illness. Schweitzer's *Psychiatric Study of Jesus* (his Strasbourg M.D. dissertation of 1913) is a herculean, but ineffective attempt to show that the purely human Jesus could be sane and yet think of Himself as the eschatological Son of man

---

[7]*History of European Morals from Augustus to Charlemagne*, II (2d ed.; London: Longmans, Green, 1869), p. 88.

who would come again at the end of the age, with the heavenly host, to judge the world. In actuality, as Dr. Winfred Overholser, past president of the American Psychiatric Association, has noted in his Foreword to the latest English edition of Schweitzer's thesis, Schweitzer has not ruled out paranoia in the case of a purely human Jesus: "Some paranoids manifest ideas of grandeur almost entirely, and we find patients whose grandeur is very largely of a religious nature, such as their belief that they are directly instructed by God to convert the world or perform miracles."[8]

The fact is that we simply cannot avoid the conclusion that Jesus was deranged if He thought of Himself as God incarnate and yet was not. Noyes and Kolb, in the latest (5th) edition of their standard medical test, *Modern Clinical Psychiatry*,[9] characterize the schizophrenic as one whose behavior becomes autistic rather than realistic, one who allows himself to "retreat from the world of reality." What greater retreat from reality than a belief in one's divinity if one is not in fact God? I know that this audience would immediately summon the "men in white coats" if I — or anyone else — seriously made the claims for himself that Jesus did! Yet, in view of the eminent soundness of Jesus' teachings, few have been able to give credence to the idea of mental aberration in Him. Indeed, the psychiatrist J. T. Fisher has asserted recently what many others have been implicitly convinced of:

> If you were to take the sum total of all authoritative articles ever written by the most qualified of psychologists and psychiatrists on the subject of mental hygiene — if you were to combine them and refine them and cleave out the excess verbiage — if you were to take the whole of the meat and none of the parsley, and if you were to have these unadulterated bits of pure scientific knowledge concisely expressed by the most capable of living poets, you would have an awkward and incomplete summation of the Sermon on the Mount. And it would suffer immeasurably through comparison. For nearly two thousand years the Christian world has been holding in its hands the complete answer to its restless and fruitless yearnings. Here

---

[8]*The Psychiatric Study of Jesus* (Boston: Beacon Press, 1958), p. 15.
[9]*Modern Clinical Psychiatry* (Philadelphia and London: Saunders, 1958), p. 401.

. . . rests the blueprint for successful human life with optimum mental health and contentment.[10]

But one cannot very well have it both ways. If Jesus' teachings provide "the blueprint for successful human life with optimum mental health," then the teacher cannot be a lunatic who totally misunderstands the nature of his own personality. Note the absolute dichotomy: if the documentary records of Jesus' life are accurate, and Jesus was not a charlatan, then He was either God incarnate as He claimed, or a psychotic. If we cannot take the latter alternative (and, considering its consequences, who really can follow this path to its logical conclusion?), we must arrive at a Jesus who claimed to be God incarnate simply because *He was God.*

Messianic Expectations

But, is there not a third way of escaping the horns of this dilemma? Could not Jesus' followers have painted a false portrait of Him — out of an intentional or unintentional desire to put Him in the best possible light? This, you will remember, is Professor Stroll's main contention: that a "messianic fever" pervaded the Jews under first-century Roman domination, and led some of them to deify Jesus of Nazareth. This interpretation, though perhaps superficially plausible, has no more to commend it than the interpretations we have just considered. It falls down on three decisive counts. (1) All types of Jewish messianic speculation at the time were at variance with the messianic picture Jesus painted of Himself, so He was a singularly poor candidate for deification. (2) The apostles and evangelists were psychologically, ethically, and religiously incapable of performing such a deification. (3) The historical evidence for Christ's Resurrection — the great attesting event for His claims to deity — could not have been manufactured. Let us take up each of these considerations in turn.

In order for the Jews of Jesus' time to have messianized Him, it would have been necessary for Jesus' teachings and conception of Himself to accord with the main outlines of the messianic hope held by His contemporaries. However, in all essential points this

---

[10]J. T. Fisher and L. S. Hawley, *A Few Buttons Missing* (Philadelphia: J. B. Lippincott, 1951), p. 273.

was not the case. Consider, for example, Jesus' attitude toward the Gentiles. Edersheim, late Grinfield Lecturer on the Septuagint at Oxford, writes in his *Sketches of Jewish Social Life in the Days of Christ*:[11]

> In view of all this [first-century Jewish antipathy toward the heathen in Palestine], what an almost incredible truth must it have seemed, when the Lord Jesus Christ proclaimed it among Israel as the object of His coming and kingdom, not to make of the Gentiles Jews, but of both alike children of one Heavenly Father; not to rivet upon the heathen the yoke of the law, but to deliver from it Jew and Gentile, or rather to fulfil its demands for all! The most unexpected and unprepared-for revelation, from the Jewish point of view, was that of the breaking down of the middle wall of partition between Jew and Gentile, the taking away of the enmity of the law, and the nailing it to His cross. There was nothing analogous to it; not a hint of it to be found, either in the teaching or the spirit of the times. Quite the opposite. Assuredly, the most unlike thing to Christ were His times.

The great Jewish scholar S. W. Baron, in his widely-acclaimed *Social and Religious History of the Jews*[12] presents a detailed discussion of "Messianic Expectations" at the time of Jesus. He writes that "Zealot activists expected the redeemer to appear sword in hand and to lead the people against Rome's military power"; that "most apocalyptic visionaries, on the other hand, expected redemption in the shape of a cosmic cataclysm, out of which would emerge a new world with the chosen people marching toward final salvation at the head of a transformed mankind"; and that even those with "less high-flown expectations" were convinced that messiah would bring back "the remnants of the lost Ten Tribes" and reunite Israel and Judah. Does this sound like the Jesus of the documents, who said, "My kingdom is not of this world"? Baron regards Jesus "as an essentially Pharisaic Jew,"[13] but the primary records present the Pharisees as His chief oppo-

---

[11]*Sketches of Jewish Social Life in the Days of Christ* (reprint ed.; Grand Rapids, Mich.: Wm. B. Eerdmans, 1957), pp. 28-29.
[12]*Social and Religious History of the Jews*, II (2d ed.; New York: Columbia University Press, 1952), pp. 58ff.
[13]*Ibid.*, p. 67.

nents. He continually set Himself above the law and refused to be bound by the legalistic traditions of the Pharisees.

As for the party of the Sadducees, no one would argue that common ground existed between Jesus and them, for they were rationalistically inclined (they denied the general resurrection of the body, the existence of angels, etc.), and though mutual hate and mistrust colored the relations between Pharisees and Sadducees, both parties were so disturbed by Jesus that they united against Him (Matthew 16:1, etc.). The single fact that official Jewry crucified Jesus for blasphemy is sufficient ground for rejecting the idea that Jesus fulfilled the messianic dreams of the time!

But what about the Essene sect of the Dead Sea scrolls, to which Professor Stroll makes reference? Millar Burrows and F. F. Bruce, among other experts on the scrolls, have shown beyond question that the Essene conception of a "Teacher of Righteousness" differed in all essential points from Jesus' messianic views. Burrows demonstrates among other things that "there is no hint of a pre-existent Messiah in the Qumran texts"; that "nowhere is there a suggestion of anything miraculous in the birth of the teacher of righteousness"; that "the saving efficacy of the death of Christ has no parallel in the beliefs of the covenanters concerning either the teacher of righteousness or the coming Messiah" (indeed, that "the idea of a suffering Messiah . . . was known at all in Judaism at that time is a debatable question"). Moreover, since the teacher of righteousness was not believed to rise from the dead until the general resurrection at the end of the age, whereas Jesus was believed to have risen directly following His crucifixion, "what for the community of Qumran was at most a hope was for the Christians an accomplished fact, the guarantee of all their hopes."

Burrows goes on to show that "the term which Jesus most commonly used in referring to Himself ['Son of man'] is one that does not occur at all in the Qumran literature as a Messianic designation," and — what is perhaps most significant of all — "there is no indication that the teacher of righteousness was considered divine in any sense."[14] To argue, then, that Jesus was deified or

---

[14]*More Light on the Dead Sea Scrolls* (New York: Viking Press, 1958), pp. 65-73. See also F. F. Bruce's *Second Thoughts on the Dead Sea Scrolls* (London: Paternoster Press, 1956), *passim*.

messianized because He fulfilled Essene messianic expectation is completely impossible on any historical ground.

Note the point to which we have arrived: if anyone deified Jesus, it must have been His own disciples — against the entire pressure of first-century Jewish ideology. But, as Burrows correctly states: "Jesus was so unlike what all Jews expected the son of David to be that his own disciples found it almost impossible to connect the idea of the Messiah with him."[15] And even when they did become convinced that He was God's anointed, could they have deified Him without cause? R. T. Herford, in discussing "The Influence of Judaism upon Jews from Hillel to Mendelssohn"[16] says: "The Jewish religion throughout the whole of the period is based upon two main principles, the assertion of the undivided unity of God and the paramount duty of obedience to His declared Will." Would then the disciples and followers of Jesus — steeped in the Jewish faith — have deified a mere man, thereby contradicting the central tenet of the Jewish faith, that "thou shalt have no other gods before me"?

Furthermore, were these early followers of Jesus psychologically or temperamentally capable of carrying out such a deification process? Certainly they — no more than Jesus Himself — were charlatans or psychotics. The picture of them we find in the documents is one of practical, ordinary people — down-to-earth fishermen, hardheaded tax gatherers, etc. — and people with perhaps more than the usual dose of skepticism (think of Peter returning to his old way of life after Jesus' death, and "doubting" Thomas). Hardly the kind of men to be swept off their feet into mass hallucination of technicolor proportions!

What did finally and irrevocably convince the followers of Jesus that He was the one He claimed to be, God incarnate? What transformed them from a shocked and broken group after the crucifixion to a company that preached Jesus' message of salvation up and down the Roman world until the empire itself, and with it the Western world, became Christian? The answer lies in the Resurrection, and a brief discussion of it will conclude our presentation.

---

[15]*Op. cit.*, p. 68.
[16]In the Oxford *Legacy of Israel* (Oxford: Clarendon Press, 1928), p. 103.

The Resurrection

Jesus was crucified in Jerusalem during the high festival of the Jewish religious year — the Passover. The city was teeming with people, and because of the involvement of mobs in the quasi-legal proceedings, it is clear that the public was well aware of what was transpiring. Owing to the fact that Jesus had claimed that He would rise again after three days, and indeed had pointed to this event as the final proof of His claims to deity (Matthew 12:38-40; John 2:18-22), the Jewish religious leaders made certain that guards were stationed at the tomb to prevent the disciples from stealing Jesus' body and maintaining that He had actually risen. However, according to the documents, Jesus did rise — bodily — and was seen again and again over a forty-day period, until He publicly ascended into heaven. The appearances are recorded with clinical detail (for example Luke 24:36-43, NEB; John 20:25-28, RSV):

> As they [the disciples] were talking . . . , there he was, standing among them. Startled and terrified, they thought they were seeing a ghost. But he said, "Why are you so perturbed? Why do questionings arise in your minds? Look at my hands and feet. It is I myself. Touch me and see; no ghost has flesh and bones as you can see that I have." They were still unconvinced, still wondering, for it seemed too good to be true. So he asked them, "Have you anything here to eat?" They offered him a piece of fish they had cooked, which he took and ate before their eyes.

> The other disciples told him [Thomas], "We have seen the Lord." But he said to them, "Unless I see in his hands the prints of the nails, and place my finger in the mark of the nails, and place my hand in his side, I will not believe." Eight days later, his disciples were again in the house, and Thomas was with them. The doors were shut, but Jesus came and stood among them, and said, "Peace be with you." Then he said to Thomas, "Put your finger here, and see my hands; and put out your hand, and place it in my side; do not be faithless, but believing." Thomas answered him, "My Lord and my God!"

The records leave no doubt that the writers were well aware of the distinction between myth and fact, and that they were proclaiming the Resurrection as fully factual. "We," they write, "have not followed cunningly devised fables, when we made known to you the power and coming of our Lord Jesus Christ, but were eyewitnesses of his majesty" (II Peter 1:16). The facticity of the Resurrection provided the disciples with the final proof of the truth of Jesus' claim to deity. It provides the historian with the only adequate explanation for the conquering power of Christianity after the death of its founder. False messiahs of the time fell into obscurity because they could not back up their claims. For example, Theudas in A.D. 44 promised a crowd that he would divide the waters of the Jordan river, and in 52-54 an unnamed "Egyptian" messiah gathered a crowd of 30,000 Jews and said that at his command the walls of Jerusalem would fall down — but both incidents ended in ignominious failure, accompanied by bloodshed at the hands of the Roman soldiery.[17] Christianity, however, flourished as a result of Jesus' *attested* claim to conquer the powers of death.

But can the modern man accept a "miracle" such as the Resurrection? The answer is a surprising one: The Resurrection has to be accepted by us just *because* we are modern men — men living in the Einsteinian-relativistic age. For us, unlike people of the Newtonian epoch, the universe is no longer a tight, safe, predictable playing field in which we know all the rules. Since Einstein, no modern has had the right to rule out the possibility of events because of prior knowledge of "natural law." The only way we can know whether an event *can* occur is to see whether in fact it *has* occurred. The problem of "miracles," then, must be solved in the realm of historical investigation, not in the realm of philosophical speculation. And note that a historian, in facing an alleged "miracle," is really facing nothing new. All historical events are unique, and the test of their facticity can only be the accepted documentary approach that we have followed here. No historian has a right to a closed system of natural causation, for as the Cornell logician Max Black has shown in a recent essay, the very concept of cause is "a peculiar, unsystematic, and erratic notion," and therefore "any attempt to state a 'universal law of causation' must prove futile."[18]

---

[17]Josephus, *Jewish War*, II, 13, 4.259; *Antiquities*, XX, 8, 6.170.

[18]*Models and Metaphors* (Ithaca, N.Y.: Cornell University Press, 1962), p. 169.

As Ethelbert Stauffer, the Erlangen historian, puts it: "What do we do [as historians] when we experience surprises which run counter to all our expectations, perhaps all our convictions and even our period's whole understanding of truth? We say as one great historian used to say in such instances: 'It is surely possible.' And why not? For the critical historian nothing is impossible."[19] If the Resurrection did occur — and the evidence for it is tremendous — then we cannot rule it out because we are unable to "explain" it by an a priori causal schema. Rather, we must go to the One who rose to find the explanation — and His explanation, though we may not like it, is that only God Himself, the Lord of life, could conquer the powers of death.

Of course, attempts have been made to "explain" the Resurrection accounts naturalistically. The German rationalist Venturini suggested in all seriousness that Jesus only fainted on the Cross, and subsequently revived in the cool tomb. This "swoon theory" is typical of all such arguments: they are infinitely more improbable than the Resurrection itself, and they fly squarely in the face of the documentary evidence. Jesus surely died on the Cross, for Roman crucifixion teams knew their business — they had enough practice! He could not possibly have rolled the heavy boulder from the door of the tomb after the crucifixion experience. And even if we discounted these immense improbabilities, what happened to Him later?

And if we agree that He died and was interred, then the occasionally alleged "explanation" that the body was stolen is no more helpful. For who would have taken it? Surely not the Romans or the Jewish parties, for they wished at all costs to squelch the Christian sect. And certainly not the Christians, for to do so and then fabricate detailed accounts of Jesus' Resurrection would have been to fly in the face of the ethic their master preached and for which they ultimately died. As J. V. Langmead Casserley pointed out in his 1951 Maurice Lectures at King's College, London, the attempts to explain away the Resurrection well demonstrate that "the assertion of the Resurrection is like a knife pointed at the throat of the irreligious man, and an irreligious

---

[19]*Jesus and His Story* (New York: Alfred A. Knopf, 1960), p. 17.

man whose irreligion is threatened will fight for his own creation, his most precious possession, like a tigress fighting for her cubs."[20]
Note well that when the disciples of Jesus proclaimed the Resurrection, they did so as eyewitnesses and they did so while people were still alive who had had contact with the events they spoke of. In A.D. 56 Paul wrote that over 500 people had seen the risen Jesus and that most of them were still alive (I Corinthians 15:1 ff.). It passes the bounds of credibility that the early Christians could have manufactured such a tale and then preached it among those who might easily have refuted it simply by producing the body of Jesus.[21] The conclusion? Jesus did rise, and thereby validated His claim to divinity. He was neither charlatan nor lunatic, and His followers were not fable-mongers; they were witnesses to the incarnation of God, and Jesus was the God to whom they witnessed.

A HISTORIAN'S APPEAL

Today, especially in university circles, agnosticism has become immensely fashionable. The days of the hidebound atheist appear to be past, but his agnostic replacement is in many ways even farther from the intellectual mainline. The atheist at least has recognized the necessity of taking a position on matters ultimate; the agnostic, however, frequently makes a demi-god out of indecision. In actuality — as Heidegger, Sartre, and other contemporary existentialists stress — all life is decision, and no man can sit on the fence. To do so is really to make a decision — a decision against decision. Historians, and indeed all of us, must make decisions constantly, and the only adequate guide is probability (since absolute certainly lies only in the realms of pure logic and mathematics, where, by definition, one encounters no matters of fact at all).[22] In these two chapters I have tried to show that the weight of historical probability lies on the side of the validity of Jesus' claim to be God incarnate, the Saviour of man, and the coming Judge of the world. If probability does in fact support

---

[20]*The Retreat from Christianity in the Modern World* (London: Longmans, Green, 1952), p. 82.
[21]See Frank Morison, *Who Moved the Stone?* (new ed.; London: Faber & Faber, 1944), *passim*.
[22]For elaboration on this point see below, chapters 7 and 8.

these claims (and can we really deny it, having studied the evidence?), then we must act in behalf of them. When Jesus said that He would spue the lukewarm out of His mouth, (Revelation 3:16), He was saying that action on His claims is mandatory. "He who is not with me is against me," He plainly taught.

And how do we act in behalf of His claims? In just one way. We come to the point of acknowledging that the ultimate problems of our existence, such as death and the self-centeredness that gives death its sting, can only be solved in His presence. We look away from ourselves to His death and Resurrection for the answers to our deepest needs. We put ourselves into His hands.

What is the result of such a personal commitment to the risen Christ? I can myself attest to it. *Freedom* — for the servant of Christ is slave to no man. In a fearfully changing world, he is solidly grounded in an unchanging Christ, and therefore is free to develop his capacities to the fullest, under God. If, again to use C. S. Lewis' words,[23] God has "closed in on you," why not let the gap be closed entirely? As Pascal so well put it, you have nothing to lose and everything to gain.

---

[23]See above, at the beginning of this chapter. For a comment by Lewis himself on these two chapters of "Jesus Christ and History," see Appendix B.

4 THE CHRISTIAN CHURCH IN McNEILL'S Rise of the West[1]

THE WRITING of universal history is an appallingly difficult task, and the ever-mounting tide of specialized monographs in the subject- and area-divisions of the historical field renders the generalist's life more difficult daily. Thus the publication of a global history by a reputable historian is an event of no mean importance. And when the work receives high acclaim from the author's own professional peers,[2] a veritable obligation is imposed upon the

---

[1]An invitational paper presented at the meeting of Evangelical Historians, held conjointly with the 79th Annual Meeting of the American Historical Association, Washington, D.C., December 28, 1964. Professor McNeill was honored guest.

[2]Reviews of *The Rise of the West* have in general been expansively commendatory. Toynbee has called it "the most lucid presentation of world history in narrative form that I know." L. S. Stavrianos of Northwestern University holds that McNeill "has demonstrated that world history is a viable and intellectually respectable field of study" (*American Historical Review*, LXIX [April, 1964], 715). British historian H. R. Trevor-Roper affirms that *The Rise of the West* is "not only the most learned and the most intelligent, it is also the most stimulating and fascinating book that has ever set out to recount and explain the whole history of mankind" (*The New York Times Book Review*, October 6, 1961, p. 1). Carter Jefferson of Rutgers calls the book "a monumental work" (*Chicago*

world of scholarship to examine it with the greatest of interest and care.

The present essay approaches *The Rise of the West* from the standpoint of Christian church history. No particular justification for such a treatment appears necessary, since few would deny that the church has loomed large in the general history of the West. If Professor McNeill is right in his over-all contention that " 'The Rise of the West' may serve as a shorthand description of the upshot of the human community to date,"[3] it should be of more than passing interest to see what role the church plays in his account of the development of this human community.

In order to prevent the discussion from degenerating to the specialist-versus-generalist level — as illustrated by the numerous tiresome critiques of Toynbee which have often proved only the tautology that no one can know everything about everything — we shall focus attention on two major and highly significant problem-areas: the origin of the church, and the subsequent development and influence of it. In the course of analyzing McNeill's approach in each of these spheres, a running critique will be offered. Having dealt in brief with particular issues, we shall attempt to isolate the general presuppositions that have influenced the total view of the church found in *The Rise of the West*. Some concluding remarks will then be in order concerning aprioristic options in the treatment of church history, and concerning the valuable lessons Christian historians can learn from McNeill's *magnum opus*.

Sunday Tribune Magazine of Books, September 8, 1963, p. 2). The most negative evaluation comes from M. I. Finley, a specialist in classical history, who argues that McNeill's treatment of Greek culture is badly wide of the mark (*New York Review of Books*, October 17, 1963, pp. 4-5). This is, however, a rather poor point of attack since McNeill's magisterial speciality was Greek historiography — and another reviewer, the historical generalist Carroll Quigley of Georgetown University, finds McNeill's treatment of "the rise of the Greeks brilliant" — the highpoint of his book! (*Saturday Review*, XLVI [August 24, 1963], 41-42).

[3]William H. McNeill, *The Rise of the West: A History of the Human Community* (Chicago: University of Chicago Press, 1963), p. 807. Hereafter *The Rise of the West* will be designated in the notes as *RW*.

PROFESSOR MCNEILL ON THE CHURCH'S ORIGIN[4]

Four pages in the 807-page text of *The Rise of the West* are devoted to the historic origin of the Christian religion in conjunction with the life and work of Jesus and the apostolic community."[5] The most noticeable characteristic of this brief treatment is its contextual location: the beginnings of Christianity are subsumed under a more general heading, "Religion," which covers the origins of the several major faiths that manifested the "high cultural tradition" of McNeill's "Eurasian Ecumene." Thus one finds parallel discussions of the rise of Christianity, Mahayana Buddhism, and Hinduism. Ostensively common elements among these three religions receive particular emphasis, while apparent differences are generally introduced as exceptions to the more obvious common characteristics. Thus, discussion of the "resemblances" between the religions precedes individual treatment of them. In this background discussion, though mention is made of Christianity's theoretically uncompromising monotheism and "pervasive historicity of outlook" (in contrast to the Indian faiths), the thrust of the presentation is the argument that Christianity, Mahayana Buddhism, and Hinduism "agreed in defining the goal of all human life as salvation," shaped an egalitarian ideal, and proclaimed "a savior God who was both a person and at the same time universal in his nature."

In *The Rise of the West*, therefore, the origin of Christianity is not discussed as a unique problem: it is regarded as one aspect of a more general religious phenomenon. The causal source of such religious manifestations as Christianity is not primarily sought in the religious realm itself; rather, other features of the historical

---

[4]An apology is doubtless warranted at the outset for the negative tone which will characterize much of the critical material in this and the following sections — particularly since Professor McNeill and I are alumni of two of the same universities (Cornell and Chicago) and since during the years I served as a history department chairman in a university, I regularly and shamelessly cribbed lecture material from his admirable *History Handbook* (rev. ed.; Chicago: University of Chicago Press Syllabus Division, 1958)! My only explanation (not excuse) is that the vital importance of the subject under discussion demands a bit of the traditional *rabies historicorum* (if not of the more terrible *rabies theologorum*).

[5]*RW*, pp. 340-44.

drama are relied upon to make Christian religious beginnings understandable:

> Important resemblances between Christianity, Mahayana Buddhism, and Hinduism may be attributed to borrowings back and forth among previously more or less independent and isolated religious traditions. But parallel invention should not be ruled out, for if the social and psychological circumstances of the submerged peoples and urban lower classes were in fact approximately similar in all parts of western Asia, we should expect to find close parallels among the religious movements which arose and flourished in such milieux.[6]

Here we see that, for McNeill, "social and psychological circumstances" in the Eurasian Ecumene constitute the essential explanatory backdrop for the religious movements, including Christianity, that originated there. Thus it becomes clear that the beginnings of Christianity are treated in *The Rise of the West* as a special case and illustration of the author's over-all thesis, well summed up by Stavrianos: "McNeill's approach is based on the propositions that human history is more than the sum of the histories of the separate civilizations, that there is a cohesion transcending peoples and continents, and that this cohesion arises from cultural diffusion."[7] Toynbee's syncretic approach to the "Higher Religions" has always stood in tension with his attempts to isolate the individual civilizations related to them; McNeill displays more consistency in maintaining an ecumenical attitude to religious origins on the basis of an ecumenical philosophy of world history.

Having opted for general social conditions in the Eurasian Ecumene as the basic interpretive factor in the rise of Christianity, McNeill is not greatly troubled by the specific difficulty facing the historian of Christian origins: how to explain, on the basis of the sources, the admittedly "enormous influence Jesus and a handful of humble Galilean country folk exercised upon subsequent human generations." Though "the birth of Christianity is one of the central dramas of human history," analyses of the phenomenon are limited by "the obscurities of early Christian history." For McNeill, "the really remarkable thing was that his [Jesus'] teach-

---

[6]*Ibid.*, p. 338.
[7]*American Historical Review*, LXIX, 713-14.

ings survived his death." The explanation must lie in the eschatological force of His message and in the subjective impact of the disciples' Pentecost experience, when they "suddenly felt the Holy Spirit descend upon them until they became absolutely convinced that their master who had just died on the cross was with them still." In the final analysis, the rise of the Christian church is to be understood in terms of the needs of the time: "Quite apart from any question of doctrinal truth or error, Christianity, Hinduism, and Mahayana Buddhism fitted men more successfully than ever before to the difficult task of living in a megalopolitan civilization."[8]

* * * * *

How does the foregoing account of Christian origins stand up under scrutiny? Not very well, in spite of its thought-provoking quality. McNeill runs into serious difficulty as a result of committing two methodological errors: he attempts to fit Christianity into a more general religious and cultural scheme instead of investigating the phenomenon on its own terms; and he neglects the primary documents concerning Christian origins in his interpretation of the beginnings of the Christian religion. Let us consider each of these problems.

The Problem of Categorizing

There is obviously nothing wrong with the grouping of historical happenings under more general heads. Indeed, the historian, as distinct from the chronicler, must employ generalizations in order to make sense out of the overwhelming mass of data for whose interpretation he is responsible. However, the historian must exercise the greatest of care in his categorizing. He must, to use Plato's expression, "cut at the joints." The only sure way to avoid forcing phenomena into procrustean beds is to subject them to full analysis on their own grounds before grouping them with other data. In the case of religious phenomena, this caution must particularly be observed, since superficial similarities often hide root differences. Indeed, the history of the field of "comparative religion" in the last fifty years is a living reminder of this point. Late nineteenth-century attempts to view the higher reli-

---

[8]*RW*, pp. 352-53.

gions of the world as little more than variations on the same
theme have been discredited as violating the uniqueness of the
individual faiths, and now students of the subject prefer to designate their field as "comparative religions" in order to illustrate the
new inductive emphasis.

The general position of contemporary theological scholarship
is that the differences between biblical religion and other world
faiths far outweigh the similarities, and that one must therefore
seek explanations for the Christian faith within the faith itself and
not by appeal to general religious or cultural conditions.[9] R. E.
Hume, translator of the Upanishads from the Sanscrit and former
Professor of the History of Religions at Union Seminary, well
expresses this approach when he sets forth the "radical dissimilari-
ties" between Jesus' teachings and the great Indian religions. The
personal God of the Bible contrasts with Hinduism's Brahma —
an impersonal, philosophical Absolute — and with Buddhism's original atheism. Jesus' high valuation of the physical world as God's
creation and His high conception of the worth of the human
personality contrasts with Hinduism's view of the world as a
temporary, worthless illusion (*maya*) and its promotion of caste.
It also contrasts with Buddhism's low regard for the material
world and desire to end the tiresome round of reincarnations
through absorption in *nirvana*. Christianity's understanding of evil
as sin against a personal and loving heavenly Father contrasts with
Hinduism's *avidya* (philosophical ignorance) and violation of
hereditary social conventions, and with Buddhism's attribution of
evil to positive activity and desire. God's vicarious, freely given
atonement for sin in the Christian faith contrasts with the impersonal power of *karma* and the absolute necessity of self-salva-
tion in the Indian religions. Christianity's physical resurrection
of Christ in time and of all men at the end of the age contrasts with
the basic soul-body dualism of the Indian faiths. And so on.[10]

---

[9]Cf. the epochal monographs, *The Old Testament Against Its Environment* by G. Ernest Wright, and *The New Testament Against Its Environment* by Floyd V. Filson (SCM Studies in Biblical Theology, Nos. 2 and
3).

[10]Robert Ernest Hume, *The World's Living Religions: An Historical
Sketch* (rev. ed.; New York: Charles Scribner's Sons, 1955), pp. 37-
40, 81-82. The above contrasts represent only a few of the significant
points discussed by Hume. It should perhaps be noted in passing that

Considerations such as these demand an evaluation of Christian origins in terms other than the general religious or social conditions of a Eurasian Ecumene.

The Primary Sources

To determine how Christianity originated, the historian must go to the primary sources dealing with the beginnings of the Christian religion: the documents comprising the New Testament, plus such collateral materials as are provided by first-century Roman and Jewish sources (Tacitus, Pliny, Josephus, *et al.*) and by the recently discovered Qumran materials. To some extent, McNeill does this — as all historians must in order to say anything significant about early Christianity. Thus he asserts that the account in Acts of the Pentecost event "still bears all the marks of authenticity."[11] But his explanatory treatment of the rise of Christianity is not inductively derived from these documents, for the New Testament materials account for·the success of Christianity after the death of its founder not on the basis of eschatological preaching or psychological assurances, but on the straightforward, objective fact of Jesus' resurrection.[12] The documents containing these claims were written by eyewitnesses or by men in contact with eyewitnesses, and the period between the recording of the

---

McNeill, like Toynbee, gives a somewhat skewed and overly "Christian" picture of Buddhism by focusing attention on its Mahayana variety, with little stress upon the Hinayana type; but the more radical differences between Christianity and Buddhism do in fact apply to Mahayana in any case.

[11]*RW*, p. 341. Cf. McNeill's *Past and Future* (Chicago: University of Chicago Press Phoenix Books, 1964), p. 35: "The sailor's life had its share of terrors for the peoples who lived around the Mediterranean in ancient times, as Paul's journeyings remind us." Hereafter this edition of *Past and Future* will be cited as *PF*.

[12]See 1 Cor. 15, where Paul, as early as A.D. 56, names specific witnesses who had seen the risen Jesus, and gives the total number at over 500 people, most still alive. As C. H. Dodd has shown in his *Apostolic Preaching and its Developments*, the resurrection forms the keynote in the sermons of the early church as given in the book of Acts; and F. F. Bruce has emphasized, in his *Apostolic Defence of the Gospel*, that the New Testament church rested its case for the truth of its message primarily on the historicity of Jesus' conquest of death. (See above, Chapter 3, for detailed discussion of this point.)

resurrection appearances and the appearances themselves was so brief that theories of communal redaction by the church hold little credibility (as we have seen in the preceding chapters).

Passages such as the following ring true only on the assumption that, in spite of disappointed hopes of an immediate eschaton and in spite of psychological disbelief and discouragement, Jesus' disciples were transformed by the sheer weight of empirical evidence for their Lord's resurrection:

> As they [the disciples] were talking, . . . there he was, standing among them. Startled and terrified, they thought they were seeing a ghost. But he said, "Why are you so perturbed? Why do questionings arise in your minds? Look at my hands and feet. It is I myself. Touch me and see; no ghost has flesh and bones as you can see that I have." They were still unconvinced, still wondering, for it seemed too good to be true. So he asked them, "Have you anything here to eat?" They offered him a piece of fish they had cooked, which he took and ate before their eyes.[13]

The eschatological-psychological explanation of Christianity's amazing growth following the death of Jesus really does little more than beg the question. For what would have motivated the disciples, in the face of their overwhelming discouragement, to create imaginary — yet closely detailed — resurrection accounts such as the one just quoted? When in A.D. 44 the pseudo-messiah Theudas failed to divide the Jordan river, his movement died. The same thing occurred when another messianic pretender in A.D. 52-54 attempted to shout down the walls of Jerusalem.[14] If Jesus had failed to rise from the dead as He promised, is there any real likelihood that His message would have become the basis of a church that eventually conquered the Roman world? Moreover, had the resurrection been a myth and not a fact, would Jesus' followers have been so foolish as to proclaim its facticity as a matter of com-

---

[13]Luke 24:36-43 (written, note well, by the same author who produced Acts, which McNeill, together with virtually all classical historians, regards as an authoritative source). Cf. also John 20:25-28. On the advancement of "miracle" claims in conjunction with a historical argument, several words will be said toward the close of the chapter.

[14]Josephus, *Jewish War*, II, 13, 4. 259; *Antiquities*, XX, 8, 6. 170.

mon knowledge — in the very Jewish communities that desperately wished to stamp out the Christian heresy?[15]

It would appear that Professor McNeill, with his usual perspicacity, has, in another connection, revealed the very difficulty that plagues his account of Christian origins:

> The Reformation without Luther, the Jesuits without Loyola, or modern science without Galileo are really unthinkable. It is a defect of historical essays such as this that the unique individual career and the strategic moment of personal thought or action can easily be obliterated by the weight of inexact generalizations.[16]

Had McNeill concentrated more fully on the primary sources for Jesus' life and on the "strategic moment of action" in that life — the resurrection that displayed His Deity — his interpretation of the origin of Christ's church would have been eminently more successful. For any explanation of the origin of the church that tends to short-circuit its founder through generalizations about the social and religious needs of the time or about the psychological state of early Christians, is doomed to failure.

THE DEVELOPMENT AND INFLUENCE OF THE CHURCH

An unsatisfying account of the church's origin does not lead *per se* to an unsatisfactory description of its subsequent history and influence. Indeed, only a particularly dull-witted church historian could miss the lucid and illuminating discussions of particular problems of ecclesiastical history interspersed throughout *The Rise of the West*. Worthy of particular note, as marvels of condensed precision in historical writing, are the author's treatments of the ecclesiology of the Patristic era; of the church in the great cultural synthesis of the High Middle Ages; and, especially, of the character and development of the Eastern Orthodox Church.[17] These sections and others like them in *The Rise of the West* show how fully

---

[15]Cf. Acts 2:22 where the apostles not only say, "We are witnesses of these things," but also, "As you yourselves also know." This point has been strongly emphasized by F. F. Bruce of the University of Manchester, one of the leading contemporary experts on the Dead Sea scrolls; see especially his *New Testament Documents: Are They Reliable?*

[16]*RW*, p. 599 (concluding the section on "The Transmutation of Europe, A.D. 1500-1650").

[17]Respectively, *RW*, pp. 405-412; 547-58; 519-24, 606-608.

McNeill benefited from the writing of his *History Handbook*: the merits of a superlative textbook are transferred to a superlatively important interpretation of world history.

An Imbalanced Summary

And yet, as the church historian moves through McNeill's fascinating narrative, a sense of disquiet grows upon him. "Suppose," he asks himself, "the material dealing strictly with the history of the church were isolated from the total narrative and put together; would a balanced summary of church history result?" The answer to this question is certainly No, particularly if one considers the last third of *The Rise of the West*, covering the period 1500 to date. McNeill's discussion of the Renaissance-Reformation[18] is a barometer of what is to follow. Contrary to usual practice, he deals first with the Reformation and then with the High Renaissance, so as to make the latter a connecting link with the secularistic, scientific *Weltanschauung* of eighteenth-century rationalism. The tacit implication of such an arrangement of material is that the Reformation — whose "theological passions" the author finds "easier to understand than to share" — deserves to be aligned with a thought world that largely passed away when the Renaissance heralded a new, anthropocentric perspective. This impression is fully supported by the spotty coverage of church history from this point on in *The Rise of the West*. Neither the Wesleys nor Whitefield are mentioned by name at all, and a passing, single-sentence reference to Methodism[19] is the only indication the reader receives of the tremendously influential eighteenth-century "awakenings," both in Europe and America, that established a permanent pattern of eleemosynary work and revivalistic faith in modern times.[20]

American church history is for all practical purposes totally disregarded, in spite of the indisputable contributions of such scholars in the field as William Warren Sweet. Though it seems

---

[18]*Ibid.*, pp. 589-98.

[19]*Ibid.*, p. 685.

[20]For an authoritative, book-length treatment of this vital subject, see A. Skevington Wood, *The Inextinguishable Blaze: Spiritual Renewal and Advance in the Eighteenth Century* ("The Advancement of Christianity Through the Centuries," VI; London: Paternoster Press, 1960).

almost unbelievable, Roger Williams, Jonathan Edwards, Timothy
Dwight, Charles Finney, Dwight Moody, and Billy Graham —
to name only a few persons who have had a powerful impact on
American religious life — are omitted entirely from McNeill's
history. What is even more amazing is the general neglect of nineteenth-century, world-wide Christian missionary expansion. Mc-
Neill's half-dozen occasional references to missions in conjunction
with other topics[21] stand in stark contrast with Kenneth Scott
Latourette's monumental seven-volume *History of the Expansion
of Christianity*, in which three full volumes are devoted to the
nineteenth century as "The Great Century" of Christian expansion![22]

When we move to the question of the church's influence
through the centuries, *The Rise of the West* provides an even less
adequate guide. True, tantalizingly brilliant suggestions appear
from time to time (generally in footnotes), such as the democ-
ratizing effect of Christianity in the Roman Empire,[23] and Christianity's contribution to the process of social differentiation within
Frankish society.[24] But vast areas of church influence, particularly
in modern times, are completely passed over: the positive impact
of the Reformation on education, science, and letters;[25] the reli-

---

[21]It is indicative that David Livingstone receives no mention in *The
Rise of the West* — though McNeill does refer to him once, *en passant*, in
Past and Future (p. 58).

[22]Only one citation to Latourette's great *History* appears in *The Rise
of the West*, and this is to Vol. I, which deals only with the first five
centuries of the Christian era (*RW*, p. 344, n. 80). McNeill cites Latourette's *History of Christian Missions in China* three times.

[23]*RW*, p. 405, n. 81.

[24]*Ibid.*, p. 445, n. 39: "Christian doctrine both exalted the powers and
sacrosanctity of the king and, by virtue of the very principle of hierarchical
ecclesiastical organization, introduced a new, non-tribal, and authoritarian
concept of social organization into the backwoods."

[25]See Emile Léonard's *Historie générale du Protestantisme* (3 vols.;
Paris: Presses Universitaires de France, 1961-1964). See also my articles,
"Luther and Libraries," *The Library Quarterly* [University of Chicago],
XXXII (April, 1962), 133-47; and "Cross, Constellation, and Crucible:
Lutheran Astrology and Alchemy in the Age of the Reformation,"
Transactions of the Royal Society of Canada, 4th ser., I (1963), 251-70
(also published in the British journal *Ambix*, June, 1963, and in French
in *Revue d'Histoire et de Philosophie Religieuses* [1966]). Both of these
articles contain numerous references to primary and secondary source
material on the subjects treated.

gious motivations for the age of discovery and exploration;[26] the synthesizing effect of Protestant theology on seventeenth-century life and thought,[27] the influence of the church on the development of modern hospitals and social service; etc. Writes Latourette of Christianity:

> It was the main impulse in the formulation of international law. But for it the League of Nations and the United Nations would not have been. By its name and symbol the most extensive organization ever created for the relief of the suffering caused by war, the Red Cross, bears witness to its Christian origin. The list might go on indefinitely.[28]

Unfortunately, however, the list does not appear — much less go on indefinitely — in *The Rise of the West*.

For McNeill, the West does not of course "rise" without the impact of the Christian church, but this impact is understood strictly in terms of McNeill's dialectic contention that "unusual instability, arising out of a violent oscillation from one extreme to another, may in fact be the most distinctive and fateful characteristic of the European style of civilization."[29] The Christian church is thus regarded as but one of the relativistic elements contributing to characteristic western "oscillation." The church produced the "transcendental, mystical" tone of the fifth and sixth

---

[26]Columbus's letter of March 14, 1493, to Ferdinand and Isabella, in which he states that he made efforts to conciliate the natives "that they might be led to become Christians" is symbolic of much of subsequent exploratory and colonization activity. William Warren Sweet, the late dean of American church historians, has made this point well in his *Religion in Colonial America* (1942) where he analyzes *in extenso* the colonization motives expressed in Richard Hakluyt's "Discourse on Western Planting." Though McNeill refers once to the "Prester John" legend (*RW*, p. 613), he apparently does not recognize in it the outworking of Christian paradise-longings in relation to exploration and colonization (cf. Elaine Sanceau, *The Land of Prester John* [New York: Alfred A. Knopf, 1944]).

[27]See the Editorial Introduction to my *Chytraeus on Sacrifice* (St. Louis: Concordia, 1962); my *Shape of the Past*, pp. 52-54; and my as yet unpublished Strasbourg dissertation for the degree of Docteur de l'Université, mention Théologie Protestante (1964).

[28]K. S. Latourette, *A History of Christianity* (New York: Harper & Row, 1953), p. 1474.

[29]*RW*, p. 412.

centuries, temporarily replacing classical "naturalism and rationalism."[30] The Christian heritage, in combination with the Greek-
Roman, created "polar antitheses" in the very heart of European
civilization — and "the prolonged and restless growth of the West,
repeatedly rejecting its own potentially "classical" formulations,
may have been related to the contrarieties built so deeply into its
structure."[31] The Reformation, interacting and colliding with the
Renaissance, "by heightening the tensions between the incompatible
inseparables at the core of European culture — the Hellenic pagan
and the Judaeo-Christian heritages — increased the variety, multiplied the potentialities, and raised the intellectual and moral energies
of Europe to a new height."[32] For McNeill, as the preceding
section of this critique has made clear, Christianity did not arise
because of its revelatory truth; therefore it is perhaps only natural
that from his relativistic viewpoint the influence of the church
should be largely restricted to its part in the Hegelian-like dialectic
antiphony that sounds throughout *The Rise of the West*.

Economic Reductionism

The problem cuts even deeper than this, however. In general,
for McNeill, the church does not so much influence the "rise of
the West" as the pattern of Western history influences it. Just as
the origin of Christianity was subsumed under, and largely explained by, more general factors (the religious needs of the Eurasian Ecumene), so the development and influence of the Christian
church is continually viewed from within the essentially non-
religious structure of the author's thesis.

This can be seen with particular clarity in McNeill's *Past and
Future*, which has correctly been termed "a kind of trial run for
The Rise of the West,"[33] and of which the author himself says in

---

[30]*Ibid.*, pp. 410-12.

[31]*Ibid.*, p. 539.

[32]*Ibid.*, pp. 588-89. McNeill's general evaluation of the Protestant Reformation reminds one somewhat of the views of Bertrand Russell (*A
History of Western Philosophy*) and Will Durant (*The Reformation*),
who somewhat gleefully picture the Protestants and the Catholics of the
time knocking each other senseless, thereby clearing the field for the rise
of the secularistic, scientific world-view in the late seventeenth century!

[33]Raymond Walters, Jr., in *The New York Times Book Review*, October
6, 1963, p. 30.

his 1964 Preface (written after the publication of *The Rise of the West*): "It remains a fact that if I were writing the chapter on the past over again today, I would wish to alter a few turns of phrase, but nothing fundamental."[34] In *Past and Future*, as in *The Rise of the West*, the over-all periodization is determined by "the methods and geographical channels of contact between alien peoples and civilizations."[35] Thus the "pedestrian epoch" (to about 2000 B.C.) is succeeded by the "equestrian period," which continues until the substitution of an "ocean centered ecumene" for the "land centered ecumene" with development of ocean-going ships (*ca.* A.D. 1500), and the latter era has, in very recent times (about 1850), been itself replaced by the age of mechanical transport over land and sea, and by a "polar centered ecumene" since the advent of practically efficient jet aircraft (*ca.* 1950).[36]

It would be beyond the scope of this paper to attempt a critique of this typology here, and we are even willing to concede the illumination that such an essentially economic thesis produces by focusing attention on the importance of potato growing and the moldboard plow[37] — Professor McNeill's Cornell Ph.D. thesis, not so incidentally, dealt with "The Influence of the Potato on Irish History"! But has not something serious gone wrong when the development of his argument in *Past and Future* permits a complete disregard of the B.C.-A.D. time division, and no mention either of the birth of Christ or of the Protestant Reformation? Evidently, a geographical-economic point-of-view has gotten out of hand, and has come to engulf historical interpretation to a degree inimical to the entire fabric of historical fact.

Such a preoccupation with the economic phase of life results continually in that grave sin of "reductionism" — the explanation of one thing by another so as to remove inherent significance from areas of life that have causal value in themselves. Thus Christianity is cited for its contribution to the European bellicosity (!)

---

[34]*PF*, p. viii.
[35]*Ibid.*, p. 15.
[36]Cf. the pictogram in *RW*, pp. 766-67.
[37]*PF*, pp. 33, 37. The moldboard plow is heavily emphasized in McNeill's *History Handbook*.

that produced, in McNeill's view, a "tough-fibered society";[38] for its supposedly pessimistic attitude to the things of this world;[39] and for its allegedly scapegoat philosophy that encourages "lines of social demarcation."[40] Reductionistic passages such as the following are by no means uncommon — and they are most definitely not balanced by religious explanations elsewhere:

> Habits of activity were inculcated by the weather itself. For most of the year, to be up and doing was the only way to keep warm. No Indian holy man could long contemplate infinity while shivering in Europe's winter; and, when the medieval monks imported Middle Eastern asceticism into Europe, it underwent a characteristic adaptation to the climate.[41]

My good friend Professor Donald Masters, F.R.S.C., has argued that the Christian historian is preserved from such reductionisms, for "regarding God as the great initiating force" in all of history, "he believes that God acts through the physical universe, but that He also communicates directly with the minds of men."[42] Dr. McNeill's relativism would seem to have left him at the mercy of a chaotic human history which must be ordered at all cost, even by the radical subordinating of vital religious factors to geographical-economic considerations.[43]

---

[38]*PF*, pp. 29-30. McNeill possibly commits a "Freudian error" when, in the course of this discussion he states that "European peasants have often turned their plowshares into swords" — exactly reversing the biblical motif!

[39]*Ibid.*, pp. 109 ff., 186 ff.

[40]*Ibid.*, pp. 170-71.

[41]*Ibid.*, p. 35.

[42]Donald C. Masters, *The Christian Idea of History* (Waterloo, Ontario: Waterloo Lutheran University, 1962), p. 15.

[43]Particularly indicative of the reductionistic element in McNeill's work is the criticism delivered by Carroll Quigley against the last third of *The Rise of the West*. Quigley, whose social-science-orientated *Evolution of Civilizations* I have analyzed in my *Shape of the Past*, pp. 86-88, wishes that McNeill had extended to the Old Regime his (McNeill's) argument that weapon development and defence needs among the Greeks largely conditioned their social and intellectual life ("The Greek miracle"). (See *Saturday Review*, August 24, 1963, pp. 41-42). Here Quigley, whose analogy between "quartz crystals" and human societies in his *Evolution of Civilizations* reduces the human drama to a sociological case-study, recognizes a certain (though incompletely developed) affinity in McNeill's reductionistic tendencies.

A PRIORI IN THE TREATMENT OF CHURCH HISTORY

How is it possible that a Latourette and a McNeill can differ so radically in their inclusion and exclusion of facts and in the interpretations they attach to the data of church history? The answer is quite obviously that they come to their subject matter with very different philosophies of history, that is to say, with very different philosophies of life; for, as the French existentialistic historian Raymond Aron has well put it: "The meaning of 'total' history is the meaning which we attach to human existence and to the succession of forms that it takes through time."[44]

What meaning does Professor McNeill "attach to human existence"? By what a prioris does he interpret the human drama? A quarter of a century ago, in writing his magisterial thesis on the presuppositional element in Herodotus and Thucydides, McNeill wisely observed:

> The issue is not, I think, between a historian with preconceptions and one without, but between a man whose preconceptions are conscious and have been examined and the man whose preconceptions are unconscious.[45]

McNeill's own a prioris are very definitely conscious and examined, though they are not always explicitly set down in his books.[46] In general, it is easy to see that he favors the rational approach to life over contemporary irrationalisms, and a "heroic optimism" concerning the fate of Western man, even though a nuclear holocaust is a live possibility in our time.[47]

But what is not so directly evident — though the present essay doubtless helps to make it so — is that McNeill's axiology is a

---

[44]Raymond Aron, "Evidence and Inference in History," in Daniel Lerner (ed.), *Evidence and Inference; the Hayden Colloquium on Scientific Concept and Method* (Glencoe, Illinois: Free Press, 1959), p. 46.

[45]W. H. McNeill, "Herodotus and Thucydides: A Consideration of the Structure of their Histories" (unpublished M.A. thesis, University of Chicago, 1939), p. 98.

[46]Cf. Trevor-Roper on *The Rise of the West*: "A critic might wish that he had, at one point, detached his general conclusions from this crowded but lucid narrative" (*New York Times Book Review*, October 6, 1963, p. 30).

[47]See the concluding sections both of *Past and Future* and of *The Rise of the West*.

thoroughgoing secular one. Perhaps the best illustration of this is the single passage in *Past and Future* where the phrase "in the fullness of time" appears:

It is an interesting coincidence, perhaps a significant one, that just as the nomadic irruption into the partial cultural vacuum of Europe at the beginning of the equestrian epoch created *in the fullness of time* the dominant world center in the epoch of ocean shipping, so the irruption of Europeans into the partial cultural vacuums of North America and of central and northern Asia during the epoch of ocean shipping has led to the establishment of the two great political states — the United States of America and the Union of Soviet Socialist Republics — which currently exhibit the most successful adaptation to the fourth of our epochs: the epoch of mechanical transport.[48]

The contrast with the original context of this allusion could hardly be greater, for St. Paul uses it in setting forth the heart of the Christian philosophy of history:

When the fullness of the time was come, God sent forth his Son, made of a woman, made under the law, to redeem them that were under the law, that we might receive the adoption of sons.[49]

When we recall that the birth of Christ is not so much as mentioned in *Past and Future*, and note that the "fullness of time" passage in that volume sets out a brief summary of McNeill's general historical thesis, we are brought to the conclusion that our author is offering an alternative historical philosophy to that proclaimed by the Christian faith: a secular, rather than a transcendent-religious, view of man's past.

This conclusion is supported further by a poignant footnote in *The Rise of the West*, where we are reminded that everyone born into the Christian religion "rejects only regretfully the comfort [the religious] explanation of man's place in the universe af-

---

[48]*PF*, p. 52 (italics ours).
[49]Galatians 4:4-5. It is perhaps worth pedantic mention that the phrase *to plērōma tou chronou* can signify only a built-in historical purpose, which is actually foreign to Professor McNeill's relativistic philosophy of history.

fords."[50] And in a recent Chicago television discussion on "The Historical Jesus," Professor McNeill, in answer to a question by Norman Ross concerning his religious viewpoint, stated that he is agnostic in relation to all religious traditions — that he feels no pressure to change his position in this regard — but (consistent with his relativism, note well!) that he does not necessarily recommend his approach to others.[51]

The essential question is, however, precisely whether one approach to historical interpretation should be recommended over another. Are we to assume, as existentialist historian Raymond Aron does, that one can never rise beyond "the plurality of systems of interpretation,"[52] or with theologian David Granskou, who in the television discussion with McNeill lamely asserted that the same facts leading McNeill to agnosticism formed the background for his faith?

The answer to such relativism (which, it is worthwhile pointing out, is uncomfortably close to philosophical solipsism) has been given, in another connection, earlier in this paper. It is the resurrection of Christ. Not without reason does Latourette conclude his seven-volume *History of the Expansion of Christianity* with the affirmation: "The Christian holds the resurrection of Jesus to be fact."[53] The facticity of that historical event on which all of Jesus' claims depended can be demonstrated by the same canons of historical method to which other, non-religious events are subject; and the result, as J. V. Langmead Casserley stated in his 1951 Maurice Lectures at King's College, London, is "like a knife pointed at the throat" of a-christian philosophies of life.[54]

If it is objected, as McNeill himself would object, that to consider seriously the historical evidence for the resurrection is to

---

[50]*RW*, p. 338, n. 76.

[51]"Off the Cuff," 12.35 a.m., December 20, 1964, Channel 7, Chicago.

[52]See his *Introduction á la philosophie de l'histoire* (2. éd.; Paris: Gallimard, 1948); and cf. my *Shape of the Past*, pp. 94-95, where his viewpoint is discussed in some detail.

[53]Vol. VII (2d ed.; New York: Harper: 1945), p. 505.

[54]Langmead Casserley, *The Retreat from Christianity in the Modern World* (London: Longmans, Green, 1952), p. 82.

admit the possibility of the miraculous,[55] the answer — strange to say — comes from *The Rise of the West* itself, where the author correctly emphasizes that the Newtonian "world machine" and "the elegant clarity of nineteenth-century physics" based upon it has been "dissolved" by the Einsteinian revolution.[56] As the late Cambridge professor C. S. Lewis has well argued in his classic refutation of Hume, the universe since Einstein has opened up to the possibility of *any* event.[57] The question is no longer what *can* happen, but what *has* happened. And an unprejudiced confrontation with the primary sources for Jesus' resurrection will lead to the conclusion so well expressed by Erlangen historian Ethelbert Stauffer:

> What do we do [as historians] when we experience surprises which run counter to all our expectations, perhaps all our convictions and even our period's whole understanding of truth? We say as one great historian used to say in such instances: "It is surely possible." And why not? For the critical historian nothing is impossible.[58]

Such an attitude is in every sense the mark of a truly modern historian. Leading as it does to the resurrected Christ, it provides an avenue beyond historical relativism to a conception of man's past which is characterized by true "fullness of time."

RECIPROCAL VALUES

If the Christian world-view is in fact true, then its perspective on history should constitute no mean asset in evaluating *The Rise of the West*. At the same time, Professor McNeill's impressive contribution to the literature of universal history cannot help but provide the Christian church historian with insights into his own task

---

[55]In the TV conversation mentioned earlier, Dr. McNeill stated that, not as a historian but simply as a twentieth-century man, he could not accept the miraculous; he admitted, however, that for him this was no more than a tenet of faith, accepted in light of the modern scientific world-view.

[56]*RW*, pp. 684, 756-58.

[57]C. S. Lewis, *Miracles* (New York: The Macmillan Company, 1947), *passim*.

[58]Ethelbert Stauffer, *Jesus and His Story* (New York: Knopf, 1960), p. 17.

and responsibilities. We shall now, in conclusion, say a few words on both aspects of this historical equivalent of a chemical "reversible reaction."

The Christian philosophy of history can do at least four exceedingly important things for McNeill's presentation of the history of mankind. First, as suggested previously, it can serve as a corrective to the geographical-economic reductionism — the creeping materialistic determinism — that not infrequently rears its head (in spite of the best humanistic intentions!) in McNeill's work.[59] Secondly, as we have also stressed by implication in the previous sections of this paper, the Christian *Weltanschauung*, focusing as it does upon God's redemptive act in Christ and the proclamation of that act through the church, protects the historian from neglecting the vital facts of church history and from overlooking their impact upon the general history of the world.

Thirdly, in line with the point just made, the Christian perspective can offer a central insight of tremendous value to McNeill's basic theme of "the rise of the West." Why, McNeill must ask, has the West displayed such long-term dynamism? His answer, as we have noted, is the "drastic instability" of the West — the "ferment of incompatibles" operative in western history. Yet such a causal motif, like Toynbee's "challenge-and-response"

---

[59] A nightmarish example of this tendency appears at the close of McNeill's 1964 Preface to his *Past and Future*: "Computers already exist that are capable of maintaining an indefinite number of bits of information about every living human being. Appropriate information fed into such a monstrous machine might in time create such an intimate and precise interaction among whole populations and individual persons as to reduce (or raise) us all to the level of the separate cells of some loosely organized creature like the Portuguese man-of-war, whose constituent parts are controlled and co-ordinated by chemical and electrical interrelations among the clustered cells that constitute the whole. We seem, in short, to be galloping toward the creation of the Leviathan of which political philosophers once dreamed — a Leviathan in which each man will have his place and proper function, calculated and assigned to him on the basis of most careful and precise statistical studies, sustained by data-storage and retrieval systems whose refinements we can only begin to imagine today. The technical means for such an evolution of humanity certainly appear to stand within our grasp" (*PF*, pp. x-xi). No one is more quickly reminded of a *particular* Leviathan — namely Hobbes's — than the Christian who reads this passage!

theory, is more a formal principle than a concrete explanation.[60] Does not the answer really lie in the "progress" idea which the linear, goal-orientated Christian view of history injected into the West, and which has constituted the underlying element in the western approach to life from that day to this?[61] McNeill is aware of the distinction between the cyclical, non-progressive, a-historical orientation of the non-Christian world and the Christian focus on Creation, Incarnation, and Last Judgment which "gave meaning and hope to ordinary terrestrial human life."[62] But he does not see the tremendous significance of this fact for his thesis. For if, as I have argued elsewhere, western "conceptions of his-torical progress — whether religious or materialistic, Christian or Marxist — take their origin ultimately from the biblical idea of history,"[63] then it is in the realm of the West's biblical faith that the explanation for our civilization's amazing vitality and urge to "rise" ought chiefly to be sought.

The fourth contribution that the Christian philosophy of history can make to McNeill's analysis of world history lies in the realm of axiology. Both *Past and Future* and *The Rise of the West* bristle with value judgments as to what is ethically worthwhile (e.g., "heroism" and "kindliness" in the face of the challenges of our day)[64] and what is significant and important in history (we "should count ourselves fortunate to live in one of the great ages of the world").[65] But how are such value judgments to be

---

[60]Cf. Gerhard Masur on Toynbee: "Toynbee still believes that the idea of 'challenge and response' constitutes a magical key to the why and how of human creativity. But is it not, after all, little more than a formal principle, like Hegel's dialectic, which cannot provide us with a canon of interpretation?" (Review of *A Study of History*, Vol. XII, in *American Historical Review*, LXVII [October, 1961], 79).

[61]Canadian philosopher George P. Grant writes: "What must be in-sisted is that the very spirit of progress takes its form and depends for its origin on the Judaeo-Christian idea of history" (*Philosophy in the Mass Age* [Vancouver: Copp Clark, 1959], p. 49). Cf. John Baillie, *The Belief in Progress* (London: Oxford University Press, 1950), *passim*.

[62]*RW*, pp. 339-40.

[63]*The Shape of the Past*, p. 42.

[64]See *PF*, p. 212. Stringfellow Barr appropriately titles his review of *The Rise of the West* "Heroically Grappling with Man's Long Saga" (*New York Herald Tribune Books*, August 11, 1963, p. 3).

[65]*RW*, p. 807.

justified? When we read in the closing paragraph of *The Rise of the West* that "good and wise men in all parts of the world have seldom counted for more" since they can help to realize "the generous ideals proclaimed by all — or almost all — the world's leaders," and that "evil men and crass vices" should not distract us, we are inclined to whisper "Amen" in our hearts. But before doing so we had better make sure that "good" and "evil" are properly defined and that "generous ideals" can be explicitly defended against those proclaimed by at least some of the world's leaders! And *why* should we rejoice to live in the present day or take its challenges upon us — why, indeed, should "the rise of the West" constitute a positive value in any sense?[66]

Questions of this kind are not answered in McNeill's writings,[67] nor, indeed, can they be answered successfully apart from a revelational absolute. Out of flux nothing but flux can come, and out of the relativism of the human situation no permanent values can be categorically established. Only if absolutes are supplied from outside the "human predicament" can man stand firmly — and the central Christian affirmation that "God was in Christ reconciling the world unto himself" signifies that the answers to man's axiological dilemma have been provided by the only One who could do so. McNeill reveals that he understands the ethical

---

[66]This same problem of ungrounded values plagues and vitiates the effectiveness of E. H. Carr's "evolving ends" philosophy of history, as set forth in his Trevelyan lectures (*What Is History?* [London: Macmillan, 1961]); Boyd C. Shafer perceptively writes of Carr's approach — and the point applies almost equally to McNeill: "Carr is persuasive. As one reads him, one agrees, quickly and easily. Later, in sober aftermath, one asks, what 'sense,' what 'direction,' whose 'sense of direction' [for the historical process]? That of Marx or Wells? of Hitler or Churchill? Gandhi or Toynbee? Mao Tse-tung or Khrushchev? Nehru or Kennedy? or that of the enlightened, liberal, hopeful professor at Trinity College [i.e., Carr himself]?" (Review of *What Is History?* in *American Historical Review*, LXVII [April, 1962], 676-77).

[67]In this glaring omission, as in the rather naïve practical relativism characteristic of his writings, does not McNeill display the typical American pragmatism — the American impatience with "theoretical" issues — that his colleague Daniel Boorstin has so well described in his book, *The Americans: The Colonial Experience* (New York: Random House, 1958) and *The Genius of American Politics* (Chicago: University of Chicago Press Phoenix Books, 1953)?

dilemma facing modern man (himself included) when he writes: "One can argue plausibly that the liberal, democratic society of the West is, in the twentieth century, living upon a humanitarian capital inherited from religious minds of past generations,"[68] and when he speculates about the possible need of a new religion in the future:

> Without religious revival on a grand scale, I should think it likely that moral lassitude and a spirit of indifference, a sense of futility, and, perhaps, a supine fatalism would increasingly gain hold of men's minds; and, having nothing much worthwhile to live for or strive for, they might even cease to propagate their kind in sufficient number to prevent a decrease in the population of the earth. Something like this frame of mind did come to possess the Greeks and Romans, and the curious demographic decay of those nations in the days of the Roman Empire may have been connected with the political and religious disintegration of their ancestral way of life.[69]

It is unfortunate that McNeill does not see that just as it was "the spirit of the Church which survived the catastrophe of the old [Roman] world, saving both itself and the best gifts of Europe,"[70] so it is the same Christian faith that continues to provide the only solid grounding for historical ideals such as are displayed in *The Rise of the West*. With McNeill's heroism and hopes we have no argument, but we wish to stress with all possible seriousness that many other minds look upon our age with existential despair, reminding us that a simple expression of ideals is hardly enough. The root question is whether justification for historical hope is possible in the face of man's all too frequent inhumanity to man.[71] The only validated positive answer remains the one

---

[68]*PF*, p. 110.

[69]*Ibid.*, pp. 174-75. However, consistent with his personal philosophy of life, McNeill immediately adds: "I do not imagine that religion alone would suffice to restore a moral soundness to mankind."

[70]So Ethelbert Stauffer effectively argues in his *Christ and the Caesars*, trans. K. and R. Gregor Smith (Philadelphia: Westminster Press, 1955), p. 286 and *passim*.

[71]M. I. Finley holds, not unreasonably, that the display of "Western power" in the Nazi period "challenges the optimism of his [McNeill's] vision and the neatness of his evolutionary pattern" (*New York Review of Books*, October 17, 1963, p. 5).

given by the resurrected Christ who not only established a focal point of salvation for human history, but also guaranteed its fulfillment at the end of the age.[72]

* * * * *

Now for the other side of the coin: What can the Christian church historian gain from *The Rise of the West?* Though secularistic wineskins will burst if they attempt to hold the Christian story, the Christian *Weltanschauung* itself is capable of incorporating all truth present in secular philosophies of life and of history. Thus, when faced by a monumental achievement such as *The Rise of the West,* the Christian historian should exhibit, not carping criticism, but reverential awe for the truths about the human condition that are revealed therein. And he should do more than this: he should permit McNeill's universal history to drive him into his study to attempt, should he have the ability, analogous productions that would display the universality of God's working in time.[73] The responsibility which Augustine discharged in the fifth century through his *Civitas Dei* falls equally upon every generation of theologians and church historians. But, regrettably, few ages seri-

---

[72]Acts 1:10-11: "While they [the apostles] looked stedfastly toward heaven as he [Jesus] went up, behold, two men stood by them in white apparel, which also said, Ye men of Galilee, why stand ye gazing up into heaven? this same Jesus, which is taken up from you into heaven, shall so come in like manner as ye have seen him go into heaven." As Carter Jefferson has correctly noted, "McNeill has avoided the apocalyptic vision that too often goes with 'universal history'" (*Chicago Sunday Tribune Magazine of Books,* September 8, 1963, p. 2); though this avoidance is commendable with respect to secular apocalypticisms, it leaves a truncated historical vision which only the Christian hope can remedy. See on this matter and on the general axiological issues discussed in the preceding section, chapter 1, "Where is History Going?"

[73]A concrete example of the significance of McNeill's universal perspective for Christian historical interpretation is suggested by Stringfellow Barr, who notes that the present planetary melting-pot of civilizations described in *The Rise of the West* can be directly correlated with the common self-awareness of peoples which the late Christian thinker Teilhard de Chardin has called the "noosphere" (*New York Herald Tribune Books,* August 11, 1963, p. 3).

ously respond to the mandate and challenge.[74] If Professor Mc-Neill is willing, in the words of his prefatory quotation, to "seek to understand, and if I can/To justify the ways of man to man," can we not raise up twentieth-century historical Miltons who will, as in days of old, "justify the ways of God to man"?

---

[74]Stavrianos is quite wrong when he claims that "globally oriented history" such as McNeill's "represents a return to the historiographic tradition of the Enlightenment, when the idea of universal history fitted in with the prevailing views regarding progress. Prior to that period Western historians had been constrained by the need to fit all historical events into a rigid Biblical context" (*American Historical Review*, LXIX [April, 1964], 713). Actually, the universal biblical frame of reference of the medieval church is the true source of global history; and the Enlightenment, with its stress on unchanging Reason, was a particularly unhistorical epoch. (See on this my *Shape of the Past*, pp. 48, 66–70.)

5. KARL BARTH AND CONTEMPORARY THEOLOGY OF HISTORY

"WHEN KARL BARTH decided to become a systematic theologian, Protestant historical scholarship lost a man who was potentially the greatest historian of doctrine since Adolf von Harnack." With these words Jaroslav Pelikan, Roland Bainton's successor as Titus Street Professor of Ecclesiastical History at Yale, introduces the 1959 American edition of Barth's *Protestant Thought from Rousseau to Ritschl*.[1] Barth's relevance to historical scholarship as well as to dogmatics is conceded by all who have even a nodding acquaintance with his writings. In the present essay an effort will be made to delineate the relationship (or lack of relationship) between theology and history in Barth's thought, and to offer a critique which will sensitize readers to the danger zones in the Barthian approach to theology of history. No apologies will be made for the negatively critical tone of the paper: in my judgment at least, based upon attendance at the University of Chicago Barth Lectures in April, 1962, there is entirely too much uncritical laudation of Barth — laudation which is as much an embarrassment to him as to others. I have always believed, and still do believe, that

---

[1] A translation of eleven chapters of *Die protestantische Theologie im 19. Jahrhundert*. (New York: Harper & Row, 1959).

out of the *rabies theologorum* truth will come if proper methodology is employed.

Christian theology has a twofold connection with history, as
we see from the magnificent proclamation with which the Epistle
to the Hebrews opens:

> God, who at sundry times and in divers manners spake in time
> past unto the fathers by the prophets, hath in these last days
> spoken unto us by his Son, whom he hath appointed heir of all
> things, by whom also he made the worlds; who being the
> brightness of his glory, and the express image of his person, and
> upholding all things by the word of his power, when he had by
> himself purged our sins, sat down on the right hand of the
> Majesty on high.

On the one hand, God works in general human history, for He
"upholds all things by the word of his power." On the other, He
has become part of man's story in a special way through prophetic
revelation and through the atoning sacrifice of Himself in the person of Jesus of Nazareth. Thus Christian theology of history must
always speak both of total history and of *Heilsgeschichte*. We
shall begin with an analysis of Barth's approach to these two fundamental problem-areas, and on this basis we shall proceed to examine the implications of his position for evangelical theology in
our day.

Barth and Total History

Pelikan, in his above-mentioned Introduction to Barth's *Protestant Thought*, says of the *Kirchliche Dogmatik*: "The many historical excursuses in *Barth's Church Dogmatics*, dealing with the
history of everything from the doctrine of the angels to the picture
of Judas Iscariot, bear witness to the breadth of his erudition and
to the depth of his understanding." But in spite of these excursuses
and in spite of its frequent references to the intimate connection
between Christianity and history, Barth's *Church Dogmatics* shows
a remarkable indifference to man's over-all temporal experience.
The following passage well captures Barth's attitude toward secular
history:

> The verdict that all have sinned certainly implies a verdict on
> that which is human history apart from the will and word and
> work of God . . . and a knowledge of the sin and guilt of man

in the light of the word of grace of God implies a knowledge
that this history is, in fact, grounded and determined by the
pride of man. . . . The history of the world which God made in
Jesus Christ, and with a view to him, cannot cease to have its
center and goal in him. But in the light of this goal and center
God cannot say Yes but only No to its corruption. . . . What is
the obviously outstanding feature of world history? . . . [It]
is the all-conquering monotony — the monotony of the pride in
which man has obviously always lived to his own detriment and
that of his neighbor, from hoary antiquity and through the ebb
and flow of his later progress and recession both as a whole and
in detail, the pride in which he still lives . . . and will most
certainly continue to do so till the end of time . . . . History . . .
constantly re-enacts the little scene in the Garden of Eden.[2]

For Barth, "the obviously outstanding feature of world history"
is its "all-conquering monotony." But how obvious is obvious?
My undergraduate professor of logic at Cornell, Max Black, whom
we affectionately called "Black Max" — and for good reason —
used to say that when the word "obvious" is employed, the point
made is, nine times out of ten, not obvious at all. Certainly "all-
conquering monotony" is not regarded as the "outstanding feature
of world history" either by the biblical writers or by the Protestant Reformers. In the Scriptures and in the writings of the Reformers one finds, not a negative but a positive attitude to history,
based upon the central conviction that total human history lies in
the hands of God. Throughout the biblical revelation this conviction is writ large: "The earth is the Lord's, and the fulness
thereof; the world, and they that dwell therein."[3] History is
eminently meaningful because God is the sovereign power in it and
over it.

Calvin well captures the spirit of the biblical approach to total
history when he writes in the final chapter of the *Institutes*:

Here is displayed His wonderful goodness, and power, and
providence; for sometimes He raises up some of His servants as
public avengers, and arms them with His commission to punish
unrighteous domination, and to deliver from their distressing

---

[2]*Church Dogmatics*, IV/1, pp. 505-508. Page references to the *Church
Dogmatics* refer to the authorized English translation.
[3]Psalm 24:1; also Exodus 9:29, Deuteronomy 10:14; I Corinthians 10:26.

calamities a people who have been unjustly oppressed: sometimes He accomplishes this end by the fury of men who meditate
and attempt something altogether different. Thus He liberated
the people of Israel from the tyranny of Pharaoh by Moses.
. . . Thus He subdued the pride of Tyre by the Egyptians; the
insolence of the Egyptians by the Assyrians; the haughtiness of
the Assyrians by the Chaldeans; the confidence of Babylon by
the Medes and Persians, after Cyrus had subjugated the Medes.
The ingratitude of the kings of Israel and Judah, and their
impious rebellion, notwithstanding His numerous favours, He
repressed and punished, sometimes by the Assyrians, sometimes
by the Babylonians. . . . Whatever opinion he formed of the acts
of men, yet the Lord equally executed His work by them, when
He broke the sanguinary sceptres of insolent kings.[4]

The contrast could hardly be greater between Barth's characteriza-
tion of history as "monotony" and Calvin's scripturally orientated
view of history as the sphere in which the "wonderful goodness,
and power, and providence" of God are dynamically displayed.

But how is such a contrast possible if, as it is commonly
claimed, Barth has attempted above all to restore a biblical and
Reformation theology to the Protestantism of the twentieth-century? The answer lies in the fact that Barth's theology originated
as an antithesis to the humanistic-liberal philosophical theologies of
the nineteenth and early twentieth centuries. And, as is commonly
the case with antitheses, the pendulum was allowed to swing too
far in an opposite direction. The nineteenth century was a time
of confident optimism in almost all spheres of life, and particularly
in philosophy of history. Hegel asserted that "world history is a
rational process" moving through "world-historical" epochs towards the inevitable goal of Freedom.[5] Marx and Engels set forth
their extraordinary philosophy of history which claimed that progression in modes of production and exchange is basic to all of life,
and will eventually usher in a millennial classless society.[6] Except
for Jakob Burckhardt, the great Swiss historian who predicted

---

[4]*Institutes*, IV xx, 30-31.
[5]See Hegel's *Lectures on the Philosophy of History*, and cf. Jean Hyppolite, *Introduction à la philosophie de l'histoire de Hegel* (Paris: Marcel
Riviere, 1948).
[6]Cf. Donald C. Masters, *The Christian Idea of History* (Waterloo,
Ontario: Waterloo Lutheran University, 1962), pp. 19-21.

that *"Führers* and usurpers" would appear in the twentieth century,[7] and Lord Acton, the editor of the original *Cambridge Modern History*, whose Catholicism led him to assert that in all human affairs "power tends to corrupt and absolute power corrupts absolutely,"[8] the last century manifested naive optimism with regard to man's history. Theological liberalism grew from the seed-bed of this nineteenth-century optimism concerning human nature. Thus one finds a typical modernist such as Shailer Mathews of the University of Chicago, asserting in his *Spiritual Interpretation of History* (1920) that "the conviction thrust upon us by history [is] that the Christian religion is in accord with the tendency of human progress."[9]

Against these varieties of anthropocentric progressivism Barth reacted violently. His 1919 *Commentary on Romans* opposed with vehemence every attempt to center attention on man, his worth, or any alleged "progress" he could make toward a humanistic "kingdom of God on earth." But in concentrating attention on the biblical affirmation of man's radical need before God, Barth lost interest in general history and in God's creative and preserving work outside the sphere of *Heilsgeschichte*. The extent to which Barth reacted against any attempt to make general human history meaningful is nowhere better illustrated than in his conflict with Brunner over "natural revelation"[10] and in his opposition to Werner Elert's theology.[11] Brunner, on the basis of biblical statements such as Romans 1:20, has trenchantly argued that there is a valid "natural theology," in the sense that all created things objectively bear the divine stamp upon them. Barth, however, absolutely refuses to see an objective divine imprint. For him,

---

[7]Burckhardt, *Briefe*, ed. F. Kaphahn (Leipzig, 1935), correspondence with F. von Preen.

[8]Cf. Gertrude Himmelfarb, *Lord Acton: A Study in Conscience and Politics* (Chicago: University of Chicago Press, Phoenix Books, 1962), pp. 161 ff.

[9]Shailer Mathews, *The Spiritual Interpretation of History* (4th ed.; Cambridge, Mass.: Harvard University Press, 1920), p. 216.

[10]See *Natural Theology: Comprising "Nature and Grace" by Professor Dr. Emil Brunner and the Reply "No!" by Dr. Karl Barth*, trans. Peter Fraenkel (London: Geoffrey Bles, Ltd., 1946).

[11]See Elert's *The Structure of Lutheranism*, Vol. I, trans. W. A. Hansen (St. Louis, Mo.: Concordia Publishing House, 1962), p. xxiii and *passim*.

revelatory faith, instead of making an existent imprint apparent, brings it about. Against Brunner[12] and Elert,[13] Barth will have nothing to do with the Classical Protestant doctrine of the *Schopfungsordnungen* (Orders of Creation), which sees all historical life — Christian and non-Christian — as governed by divinely-established structures (the family, the state, etc.). In opposing optimistic anthropologies and modernist theologies that disregarded the central Christian doctrine of redemption, Barth went to the other extreme of focusing virtually all of his attention on the Christ-event, thereby ignoring the creative action of God in general human history.

Thus Barth's view of total history as "all-conquering monotony" relates to what critics have well called his "unitarianism of the Second Person" — his absorption of all theology into Christology. No one can deny that a christless modernism required a radical corrective, but two wrongs have never made a right. Particularly in our day, when the popularity of Toynbee's *A Study of History* reveals the desire of non-Christian and Christian alike for a meaningful interpretation of general history, we must look beyond Barth for a full-orbed, biblically Trinitarian concept of man's past.[14]

BARTH AND "HEILSGESCHICHTE"

Barth's concern is not with the alleged "monotony" of general history but with the significant events of salvation-history. Since God's revelation of Himself in Jesus Christ is the focal point of Barth's theological efforts, we must now see how he relates time and eternity in the drama of salvation.

In the *Commentary on Romans* one encounters a remarkable passage which serves as a key to Barth's theology of history as it applies to the plan of redemption:

---

[12]Emil Brunner, *The Divine Imperative*, trans. Olive Wyon (Philadelphia: The Westminster Press, 1947).

[13]Werner Elert, *The Christian Ethos*, trans. C. J. Schindler (Philadelphia: Muhlenberg Press, 1957).

[14]I am attempting such an interpretation in my series, "History in Christian Perspective," the first volume of which has already appeared under the title, *The Shape of the Past: An Introduction to Philosophical Historiography* (Ann Arbor, Mich.: Edwards Bros., 1962).

The entrance of sin into the world through Adam is in no strict sense an historical or psychological happening. The doctrine of Original Sin, as it has been generally understood in the West, would not have been to Paul an "attractive hypothesis" (Lietzmann); it would have been just one of the many historical and psychological falsifications of his meaning. The sin which entered the world through Adam is, like the righteousness manifested to the world in Christ, timeless and transcendental.[15]

To Barth, the fall into sin and the redemption from sin must be regarded, not from the standpoint of *Historie* (i.e., not as facts capable of discovery by a neutral historical investigator) but from the viewpoint of *Geschichte* (i.e., as revelational events, which can never be identified with *Historie* as such). The events of salvation-history always have a hiddenness about them that eludes the "objective" historian. Thus Barth never tires of condemning the theologians of Protestant Orthodoxy for asserting that revelation took place directly in history — that Adam fell in history, that Christ's redemptive act was an historical event in the full sense of the term, that the historic Scriptures are in fact revelation. The Orthodox made the tragic error, according to Barth, of pointing to history and saying, "*There is* revelation" — an "*es gibt*" which is in the final analysis "profane."[16] When we speak theologically, cautions Barth, "historical does not mean fixable as historical or fixed as historical. Historical does not therefore have its usual meaning of 'historical.' "[17]

But what about Barth's opposition to Bultmann, as expressed in his 1952 critique of the latter? Is it not true that Barth strongly defends the facticity of the resurrection over against Bultmann's demythologizations?[18] Cornelius Van Til, in his latest book, *Christianity and Barthianism*, correctly sees the fallacy in this line of argumentation:

---

[15]Barth, *The Epistle to the Romans*, trans. E. C. Hoskyns (London: Oxford University Press, 1933), p. 171.

[16]*Church Dogmatics*, I/1, p. 44.

[17]*Ibid.*, p. 373.

[18]Cf. Gustaf Wingren, *Theology in Conflict: Nygren — Barth — Bultmann*, trans. E. H. Wahlstrom (Philadelphia: Muhlenberg Press, 1958), pp. 137 ff.

What Barth considers to be the objective basis for the faith is found in *his* Christ, and in the resurrection of *his* Christ. And *this* resurrection of *this* Christ does not follow upon his death as one event in time follows another . . . On Barth's view, there would be no true objectivity for the gospel message if the resurrection were directly identified with a fact of history, following upon the death of Christ as another fact of history, for then the revelation of God in the resurrection would no longer be divine revelation. Then revelation no longer would be *hidden* as well as revealed. Therewith all the evils of a natural theology and of a self-enclosed anthropology would have returned. If Barth's idea of the objectivity of the gospel is to be maintained, then, on his own view, that of the Reformation must be rejected. Barth answers Bultmann, as he answered Romanism and all others, in terms of his Christ-Event, and this answer is based on a purely subjective foundation. We cannot walk down this incline of subjectivism for some distance and then arbitrarily stop. Bultmann and Barth stand together in their common opposition to the gospel of grace as founded on the Christ of the Scriptures. We dare not follow Barth any more than we dare follow Bultmann.[19]

These are exceedingly strong words, and Van Til's evaluation of Barth has deeply troubled many evangelicals of our day. A prime example is Edward John Carnell, who wrote following the Barth Lectures at Chicago: "I felt actual physical pain when I read in *Time* magazine that Cornelius Van Til, one of my former professors, had said that Barthianism is more hostile to the Reformers than is Roman Catholicism. I propose that Van Til ask God to forgive him for such an irresponsible judgment."[20]

But how "irresponsible" is Van Til's judgment, in fact? The essence of the Christian message is that *ho Logos sarx egeneto* (John 1:14), the Word became flesh — *historical* flesh is meant — and that He actually died and factually rose on the third day. The New Testament writers seem to go out of their way to assert the full facticity of the gospel events. John says that the Apostolic church heard, saw with its eyes, and handled with its hands the

---

[19]Cornelius Van Til, *Christianity and Barthianism* (Grand Rapids, Mich.: Baker Book House, 1962), pp. 444-45.

[20]Edward John Carnell, "Barth As Inconsistent Evangelical," *Christian Century*, LXXIX (June 6, 1962), 714.

Word of life (I John 1:1), and he climaxes his Gospel with the "doubting Thomas" incident in which Thomas affirms the Deity of Christ after factually encountering Him risen from the dead. Luke claims that his record of Christ is based upon the accounts of eyewitnesses (Luke 1:2), and he goes to the trouble of noting that Jesus demonstrated the corporeality of His resurrection by eating before the eyes of His disciples, who had mistakenly taken Him for a ghost (Luke 24:36-43). And Paul rested the entire truth of Christianity on the facticity of the resurrection, affirming that over five hundred people had seen the risen Christ (I Corinthians 15:4-6). The Pauline assertion that Christ "was delivered for our offenses and was raised again for our justification" (Rom. 4:25) must mean, if it means anything, that apart from a truly historical, *historisch* (not merely *geschichtlich*) death and resurrection, we would still be in our sins, subject to God's wrath. Moreover, in light of the Adam-Christ parallel in Romans 5 the factual historicity of Adam's fall is likewise essential to the Christian message.[21] Barth's "denial of the objective existence of evil"[22] certainly connects with his unhistorical view of the fall; and where the human disease is not objectively identifiable, neither can the divine remedy have objective reality.[23]

Thus we should perhaps not be too quick to condemn Van Til's evaluation of Barth. Perhaps he has seen more clearly than others the implications of Barth's separation of history and theology. The great Cambridge historian Herbert Butterfield has said: "It would be a dangerous error to imagine that the characteristics of an historical religion would be maintained if the Christ of the theologians were divorced from the Jesus of history."[24] In Barth's theology of history just such a divorce has taken place.

---

[21]See my article, "Some Comments on Paul's Use of Genesis in his Epistle to the Romans," *Evangelical Theological Society Bulletin*, IV (April, 1961), 4-11.

[22]Wingren, *op. cit.*, pp. 117 ff. Cf. my report, "Barth in Chicago: Kerygmatic Strength and Epistemological Weakness," *Dialog, A Journal of Theology*, I (Autumn, 1962), 56-57.

[23]See further on Barth's anti-and meta-historical tendencies, Walter Köhler's *Historie und Metahistorie in der Kirchengeschichte* (1930), and Robert P. Lightner, *Neo-evangelicalism* (Findlay, Ohio: Dunham, 1961), p. 117.

[24]Herbert Butterfield, *Christianity and History* (London: Collins Fontana Books, 1957), p. 168.

DEPTH ANALYSIS

We have found Barth's theology of history wanting both in the realm of general historical interpretation and in the sphere of *Heilsgeschichte*. But how can this be, when Barth again and again states his desire to recover the original purity of both the biblical writers and the Reformers? A motivational factor is evidently at work which we have not yet considered.

This factor is suggested in Barth's exceedingly strange and complex book, *Anselm: Fides Quaerens Intellectum*, which purports to rescue Anselm's so-called "ontological" proof of the existence of God from the misinterpretations put upon it by critics through the centuries. In fact, the resultant commentary gives the reader far more Barth than Anselm; but this need not concern us here. What does concern us is the conception of theology that Barth sets forth by way of Anselm. At the end of this book, Barth summarizes as follows:

> The Proof as Anselm wanted to conduct it and had to conduct it is finished. He himself reminds us again of what he understands by proof. Not a science that can be unravelled by the Church's faith and that establishes the Church's faith in a source outside of itself. It is a question of theology. It is a question of the proof of faith by faith which was already established in itself without proof.[25]

Here we have a statement of one of the most central principles of Barth's theology: that theology is an autonomous realm in the sense that no bridge exists between it and other realms of human knowledge or experience. Christianity can have no apologetic, for an apologetic would remove the "hiddenness" of revelation. Thus theology must be distinguished from history, for history is not hidden, but open to investigation. In Bultmann's "circularity" principle we see this same approach made even more explicit.[26]

---

[25]Barth, *Anselm: Fides Quaerens Intellectum; Anselm's Proof of the Existence of God in the Context of his Theological Scheme*, trans. I. W. Robertson (Richmond, Va.: John Knox Press, 1960), p. 170.

[26]On Bultmann's "circularity," principle, see Armin Henry Limper, "Hermeneutics and Eschatology: Rudolf Bultmann's Interpretation of John," Chapters 13-17 (unpublished Ph.D. dissertation, University of Chicago, 1960).

When Bultmann relativizes and existentializes both general history (by saying that "always in your present lies the meaning in history"[27]) and *Heilsgeschichte* (by saying that "Jesus rose in the kerygma"[28]), he is simply carrying Barth's position to its appropriate conclusion. A dualism between earth and heaven — between history and theology — between Jesus and the Christ — between the Bible and Revelation — becomes essential; and with it, inevitably, comes a denial of Incarnation, the Word actually made flesh.

But why this preoccupation with an alleged "hiddenness" of revelation? We have seen that the biblical writers go to the greatest length to declare the *openness* of the revelation given by God through the prophets and His Son. Indeed, the declaration of Paul before Agrippa could be taken as the theme of the Apostolic preaching: "This thing was not done in a corner" (Acts 26:26). The Barthian concentration on "hiddenness," with its resultant dualism, stems, I believe, from fear — fear of intellectual attack from the steadily growing "post-Christian" forces of our day. Barth is intensely aware of the victories of science over traditional theology in the last two centuries,[29] and he is unable to reject the higher-critical revisionism which has conditioned virtually all of contemporary biblical scholarship. He regards the Reformation identification of *Historie* with *Geschichte* as hopelessly pre-Kantian; to maintain this identification today, he feels, is to invite the decimation of the Christian faith by its critics.

How then does Barth deal with the unbeliever? In *No!* he says that experience has led him to treat "unbelievers" (the quotation marks around "unbelievers" are his) "as if their rejection of 'Christianity' was not to be taken seriously."[30] Barth makes the same point in his work on Anselm: "Perhaps Anselm did not know any other way of speaking of the Christian *Credo* except by addressing the sinner as one who had not sinned, the non-Christian as a

---

[27]Rudolf Bultmann, *The Presence of Eternity: History and Eschatology; the Gifford Lectures 1955* (New York: Harper & Row, Inc., 1957), p. 155.

[28]Rudolf Bultmann, *Das Verhältnis der unchristlichen Christusbotschaft zum historischen Jesus* (2d ed.; Heidelberg: Carl Winter, 1961), p. 27.

[29]Cf. Andrew Dickson White's *A History of the Warfare of Science with Theology in Christendom* (2 vols., reprint ed.; New York: Dover Publications, Inc., 1960).

[30]*Natural Theology* (*op. cit.*), p. 127.

Christian, the unbeliever as believer, on the basis of the great 'as if' which is really not an 'as if' at all, but which at all times has been the final and decisive means whereby the believer could speak to the unbeliever."[31] Barth's fear of being unable to defend the Christian revelation historically has thus led him to the point where, ostrich-like, he ignores the existence of unbelief and denies the ontological existence of evil; he merely proclaims a "transhistorical" gospel to those who — even though they vehemently deny it — are "believers" already. To be sure, Barth has removed the Christian faith from criticism and from the necessity of apologia — but at a frightful cost — at the cost of the Incarnation which lies at its very center, at the cost of the realistic, biblical doctrine of sin, and at the cost of any meaningful attempt to relate the gospel to general human history. He has turned the historic Christian faith into a timeless, unsupportable religion of the order of Buddhism, Hinduism, and their theosophical counterparts.

And, ironically, the reaction of the unbeliever has been exactly the opposite of what Barthianism claims it should be. Let us hear the recent evaluation by the Jewish scholar Samuel Sandmel, in his article, "The Evasions of Modern Theology," in the Phi Beta Kappa journal, *The American Scholar*:

> In the Bible there is set forth on many, many pages the conviction that God is revealed in history. The Bible knows nothing of trans-history, and, indeed, the very idea is one hundred and eighty degrees removed from what the Bible says. It is the shabbiest kind of learning that dares to call trans-history biblical. And since the word is mongrel, for *trans* is Latin and *history* is Greek, a supposedly better term, *metahistory*, is offered. It too is not biblical. Is trans-history or metahistory an explanation, or is it an evasion? . . . Does the modern theologian enter the arena of the intellectual combat with the secular historian? Is he grappling with a genuine issue, and setting it into a convincing array of ideas and propositions? Or does he simply abandon the field to his adversary? In my judgment the modern theologian is guilty of evasion. And, I would add, the theologian is at this point throwing away even the bare possibility of communicating with the layman, for to most of us the word history has had a particular import; the word trans-

---

[31]Barth, *Anselm*, p. 71.

history seems to me to be more a barrier to, than a vehicle of, communication.[32]

Clearly the Barthian theology has sold its birthright for a mess of pottage when it has lost both the historical center of the Christian faith and the ability to convey a meaningful gospel to the un-believer of our day. History can be removed from Christian theology only by the total destruction of theology itself.

THE PROBLEM IN EVANGELICAL CIRCLES

At this point those of us who regard ourselves as "evangelicals" no doubt breathe a sigh of relief, and thank God that we are "not as other men are, dualists, metahistoricizers, opponents of the biblical apologetic — or even as this Karl Barth." But is this really the case? Has Barth's influence passed us by? I do not believe so, and I shall present some brief but sobering examples of the ease with which we uncautiously slip into the Barthian methodology.

First, we have found that Barth refuses to see meaning in general human history — that he tends to ignore the creative ac-tivity of God throughout the history of mankind. This hesitancy to apply the biblical message to total history is due, we have sug-gested, not only to the Barthian reaction to the progressivistic-optimistic philosophies of history characteristic of modernism, but also to a fear of subjecting the Christian faith to secular criticism. But what about contemporary evangelicals? Have we produced a twentieth-century equivalent of Augustine's *City of God?* or an interpretation of general history comparable to Toynbee's? The bibliography to the chapter on "Philosophy of History" by Earl E. Cairns in *Contemporary Evangelical Thought* lists five authors: John Baillie, Herbert Butterfield, Otto Piper, Eric C. Rust, and Toynbee, and a note informs us: "In lieu of a satisfactory Evan-gelical bibliography in Philosophy of History, the above volumes, representative of diverse viewpoints, are included to suggest im-portant contemporary literature in this field."[33]

Moreover, one finds in such contemporary evangelical writers as Bernard Ramm careful strictures of the following kind: "Con-

---

[32]*The American Scholar*, XXX (Summer, 1961), 377.

[33]*Contemporary Evangelical Thought*, ed. Carl F. H. Henry (Great Neck, N.Y.: Channel Press, 1957), p. 315.

cerning the moral interpretation of secular history (or even church history) the Christian walks the same tightrope of probability that the secular historian does."[34] This statement has an element of truth in it, surely, since no Christian historian is God, but are we not too quick in acknowledging our fallibility and too slow in affirming the absolute relevance of biblical truth to the understanding of history? I think Ramm totally in error when he says that "the reality of historical revelation does not put the Christian in a superior position to write the philosophy of history."[35] The Christian historian is in fact the *only* historian who *can* write the philosophy of history, because only he has a revelational perspective which is not conditioned by his own finite stance in history.

In my book, *The Shape of the Past*, I have pointed out that secular historiography in our day has reached a philosophical impasse in at least four respects: (1) it is unable to arrive at a satisfactory and defensible conception of human nature; (2) it is unable, for want of an absolute axiology, to determine levels of significance among historical events; (3) it is unable to set out patterns of total history, since neither the origin nor the goal of history is known; and (4) it is unable, having no doctrine of regeneration, to tell the historian how to put into practice Croce and Collingwood's paramount dictum that the historian must re-experience the past, for re-experiencing requires a radical change in the egocentric personality of the historian, who tends to read his own personality back into the past instead of "losing himself" in order to "find" the people of past ages. Only the Christian faith provides a way out of this fourfold historiographical graveyard, for only Christianity offers the historian (1) a reliable, absolute conception of human nature, (2) a criterion of historical importance (the Cross), (3) a knowledge of the origin and goal of history, and (4) a means of regeneration for the historian himself. Thus evangelicals have a holy responsibility to lead present-day historiography out of its naturalistic blind alley; and if they neglect this task they are like the unheeding priest and Levite who "passed by on the other side" when radical need cried out to them on the way from Jerusalem to Jericho.

---

[34]Bernard Ramm, *Special Revelation and the Word of God* (Grand Rapids, Mich.: Wm. B. Eerdmans, 1961), p. 98.
[35]*Ibid.*, p. 97.

In reviewing the Jesuit M. C. D'Arcy's *Meaning and Matter of History: A Christian View*, E. Harris Harbison of Princeton has noted that D'Arcy's cautious willingness merely to use Christian insights in "enlarging our vision of human efforts and human achievements" is a far cry from Augustine's forthright vindication of God's action in bringing about Rome's collapse.[36] Perhaps we deserve this same criticism; and I suggest that the Barthian fear of becoming vunerable to the world's attacks lies at the root. Whenever we hesitate to interpret general history by the revelational insights of Scripture — for fear of subjecting the faith to attack — we travel along the Barthian road.

"Yet certainly there is no metahistoricizing of divine revelation among evangelicals," we say with confidence. This confidence may waver a bit, however, in contact with Ramm's above-quoted book, *Special Revelation and the Word of God*, where the author again and again lashes out against a type he calls "the rationalistic fundamentalist"; this is the person who "wants a Bible that is better than the famous Cambridge historical series" — who "wants the kind of rational religious certainty which can emerge from solid, hard, historical factuality."[37] For Ramm, "only if there were no presence of the Holy Spirit or of God or of the community of the covenant could we think of historical revelation in terms of documented court evidence."[38] In effect, Ramm is here arguing a "circularity" principle which has more than a little in common with Barth and Bultmann, for he is saying that the Scripture does not have demonstrable reality as historical revelation apart from the covenantal community and the *testimonium* (internal witness) of the Spirit. In actuality, however, the reality of historical revelation in Scripture is fully objective — and the Spirit and the community *bear witness* to this fact; they do not in any sense bring it about.

Even more disturbing is the approach to the resurrection of Christ taken by George Eldon Ladd in a recent issue of the new

---

[36]E. Harris Harbison, Review of *The Meaning and Matter of History: A Christian View* by M. C. D'Arcy, *History and Theory*, I (1960), 86-89.
[37]Ramm, *op. cit.*, p. 99.
[38]*Ibid.* See also Ramm's *The Witness of the Spirit* (Grand Rapids, Mich.: Eerdmans, 1960), *passim*.

theological journal *Dialog*.[39] Professor Ladd was requested by the editor of *Dialog* to provide an "evangelical" comment on the previous issue of the magazine, which was devoted to the general subject of "Death and Resurrection." Articles in that issue of *Dialog* (e.g., Robert Scharlemann's "Shadow on the Tomb" and Roy A. Harrisville's "Resurrection and Historical Method") parroted the Barthian metahistorical approach to the resurrection — refusing to accept the resurrection as objective *Historie*. I am myself personally acquainted with the editor of *Dialog*, and I know him to be fully committed to the metahistorical approach. He told me that he had been surprised to find Professor Ladd's contribution in full accord with the thrust of the resurrection issue of *Dialog*. I too was surprised — and pained. Ladd writes:

> The New Testament does not share the modern idea of history, and it does not represent the resurrection of Jesus as an "historical" event in the modern critical sense of this word. It was an event without historical cause. . . . The resurrection is also without historical analogy. . . . The basic problem for the modern theologian is this. Shall we insist upon a definition of history broad enough to include such supra-historical events as the resurrection; or shall we accept the modern view of history as a working method but insist that there is a dimension within history which transcends historical control? The latter is the method of Karl Barth; and . . . it appears to be the only adequate explanation which satisfies the data of redemptive history.

Here Dr. Ladd makes Barth's very mistake. He creates a metahistorical category of interpretation for the resurrection in order to preserve its theological truth from historical criticism. What he should do is to distinguish between truly empirical historical method (which simply collects and analyzes the data of the past — and never excludes phenomena because causal linkages cannot be established or because of the uniqueness which is, after all, characteristic of all historical events), and the Historicism which grew out of nineteenth-century historical Positivism and which passes for "objective, critical history" in Barthian circles

---

[39]George Eldon Ladd, "The Resurrection and History," *Dialog*, I (Autumn, 1962), 55-56.

today.[40] Historicism refuses to regard the resurrection as history because of the absence of human causation and because of its uniqueness; but this is no more than the result of rationalistic pre-suppositionalism concerning the nature of the universe (all events must have natural causes; all events must be analogously related to other events). Ladd accomplishes nothing by appealing, à la Barth, to a "supra-history," for, as we have seen, this inevitably weakens the central Christian truth of Incarnation, and, in any case, meta-history has no meaning to the non-Christian since it is beyond the possibility of investigation.

The weakness in the "mediating evangelical" approach here described is particularly evident in Ramm's summary assertion that "a fanatical *'objectivizing'* of Scripture can be as detrimental to its proper understanding as a frightful *'subjectivizing.'* "[41] In point of fact, *there are no degrees of objectivity;* either Scripture and the events of salvation-history recorded in it are objective or they are not. If they are not, then we must move beyond Barth's ambiguous, intermediate position to Bultmann's mythical approach (since Barthian "metahistory" is not amenable to any adequate epistemological test). But if the events of *Heilsgeschichte* are ob-jective (as Ramm and Ladd of course believe), then we must cease to speak in terms of metahistory and courageously use the language of objective facticity. What are we afraid of? The events of *Heilsgeschichte* will not dissolve under the searchlight of proper historical investigation. Our responsibility is to make sure that in the use of historical method scientistic, historicistic presuppositions (e.g., Bultmann's a priori — completely inappropriate in an age of Einsteinian relativity — that historical explanation must always take place within the unbroken nexus of "natural" causes) are not surreptitiously smuggled into the picture disguised as objective historical method and allowed to determine the results of the in-vestigation.

Conclusion

We must face the issue squarely: there is no *tertium quid.* Either the events of *Heilsgeschichte*, such as the resurrection, are in the full sense *Historie* or they are not. If they are not, then of

---

[40]Cf. the parallel distinction between true scientific method and scientific Positivism or Scientism (see my *Shape of the Past*, pp. 141, 265-68).

[41]Ramm, *Special Revelation and the Word of God*, loc. cit.

course they are not subject to attack (as is likewise the case with the timeless doctrines of Eastern mysticism, such as *karma*). But then the affirmation that "the Word became flesh" has only mythical significance, and we are still in our sins. But if the gospel events are *Historie*, then we must acknowledge the unpleasant fact that they must be defended as such against the barbs of a hostile world. Doubtless, when, like Paul, we proclaim the historical facticity of the resurrection and other saving-events, some will mock, and others will say, "We will hear thee again of this matter" (Acts 17:31-32). But God help us if in our darkling age we do not proclaim the incarnational truths of the faith once delivered — historically — to the saints.

And if I am right that it is fear of criticism which leads to the Barthian divorce between theology and history and to all its attendant evils? Then perhaps even a pagan can give us needed advice. Pericles, in his magnificent Oration on the Athenian Dead, told his countrymen that their political freedom depended squarely upon their courage: "We rely, not on secret weapons, but on our own real courage. . . . Make up your minds that . . . freedom depends on being courageous."[42] Not only political freedom rests on courage; so also does spiritual freedom. If we would introduce a sin-enslaved post-Christian age to freedom in Christ, we must not rely upon the "secret weapons" of metahistory, but on the courage to reiterate and defend in our day the Apostolic (and Reformation) proclamation:

> Having therefore obtained help of God, I continue unto this day, witnessing both to small and great, saying none other things than those which the prophets and Moses did say should come: that Christ should suffer, and that he should be the first that should rise from the dead, and should shew light unto the people, and to the Gentiles. And as he thus spake for himself, Festus said with a loud voice, Paul, thou art beside thyself; much learning doth make thee mad. But he said, I am not mad, most noble Festus; but speak forth the words of truth and soberness. For the king knoweth of these things, before whom also I speak freely: for I am persuaded that none of these things are hidden from him; for this thing was not done in a corner (Acts 26:22-26).

---

[42]Thucydides, *History of the Peloponnesian War*, trans. Rex Warner (Harmondsworth, England: Penguin Books, 1954), pp. 118, 121.

6. TILLICH'S PHILOSOPHY OF HISTORY*

DURING a recent evening of bibliomaniacal revelry, Robert Al-
lenson, president of the distinguished firm of theological book-
sellers in Naperville, Illinois, told me the following story about
Tillich — a story that he had heard during his student days at
Union Theological Seminary. Reinhold Niebuhr, deep in conversation and oblivious to all else, was descending a staircase, while
Tillich was coming up the same stairs. As they passed, the student with Niebuhr asked him: "But what about Dr. Tillich's view
on the subject?" "You mean that damned pantheist?" replied
Niebuhr with a chuckle. Several weeks later, as spring was coming on, Niebuhr found Tillich, who was a great lover of nature,
on his hands and knees in the quadrangle sniffing a crocus. "Ah,
Professor Tillich," he called out, "what are you doing?" Tillich,
without changing his position, looked up and said: "It is zee
damned pantheist worshipping zee flowers."

This tale, perhaps better characterized as *Geschichte* than *Historie*, provides a most appropriate starting-point for our discussion of Tillich's philosophy of history, for it reminds us of the
extent to which Tillich's views have been subject to facile generali-

---

*An invitational paper presented on November 11, 1966, at the annual
Philosophy Conference sponsored by the philosophy faculty of Wheaton
College, Wheaton, Illinois (Arthur F. Holmes, director).

zation and superficial criticism. The centrality of Tillich's historical understanding to his entire theological endeavor makes it
imperative that as we study this aspect of his thought we avoid
labels, epithets, and the preconceptions that so readily give rise to
them, and instead try sensitively to discover the root concerns that
informed his views of historical reality.

Some justification for a paper on Tillich's philosophy of history
seems in order when the mass of Tillich literature is growing daily,
and when valuable analyses of his approach to history have already been done from a variety of theological perspectives.[1] Yet
after one has granted the genuine contributions offered by previous
studies of Tillich's philosophy of history, two highly significant
considerations undeniably demand a new and different approach.
The first is the striking "last stage" of Tillich's thought, char-

---

[1]Especially noteworthy are: (1) James Luther Adams, "Tillich's Interpretation of History," in Charles W. Kegley and Robert W. Bretall (eds.),
The Theology of Paul Tillich (New York: The Macmillan Company,
1952), pp. 294-309 (with Tillich's reply to Adams and to other critics of
his historical position, pp. 345-48); (2) John W. Sanderson, Jr., "Historical
Fact or Symbol? The Philosophies of History of Paul Tillich and Rien-
hold Niebuhr," *Westminster Theological Journal*, XX (May, 1958), 158-
69, and XXI (November, 1958), 58-74; (3) William Wright Paul, "Paul
Tillich's Interpretation of History" (Ann Arbor, Michigan: University
Microfilms [AC-1 No. 59-3124], 1959; (4) George H. Tavard, *Paul Tillich
and the Christian Message* (New York: Chas. Scribner's Sons, 1962), es-
pecially chap. v. ("Christology As History"), pp. 82-112; (5) Robert D.
Knudsen, "Symbol and Myth in Contemporary Theology, with Special
Reference to the Thought of Paul Tillich, Reinhold Niebuhr, and Nicolas
Berdyaev" (Roslyn, Pa.: The Author, 1963), *passim* (mimeographed and
stylistically revised version of the author's 1952 S.T.M. thesis submitted at
Union Theological Seminary, New York); (6) J. Heywood Thomas,
Paul Tillich: An Appraisal ("The Library of Philosophy and Theology";
London: SCM Press, 1963), especially chaps iii ("Christology and Histori-
cal Criticism"), pp. 78-90, and vii ("History and the Kingdom of God"),
pp. 150-71; (7) Avery R. Dulles, S.J., "Paul Tillich and the Bible," in
Thomas A. O'Meara and Celestin D. Weisser (eds.), *Paul Tillich in
Catholic Thought* (Dubuque, Iowa: Priory Press, 1964), pp. 109-32 (with
Tillich's reply as to the relation between the Jesus of history and the
Christ of faith, pp. 309-10); (8) James Luther Adams, *Paul Tillich's
Philosophy of Culture, Science, and Religion* (New York: Harper, 1965),
passim; and (9) Bruce J. R. Cameron, "The Historical Problem in Paul
Tillich's Christology," *Scottish Journal of Theology*, XVIII (September,
1965), 257-72.

acterized by his intense interest in the history of religions and his unwitting influence on death-of-God thinking during the final year of his life. ("Faithful to his vocation and his destiny," said religious phenomenologist Mircea Eliade at the Tillich Memorial Service of the University of Chicago Divinity School on October 29, 1965, "Paul Tillich did not die at the end of his career, when he had supposedly said everything important that he could say. On the contrary, he died at the beginning of another renewal of his thought. Thus his death is even more tragic, for theologian and historian of religion alike. But it is also symbolic."[2]) Secondly, recent applications of the insights of analytical philosophy to philosophy of history[3] have provided a technique by which a keener examination of Tillich's historical thinking now becomes possible to historian and theologian alike. The present essay, therefore, while endeavoring to present a synoptic view of the general development of Tillich's theology of history, will come to focus on the revolutionary last years of his career, and will seek to offer a responsible analytical critique of his fully matured outlook on the relations between history and religious belief.

Ultimate Concern and Theonomous History

A proper beginning is made at the keystone of Tillich's entire theological endeavor — a keystone which was put in place early in his life and which in so many and variegated ways, conditioned all his subsequent thinking. I refer to his passionate desire to create a theology and arrive at a historical understanding of Christianity which would stand in opposition to all forms of idolatry.

We first meet our theologian in post-World War I Germany —a Germany smarting under military defeat and overwhelming war reparations, further weakened by the inept Weimar Republic, and open to the totalitarian panacea about to be offered by National Socialism.[4] In the autobiographical section (Part One) of

---

[2]Mircea Eliade, "Paul Tillich and the History of Religions," in *The Future of Religions* by Paul Tillich (New York: Harper & Row, 1966), pp. 35-36.

[3]E.g. Arthur C. Danto, *Analytical Philosophy of History* (Cambridge: Cambridge University Press, 1965).

[4]Cf. Karl Hennig, "Paul Tillich: Leben und Werk," in *Der Spannungsbogen. Festgabe fuer Paul Tillich zum 75. Geburtstag* (Stuttgart: Evangelisches Verlagswerk, 1961), pp. 171 ff.

The Interpretation of History,[5] Tillich describes his reaction to that situation. He established his political position "on the boundary"[6] between the individualistic autonomy debilitating the Weimar government and the rising dictatorial heteronomy that would engulf Germany under Hitler. For Tillich, both autonomous individualism and heteronomous authoritarianism were demonic. He opted instead for a "theonomous" orientation: a religious socialism that would avoid these idolatrous extremes. Thus, until Reinhold Niebuhr and others at Union Theological Seminary engineered his emigration from the Third Reich in 1933, he served as one of the outstanding members of the German Christian-Socialist party.

Out of this political philosophy, Tillich developed a striking interpretation of history, involving the dialectic interaction of theonomous, heteronomous, and autonomous motifs. He writes:

By analyzing the character of "historical" time, as distinguished from physical and biological time, I developed a concept of history in which the movement toward the new, which is both demanded and expected, is constitutive. The content of the new, toward which history moves, appears in events in which the meaning and goal of history become manifest. I called such an event the "center of history"; from the Christian viewpoint the center is the appearance of Jesus as the Christ. The powers struggling with one another in history can be given different names, according to the perspective from which they are viewed: demonic-*divine*-human, sacramental-*prophetic*-secular, heteronomous-*theonomous*-autonomous. Each middle term represents the synthesis of the other two, the one toward which history is always extending itself — sometimes creatively, sometimes destructively, never completely fulfilled, but always driven by the transcendent power of the anticipated fulfillment. Religious socialism should be understood as one such move toward a new theonomy. It is more than a new economic system. It is

---

[5]Paul Tillich, *The Interpretation of History*, trans. Rasetzki and Talmey (New York: Scribner, 1936); Part One of this work has just been reissued under the title, *On the Boundary: An Autobiographical Sketch* (New York: Charles Scribner's Sons, 1966).

[6]With the "boundary" motif in Tillich's thought, cf. Helmut Thielicke, "Paul Tillich — Wanderer zwischen zwei Welten," in *Der Spannungsbogen*, pp. 9-24.

a comprehensive understanding of existence, the form of the theonomy demanded and expected by our present Kairos.[7]

Tillich views the history of western Christendom by way of this typology:[8] The early Middle Ages exhibited theonomy, for both corporate and individual power were subordinated to an ultimate, divine perspective. In the later medieval period, the ecclesiastical system came to overshadow everything, and a heteronomy resulted. The Renaissance constituted an individualistic, autonomous over-reaction to the stifling medieval heteronomy. The early Reformation endeavored to restore the theonomous perspective of early Christianity, but, in the later years of the Reformation era, Protestant ecclesiastical controls coupled with the absolutistic powers of rising national states created a new heteronomy. The eighteenth-century "Enlightenment" chose the path of rationalistic autonomy, thus over-reacting to heteronomy as had the Renaissance in relation to medieval civilization.[9] For Tillich, the breakdown of autonomy after World War I offered two alternatives: return to a totalitarian heteronomy, as exemplified by Nazi (or Communist) rule, or commitment to a theonomous way of life, where the Ultimate is not identified with any earthly power, whether corporate or individual, but stands in judgment on all of man's decisions. A Christian socialism seemed, in Tillich's view, the best means of achieving such a theonomous goal.

What evaluation do we place on this theology of history? In spite of its obvious leanings toward over-generalization (a built-in danger in any historical typology!), and in spite of the naïveté of its socialism (why cannot the social body become a demonic heteronomy no less all-embracing than the traditional national

---

[7]Tillich, *On the Boundary*, pp. 80-81.

[8]I have discussed and schematically diagrammed Tillich's theonomy-heteronomy-autonomy view in my book, *The Shape of the Past: An Introduction to Philosophical Historiography* ("History in Christian Perspective," Vol. 1; Ann Arbor, Michigan: Edwards Brothers, 1962), pp. 127-31.

[9]Cf. Tillich, "A History of Christian Thought: A Stenographic Transcription of Lectures Delivered during the Spring Term, 1953 at Union Theological Seminary," ed. Peter H. John, pp. 234-41. ("These lectures are intended for private use of present and former students of Dr. Tillich and are not to be quoted for publication without his permission"—Foreword.)

state?), Tillich's interpretation gives striking expression to one of the most fundamental themes of Christian philosophy of history: God's transcendence over history. This theme, stressed alike by the Old Testament prophets and the Protestant Reformers, is in essence the application to history of the First Commandment: "I am the Lord thy God, which have brought thee out of the land of Egypt, out of the house of bondage. Thou shalt have no other gods before me." In the greatest of contemporary theological interpretations of history, Eric Voegelin's still unfinished *Order and History*, one can see how Tillich's theonomy motif has borne exceedingly rich fruit. As I have noted elsewhere, Tillich taught Voegelin to see "the central demonic temptation of our time: the attempt to create God in man's own image — in the image of his political, social, and religious theories and projects." Both cry to our age what Luther cried to his: "Let God be God!"[10]

Yet Tillich never developed his historical philosophy in detail. *The Interpretation of History* was the only book-length work of the subject he was to write, and when, a few years before his death, the American Theological Library Association requested permission to reprint it photolithographically in a limited edition for libraries unable to obtain it, Tillich refused. Though the autobiographical section of the book was reissued in 1966,[11] the substantive portion of it, applying Tillich's typology to historical epochs, remains out of print. Why? For one thing, as Tillich himself tells us in his contribution to *Christian Century's* "How My Mind Has Changed" series, he moved "beyond religious socialism" after coming to the United States,[12] and did not find the political climate of the present an incentive toward more extensive interpretation of the past.

> Since the early twenties I have made a distinction between periods in which historical opportunities are predominant and those in which historical trends determine the outcome. While I felt that the years after World War I were years of opportunity, I feel that those following World War II have been years of trend. This also is only relatively true, but it has a somewhat

---

[10]Montgomery, *op. cit.*, pp. 135-36; I treat Voegelin in detail on pp. 131 ff.

[11]See above, note 5.

[12]Cf. Hanns Lilje, "Paul Tillichs Bedeutung fuer das amerikanische Geistesleben," in *Der Spannungsbogen*, pp. 149-69.

paralyzing influence on political passion. And since I believe that the key to history is historical action, my desire to concentrate on the problems of an interpretation of history was also diminished.[13]

Here Tillich makes quite clear that it has been the present which has driven him to any historical interests that he has had, not the reverse, and it is not difficult to relate this present-time orientation to Tillich's profound concern with philosophical and religious existentialism, which is at root a present (rather than past) oriented world-view.[14] But Tillich quite rightly claims that he "was never an existentialist in the strict sense of the word."[15] Indeed, his entire theological endeavor can be understood as an attempt to stiffen and shore up existentialism through a firm ontology — or, expressed otherwise, an attempt to provide an apologetic bridge for the existentially immersed modern man to cross over to an ontologically justifiable religious position. Existential questions, according to Tillich's famous "principle of correlation," can be answered only by proper ontological understanding. The most basic reason, then, for Tillich's lack of continuing interest in historical interpretation will be found to lie in the nature of his ontological commitment. To this we shall now give our attention.

BEING ITSELF AND HISTORY UNDER THE PROTESTANT PRINCIPLE

Tillich's profound concern with theonomy — with the elimination of all forms of idolatry through focus on the only Ultimate Concern that is truly ultimate — led him to condemn the identification of the Absolute with anything in the phenomenal world. Thus in his autobiography he wrote:

---

[13]Tillich, in Harold E. Fey (ed.), *How My Mind Has Changed* (New York: Meridian Living Age Books, 1961) pp. 165-66.

[14]Cf. Rudolf Bultmann's characteristic statement at the close of his Gifford Lectures: "Always in your present lies the meaning in history." *The Presence of Eternity: History and Eschatology* (New York: Harper & Row, 1957), p. 155.

[15]*How My Mind Has Changed*, p. 165. Cf. Tillich's exceedingly valuable essay, "Existential Philosophy: Its Historical Meaning," in his *Theology of Culture*, ed. Robert C. Kimball (New York: Oxford University Press, 1959), pp. 76-111.

My fundamental theological problem arose in applying the relation of the absolute, which is implied in the idea of God, to the
relativity of human religion. Religious dogmatism, including
that of Protestant orthodoxy and the most recent phase of what
is called dialectical theology, comes into being when a historical
religion is cloaked with the unconditional validity of the divine,
as when a book, person, community, institution, or doctrine
claims absolute authority and demands the submission of every
other reality; for no other claim can exist beside the unconditioned claim of the divine. But that this claim can be grounded
in a finite, historical reality is the root of all heteronomy and
all demonism. The demonic is something finite and limited
which has been invested with the stature of the infinite.[16]

But, if nothing "finite and limited" can be identified with the
Ultimate, where do we find it? What criteria do we employ?
Tillich refuses to start the search for the Ultimate in the realm of
epistemology, for, he claims, every epistemology presupposes an
ontology. The start must therefore be made at the point of ontological reality itself. "Being itself" is both the beginning and the
end of the search for the Ultimate, for it *is* the only Ultimate and
the only proper object of theonomous faith.[17] Nothing — no
existent thing, idea, or person — can be identified with Being itself
without committing the root sin of idolatry. Thus religious doctrines, affirmations and beliefs must be regarded as *symbolic* of
Being itself and not confused with ultimate truth. For Tillich,
religious phenomena, whether Christian or non-Christian, can never
attain a status beyond the symbolic; that is to say, though they
"participate" in ontological reality, they always point beyond themselves to that Being which is not another existent thing, but the
ground of all that is.[18] Here we arrive at Tillich's most fundamental operating rule, the "Protestant principle," by which he

---

[16]*On the Boundary*, p. 40.
[17]"The God who is *a* being is transcended by the God who is Being
itself, the ground and abyss of every being," Tillich, *Biblical Religion and
the Search for Ultimate Reality* (Chicago: University of Chicago Press,
1955), p. 82.
[18]See Tillich's essays, "The Meaning and Justification of Religious Symbols" and "The Religious Symbol" in Sidney Hook (ed.), *Religious Experience and Truth* (New York: New York University Press, 1961), pp.
3-11, 301-21.

scores all attempts to elevate the symbolic to the level of ultimacy. As the Reformers condemned late medieval Romanism for heteronomously absolutizing the visible Church and identifying it with the divine will, so we must unqualifiedly reject *all* historical identifications of the Absolute with religious phenomena. "Where the myth is taken literally," writes Tillich, "God is less than the ultimate, he is less than the subject of ultimate concern, he is not God in the infinite and unconditional sense of the great commandment."[19]

Tillich's ontological orientation had a predictable effect on his historical interests: it shifted him away from history, which at best can provide only symbols and myths of ultimacy, and directed his gaze to the purity of unconditioned Being itself. Thus one finds remarkably little stress placed on ecclesiology in Tillich's thought, and a tendency to depreciate the "Church manifest" in favor of a "Church latent" which is not "a specifiable or identifiable historical group," but is composed of "those groups within paganism, Judaism or humanism which also reveal or actualize the New Being";[20] for Tillich this concept of a "latent" Church "precludes the possibility of ecclesiastical arrogance"[21] by exposing to criticism the idolatrous and presumptive claims of the empirical churches. But, even more important, Tillich's ontological commitment demanded a radical reinterpretation of the place of the historical Christ in Christian theology.

In *The Interpretation of History* it had been evident that Tillich was fully convinced by the rationalistic arguments of Lessing against historical certainty, and by the negative judgments of nineteenth-century biblical criticism on the worth of the New Testament accounts of Jesus. There Tillich wrote that, consistent with an aim held as far back as his doctoral studies in 1911, he was attempting "to answer the question, how the Christian doctrine might be understood, if the non-existence of the historical Jesus should become historically probable."[22] In the second volume of

---

[19]Tillich, "Where Do We Go from Here in Theology?" *Religion in Life*, Winter, 1955-56.

[20]Thomas, *op cit.*, p. 140.

[21]*Ibid.*, pp. 140-41. Tillich treats the "Church latent" in conjunction with several topics discussed in the third volume of his *Systematic Theology*.

[22]*The Interpretation of History*, p. 33.

his *Systematic Theology*, the volume dealing with Christology, Tillich reaffirmed his conviction that "faith cannot rest on such unsure ground" as historical research into the life of Jesus.[23] A year before his death, in a foreword to the English translation of a seminal work by his teacher Martin Kähler, Tillich made clear that the years had not altered his viewpoint. "I do believe that one emphasis in Kähler's answer is decisive for our present situation, namely, the necessity to make the certainty of faith independent of the unavoidable incertitudes of historical research."[24]

But how is it possible to avoid "the incertitudes of historical research" when a historical incarnation of God in Christ appears central to the Christian proclamation? Tillich's answer is to regard the Christ-event, not from the standpoint of *de facto* divine incarnation (this would have all the earmarks of idolatrous identification of Being itself with the finite and would violate the Protestant principle), but from the viewpoint of religious symbol. Jesus, understood symbolically *as* the Christ, is the most fundamental religious symbol of all, for in his death on the cross we have the great *Kairos* — the decisive event *par excellence* — which symbolizes the judgment of Being itself on all human pretensions and idolatrous expressions.[25] Indeed, Jesus conceived as the Christ may be termed the "New Being," since in Him we see the dichotomy between man's essence and existence mended, and insight is given into the true nature of Being, which is Eros or self-realizing love.[26] But, having said all of this, we must always be on our guard against absolutizing the historical Jesus or basing our faith upon a historical foundation; indeed, the best evidence that the Christ-event constitutes the greatest of all religious symbols is that it judges even itself!

---

[23]*Systematic Theology* (3 vols.; Chicago: University of Chicago Press, 1951-1963), II, 113.

[24]Tillich, "Foreword" to Martin Kähler, *The So-Called Historical Jesus and the Historic, Biblical Christ*, trans. Carl E. Braaten (Philadelphia: Fortress Press, 1964), p. xii. (This translation is limited to the first and second essays in the 1896 ed. of Kähler's book.)

[25]Cf. Tillich's article, "Kairos," in Halverson and Cohen (eds.); *A Handbook of Christian Theology* (New York: Meridian Living Age Books, 1958), pp. 196-97.

[26]See Tillich's *Love, Power, and Justice* (New York: Oxford University Press, 1954), *passim*.

Every type of faith has the tendency to elevate its concrete symbols to absolute validity. The criterion of the truth of faith, therefore, is that it implies an element of self-negation. That symbol is most adequate which expresses not only the ultimate but also its own lack of ultimacy. Christianity expresses itself in such a symbol in contrast to all other religions, namely, in the Cross of the Christ. Jesus could not have been the Christ without sacrificing himself as Jesus to himself as the Christ. Any acceptance of Jesus as the Christ which is not the acceptance of Jesus the crucified is a form of idolatry. The ultimate concern of the Christian is not Jesus, but the Christ Jesus who is manifest as the crucified. The event which has created this symbol has given the criterion by which the truth of Christianity, as well as of any other religion, must be judged. The only infallible truth of faith, the one in which the ultimate itself is unconditionally manifest, is that any truth of faith stands under a yes-or-no judgment.[27]

The stage was therefore set for Tillich's analysis of "history and the Kingdom of God" in the third and final volume of his *Systematic Theology*. There he states that in regard to the question of history's meaning "the subject-object character of history precludes an objective answer in any detached, scientific sense,"[28] and that historical interpretation is subject to the "theological circle"[29] interlocking the observer with what he observes, so that "it is an unavoidable circle wherever the question of the ultimate meaning of history is asked."[30] In the absence of any possibility of arriving at objective historical meaning (to do so would raise history to the level of ultimacy, thus violating the Protestant principle!), Tillich affirms that the ambiguities of history are best understood and overcome through the symbol "Kingdom of God."

The Kingdom of God may appear through a political system, a revolution, a church, or an individual, and whenever it does

---

[27]Tillich, *Dynamics of Faith* (New York: Harper Torchbooks, 1958), pp. 97-98.
[28]Tillich, *Systematic Theology*, III, 349.
[29]I have dealt in some detail with the issue of the "theological circle" in my paper, "Lutheran Hermeneutics and Hermeneutics Today," in *Aspects of Biblical Hermeneutics* ("Concordia Theological Monthly. Occasional Papers," No. 1; St. Louis, Missouri, 1966), pp. 78-108.
[30]Tillich, *Systematic Theology, loc. cit.*

appear it heals the conflicts of history — but it heals them only fragmentarily. For the ultimate and final answer to history is not found in history, but at the end of history. This answer is the salvation of God, called by Tillich "universal essentialization," which means that all being, man included, is raised to un-ambiguous unity with the ground and power of being, and therein finds its fulfillment.[31]

Since Tillich views evil as a negative — as the absence of being — he holds that it has no actual ontological existence; "universal essentialization" therefore precludes the eternal damnation of any-one.[32] Indeed, it is vital to see that when Tillich employs tradi-tional eschatological terminology (general resurrection, last judg-ment, etc.), he does not refer to concrete historical happenings at the end of the age; he regards these doctrines as symbols of man's present relationship to the ground of his being. Thus he "can discuss the resurrection of the body without reference to the Resurrection of Christ as either norm or criterion."[33] A la Schell-ing's concept of the "becomingness of God," Tillich sees Being itself as engaged in "the eternal conquest of the negative."[34] He diagrams[35] the relation between eternity and time not in terms of the traditional biblical concept of linear, historical progression,[36] viz.

CREATION ●————————→————————→————————● LAST JUDGMENT
INCARNATION

---

[31]Alexander J. McKelway, *The Systematic Theology of Paul Tillich* (Richmond, Virginia: John Knox Press, 1964), p. 249.

[32]"Absolute judgments over finite beings . . . are impossible, because they make the finite infinite" (Tillich, *Systematic Theology*, III, 407).

[33]McKelway, *op. cit.*, p. 245, n. 11.

[34]Tillich, *Systematic Theology*, III, 405. On the profound influence of Schelling's *Lebensphilosophie* on Tillich's ontological thought, see John H. Randall, Jr., "Tillich's Systematic Theology, vol. III," *Union Seminary Quarterly Review*, XIX (May, 1964), 356 ff.

[35]See Tillich, *Systematic Theology*, III, 420.

[36]As presented, e.g., in my *Shape of the Past*, pp. 42, 45.

but in such a way as to affirm that "fulfillment is going on in every moment here and now beyond history, not some time in the future, but here and now above ourselves":[37]

ETERNITY

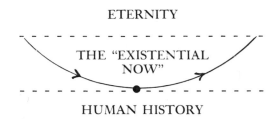

HUMAN HISTORY

Kenneth Hamilton has well captured the symbolical spirit of Tillich's understanding of the Kingdom of God and its eschatological fulfillment:

> *Allegory*: Christ will deliver up the Kingdom to the Father, and God will be all in all.
>
> *Reality*: Universal participation in the Ground of Being can come only in essentialization, where the Absolute gathers into itself all that is positive in the movement from essence to existence, thus fulfilling itself through the world-process.[38]

Tillich's endeavor to provide an ontological answer to man's existential predicament led him — as our analysis of his views of Christ and the Kingdom has well demonstrated — to a basically non-historical interpretation of the Christian faith. It should not come as a surprise, therefore, that in spite of Tillich's opposition to "suprahistorical" views of salvation-history,[39] and in spite of his

---

[37]Tillich, "The Decline and the Validity of the Idea of Progress," in his *The Future of Religions*, p. 79. Cf. Tillich's theme of "the eternal now," which served as the title of one of his important sermons and was chosen by him as the title for the entire published sermon collection in which it appeared: *The Eternal Now* (New York: Charles Scribner's Sons, 1963).

[38]Kenneth Hamilton, "Paul Tillich," in Philip Edgcumbe Hughes (ed.), *Creative Minds in Contemporary Theology* (Grand Rapids, Michigan: Eerdmans, 1966), p. 478. Cf. Hamilton's book-length treatment of Tillich: *The System and the Gospel: A Critique of Paul Tillich* ("The Library of Philosophy and Theology"; London: SCM Press, 1963).

[39]See Tillich's *Systematic Theology*, III, 363. On the dialectical concept of "suprahistory" ("metahistory," *Geschichte*), see above, chapter 5.

caveats against the historical indifferentism of the Eastern religions,[40] his last years saw him being drawn more and more into the orbit of non-historical Oriental thought. From May to July of 1960, Tillich visited Japan, and in retrospect he described the religious effect his Eastern experience had upon him:

> They have confirmed my theological conviction that one cannot divide the religions of mankind into one true and many false religions. Rather, one must subject all religions, including Christianity, to the ultimate criteria of religion: the criterion of a faith which transcends every finite symbol of faith and the criterion of a love which unconditionally affirms, judges, and receives the other person.[41]

> The fact that so many highly educated people [in the West] prefer Zen to Christianity seems to me to stem from their aversion to the "objectified" and literally interpreted Christian symbols. The necessity of "demythologizing" in the sense of "deliteralizing" or "deobjectifying" has become more ugent for me in light of these observations and of the whole impact of Eastern wisdom on me. And Eastern wisdom, like every other wisdom, certainly belongs to the self-manifestations of the Logos and must be included in the interpretation of Jesus as the Christ, if he is rightly to be called the incarnation of the Logos.[42]

On his return to the United States, Tillich delivered at Columbia University the American Bampton Lectures for 1961, subsequently published under the title, *Christianity and the Encounter of the World Religions*.[43] There Tillich himself drew many of the parallels between Eastern religious thought and his own ontological version of Christianity that Professor Yoshinori Takeuchi of Kyoto had earlier noted in his Festschrift essay for Tillich.[44] Mircea

---

[40]See e.g., his 1939 essay, "Historical and Nonhistorical Interpretations of History: A Comparison," in his *The Protestant Era*, trans. James Luther Adams (Chicago: University of Chicago Press, 1948), pp. 16-31.

[41]*How My Mind Has Changed*, p. 161.

[42]*Ibid.*, pp. 163-64.

[43]*Christianity and the Encounter of the World Religions* (New York: Columbia University Press, 1963).

[44]Takeuchi, "Buddhism and Existentialism: The Dialogue between Oriental and Occidental Thought," in Walter Leibrecht (ed.), *Religion and Culture: Essays in Honor of Paul Tillich* (New York: Harper & Row, Inc., 1959), pp. 291-318.

Eliade, in memorializing Tillich, noted that the Bampton Lectures signified "only the beginning of a new phase in Paul Tillich's thought"[45] — a phase marked by his proposal at the University of Chicago Divinity School of a joint seminar on History of Religions and Systematic Theology. This took place in the winter and autumn quarters of 1964. Eliade describes Tillich's contribution to it in terms that well characterize the religious ontologist whose interests had always extended beyond the historical confines of Christian faith:

> Paul Tillich would never have become a historian of religions nor, as a matter of fact, a *historian* of anything else. He was interested in the existential meaning of history — *Geschichte*, not *Historie*. When confronted with archaic, traditional, and oriental religions, he was interested in their historical concreteness and immediacy, not in their modifications or changes or in the results of the flowing of time. He did not deny the importance of the temporal flux for the understanding of the history of specific religious forms — but he was primarily interested in their structures; he deciphered their meaning in grasping their structures.[46]

Tillich's last public lecture was delivered on October 12, 1965, on the subject, "The Significance of the History of Religions for the Systematic Theologian." In it he interrelated his new appreciation for the non-historical religions of mankind with his ontologically conceived, essentially non-historical interpretation of Christianity; his hope was that out of them a "Religion of the Concrete Spirit" might arise. Tillich's remarks, quoted *in extenso*, provide a fitting close to his career as well as an appropriate base for the criticism of his philosophy of history in the subsequent sections of this paper.

> It might well be that one can say the inner *telos*, which means the inner aim of a thing, such as the *telos* of the acorn is to become a tree — the inner aim of the history of religions is to become a Religion of the Concrete Spirit. But we cannot identify this Religion of the Concrete Spirit with any actual religion, not even Christianity as a religion. . . . We can see the whole history of religions in this sense as a fight for the Religion of the Concrete Spirit, a fight of God against religion within religion. And

---

[45]Eliade, in Tillich's *The Future of Religions*, p. 32.
[46]*Ibid.*, p. 33.

this phrase, the fight of God within religion against religion, could become the key for understanding the otherwise extremely chaotic, or at least seemingly chaotic, history of religions. . . . I must say that my own *Systematic Theology* was written before these seminars and had another intention, namely, the apologetic discussion against and with the secular. Its purpose was the discussion or the answering of questions coming from the scientific and philosophical criticism of Christianity. But perhaps we need a longer, more intensive period of interpenetration of systematic theological study and religious historical studies. Under such circumstances the structure of religious thought might develop in connection with another or different fragmentary manifestation of theonomy or of the Religion of the Concrete Spirit. This is my hope for the future of theology.[47]

THE TILLICHIAN DILEMMA

Shortly after Tillich's death, *The Christian Century* published an article titled, "After Tillich, What?" Its author concluded his evaluation as follows: "Tillich solved the problem of reflection and doubt not by equating the absolute with the whole content of a system of thought or of religious feeling, but by identifying it with a paradoxical object — one whose objectivity can be grasped only in its self-cancellation and whose power is exercised by its self-negation. . . . To have seen this is Tillich's enduring contribution."[48] In point of fact, to have "seen" this is Tillich's quandary — a dilemma which makes Robert Benchley's "ten years in a quandary" seem like a mild experience indeed.

As we have emphasized, Tillich was concerned throughout his career with the issue of idolatry: he wished above all to have an ultimate concern that was in fact ultimate (Being itself), and he endeavored mightily to develop a methodology (the Protestant principle) which would crush all attempts to absolutize the non-ultimate. But, in this case, where does ultimacy lie? With Being itself or with the Protestant principle? With "the absolute" or with

---

[47]Tillich, "The Significance of the History of Religions for the Systematic Theologian," in his *The Future of Religions*, pp. 87-88, 91.

[48]Robert P. Scharlemann, "After Tillich, What?" *The Christian Century* LXXXII (December 1, 1965), 1480. Scharlemann's muddy neo-Tillichian thinking has been scored by John Hick in an exchange in *Theology Today*, XXII (January 1966), 513-29; XXIII (April, 1966), 139-40.

its "self-negation"? This quandary was brought into sharp focus by Thomas J. J. Altizer, in his 1963 review of Tillich's *Christianity and the Encounter of the World Religions*, where he asserted that had Tillich applied his Protestant principle consistently — by refusing to give ultimacy even to Being itself — he could have become the progenitor of a new theonomous age: "Potentially Tillich could become a new Luther if he would extend his principle of justification by doubt to a theological affirmation of the death of God."[49] Tillich, however, was horrified at such a suggestion. In the heated argument with death-of-God theologians shortly before his death (Mrs. Tillich connects his fatal heart attack with it)[50] Tillich refused to give the Protestant principle a critical function in relation to Being itself. Though his writings had never set limits on the application of the principle (even Jesus, as we noted, was judged by it), and even though no revelational limit to its use could be appealed to (since revelation had also been subordinated to it), Tillich found himself unwilling to allow the principle to destroy his own ultimate concern.[51] Like the sorcerer's apprentice, he perhaps became dimly aware too late of having conjured up a critical methodology that even he was incapable of controlling. Like a modern King Midas (to change the simile) he had acquired a power that was now systematically and logically destroying that which he loved most.

But suppose — by what Franz Pieper called the "happy inconsistency" so characteristic of modern theologians[52] — the Protestant principle is kept in subordination to Being itself; is Tillich better off? Can Being itself survive as an ultimate concern? The answer is *Yes* only if Being itself is given no descriptive content whatever, i.e., if it is understoood in a purely formal sense only.

---

[49]Altizer, in *The Christian Scholar*, XLVI (Winter, 1963), 362. Cf. my book, *The 'Is God Dead?' Controversy* (Grand Rapids, Michigan: Zondervan Publishing House, 1966), pp. 23-24 and *passim*.

[50]So reports Dr. Jürgen Winterhager, professor of ecumenics at Berlin.

[51]Cf. Tillich's sermon, "Our Ultimate Concern," in his *The New Being* (New York: Scribner, 1955), pp. 152-60; and D. Mackenzie Brown (ed.), *Ultimate Concern: Tillich in Dialogue* (New York: Harper & Row, Inc., 1965), *passim*.

[52]Franz Pieper, *Christian Dogmatics*, trans. and eds. T. Engelder, J. T. Mueller, and W. W. F. Albrecht (4 vols.; St. Louis, Missouri: Concordia Publishing House, 1950-1957), II, 557.

Why? Because the moment any characteristics are given to it, then these fall under the axe of the Protestant principle, which preserves Being itself from idolatrous, anthropomorphic contamination. *Everything* predicated of Being itself (even love) must be regarded symbolically in order to avoid absolutizing finite values.[53] Under these circumstances, though Tillich insists that religious symbols do "participate" in the ultimate reality to which they point, no meaningful criteria can possibly determine whether an alleged symbol is in fact truly symbolic of Being itself. Otherwise stated, there is no way of knowing which aspects of a symbol only point to the absolute and which actually participate in it — or indeed, if any genuine participation occurs at all.[54]

And if we do take Being itself in a purely formal sense? Then we indeed have an irrefutable concept — but its irrefutability is a Pyrrhic victory, since it is achieved at the cost of draining away all substantive knowledge. As Williard van Orman Quine has well stated:

> A curious thing about the ontological problem is its simplicity. It can be put in three Anglo-Saxon monosyllables: "What is there?" It can be answered, moreover, in a word — "Everything" [or Being itself!] — and everyone will accept this answer as true. However, this is merely to say that there is what there is.[55]

Paul Edwards, in a trenchant essay on "Professor Tillich's Confusions," delivers the *coup de grâce*: "Tillich's theology is indeed safe from anti-theological arguments, . . . but only at the expense of *being compatible with anything whatever*. All of us normally regard this, as I tried to show, as a reason for calling a sentence meaningless or devoid of cognitive content."[56]

---

[53]"There can be no doubt that any concrete assertion about God must be symbolic, for a concrete assertion is one which uses a segment of finite experience in order to say something about him" (Tillich, *Systematic Theology*, I, 239).

[54]This point has been made by a number of Tillich's critics in the symposium edited by Sidney Hook (*op. cit.*).

[55]Willard van Orman Quine, "On What There Is," in his *From a Logical Point of View* (2d ed.; New York: Harper Torchbooks, 1963), p. 1.

[56]Paul Edwards, "Professor Tillich's Confusions," *Mind*, LXXIV (April, 1965), 197 (Edwards' italics).

REMEDY: HISTORY THE FUNDAMENT OF FAITH

Whether Being itself or the Protestant principle serves as the ultimate reference point in the Tillichian world-view, the result is the same: total absence of religious content. Neither the purely analytical concept of Being nor the purely critical Protestant principle can offer any substantive answers to ultimate questions such as those concerned with the meaning of history. To avoid heteronomous and autonomous idolatries, we must be able to distinguish true theonomy from them; but the formality of Tillich's system precludes the possibility of our doing so. The crucial events (*kairoi*) of history must be identified and related to the great *Kairos* — the Christ-event — but the symbolical character of the latter leaves us without clear criteria for recognizing *kairoi* and, equally important, for distinguishing divine from demonic *kairoi*. And the Kingdom of God hardly solves the ambiguities of history when the operations of Being itself cannot be unambiguously specified.

Where does the root difficulty lie in Tillich's remarkable system? Precisely at the epistemological point: Tillich consistently refuses to face the verification question. In the spirit of such metaphysical philosophers of history as Kant and Hegel,[57] he does not see that the attempt to produce a philosophy of maximum generality results in a formal *Weltanschauung* that says nothing because it says everything. Over much of Tillich's labors the remark could be posted that Wolfgang Pauli wrote on a paper submitted to him by a fellow physicist: "This isn't right. This isn't even wrong"! Tillich missed the vital insight offered by contemporary analytical philosophy[58] in its distinction between analytic (purely formal) and synthetic (content) judgments; only the latter, based

---

[57]See my *Shape of the Past*, pp. 67-68, 70-71; and cf. Tillich's own remarks in *How My Mind Has Changed*, p. 168. It should not be necessary to point out that for all this Tillich was no orthodox Kantian or Hegelian (see *The Future of Religions*, pp. 85-86).

[58]Of more than humorous interest is Tillich's passing comment: "I once said to a Logical Positivist that I would like him to attend my lectures and to raise his finger if something is said that lacks rationality. He answered that he could not accept this task because he would have to raise his finger during the whole lecture" (*The Theology of Paul Tillich*, eds. Kegley and Bretall, p. 330).

on experiential investigation of the world, can provide substantive knowledge of reality. If one intends, therefore, to speak of religious or historical meaning, he must offer concrete evidence in behalf of his claims — or, at minimum, show that his views are not compatible with all negative evidence! Granted, only a high level of probability can ever be adduced in support of such synthetic claims; but to demand absolute certainty is to obtain pure formality and thus no knowledge of the world at all.

In trying to elevate religious truth about the "incertitudes" of history, Tillich was attempting the impossible. All our verifiable knowledge of the world, present or past, is based on the sifting of experiential data, and just as in ordinary life we must constantly jump the gap between probability and certainty by faith, so in the religious realm we have no right to demand — much less any expectation of acquiring — a certainty transcending the probabilities of historical evidence.[59] Ian Ramsey has recently resuscitated Butler and Newman in effectively making our point:

> Butler reminded us that a total devotion to duty — shown, for example, by leaping into a river to save a drowning child — could *and reasonably*, be associated with many empirical uncertainties and probabilities: we might be mistaken about the strength of the current, about our swimming ability, or whether in fact that floating heap was a child, and so on. But acknowledging these uncertainties Butler claimed that we should nevertheless think a man in a literal sense distracted — not himself — who failed to respond to the moral challenge displayed by such a situation of great consequence. For Butler this moral response reared on probabilities, this total devotion, and (in Newman's phrase) this "real assent" is reasonable, as being that which any "reasonable" man, anyone deserving to be called a person, would in similar circumstances display. "Probability" in this special sense is (said Butler) the "guide of life." So our Christian con-

---

[59]Tillich's inability to grasp this vital fact was clearly brought out in his interview with Ved Mehta shortly before his death. Mehta: "I asked Tillich whether . . . he thought Christ really performed miracles or whether he thought the miracles were 'mythological,' in Bultmann's sense." "I think there is good evidence for some of those healings that He did," he [Tillich] replied equably. "But in history, of course, you never have definite evidence for anything" (Ved Mehta, "The New Theologian I," *The New Yorker* XLI [November 13, 1965], 128).

victions based on historical uncertainties are in principle reasonable as being one with the rest of life.[60]

How unfortunate that Tillich uncritically absorbed the negative
nineteenth century criticism of the New Testament records and
never made an effort to distinguish truly inductive historical method
from the rationalistic, anti-miraculous historicism that passed itself
off as scientific history.[61] Had he made this distinction, he would
have found the New Testament documents fully capable of sus-
taining the truth-claims of the Christian faith,[62] and he would not
have been led into a quixotic endeavor to ground religious belief
in formalistic ontology. Tragically, his focus shifted from the
facts of history to the tautologies of Being, until he was incapable of saying anything concrete about either history or faith.
When the *Systematic Theology* reaches its terminal sections on the
Kingdom of God and eschatology, the reader is uncomfortably
reminded of Wolcott Gibbs' evaluation of Alexander Woollcott:
"He wasn't exactly hostile to facts, but he was apathetic about
them." In Tillich's "hope for the future of theology," a "Religion
of the Concrete Spirit," one finds the exact opposite of factual
concreteness: a transparent wraith of a religion, capable of interpretation in any direction one wishes — the parent of Altizer's
mystical "third age of the Spirit"[63] and of the secular theologians'

---

[60]Ian T. Ramsay, *Christian Discourse: Some Logical Explorations* (London: Oxford University Press, 1965), pp. 23-24.

[61]This is Alan Richardson's primary criticism of Tillich's theology of
history; see Richardson's *History Sacred and Profane; Bampton Lectures
for 1962* (London: SCM Press, 1964), pp. 127-31.

[62]See below, chapter 8. Argues George H. Tavard (*op. cit.*, pp. 111-
12): "Tillich is right in being sceptical of the historians' efforts to re-
write the story of Jesus — but for the wrong reason. Historians cannot
re-write the story because it is already written: the historical value of
the New Testament is plain enough. Historians have not been able to
make its reliability improbable. Tillich has simply not been radical enough
in criticizing liberal theology. He has not seen that the historians who
doubt the value of the records have failed to establish their point. Here,
Paul Tillich remains a child of his generation, a victim of the historicism
of the last century."

[63]See Montgomery, *The 'Is God Dead?' Controversy*, p. 26.

"God of the present," who is conveniently identified with the social action favored at the moment.[64]

Herbert Butterfield's warning still stands: "the Christ of the theologians" must not be "divorced from the Jesus of history."[65] Had Tillich approached religious and historical truth-questions from the standpoint of the Jesus of the primary documents, he would have found the answer to his quest. Claiming to be no less than God incarnate and verifying that claim by His resurrection, Jesus demonstrated that the ultimate could and did enter the phenomenal world — that those who had seen Him had seen the Father (John 14:6-9) — and that therefore His Word stood in judgment and in grace over everything else. The true preservative against idolatry is, then, not a Protestant principle (or any other principle) that judges Jesus, but acknowledgment that Jesus and Jesus alone is the Way, Truth, and Life. Whereas the Protestant principle leads logically to a negation of ultimacy itself, Jesus is the door leading the believer into the Father's Kingdom. Now the characteristics of God's reign become clear through the teachings, the life, and the death of His only Son; and a literal Incarnation of God becomes the empirical center of history, the key to its meaning, and the earnest of eschatological fulfillment at the time of Christ's return.[66]

Only if God did in fact enter the world in Jesus can Tillich's theonomous perspective on the total historical drama come to fruition. For apart from a *de facto* relevation of God in history, what Danto calls "substantive philosophy of history" is in principle impossible, since it always implies a stance outside of time by which the philosopher views "the present and the past in the perspective of the future (indeed of the ultimate future, for there must be an end to every story)."[67] Wittgenstein was quite right that "the sense of the world must lie outside the world."[68] How to find it

---

[64]Cf. James McCord's opinion, described in *Time*, August 5, 1966, pp. 69-70, that "we are on the threshold of a whole new era in theology," characterized by emphasis on the Holy Spirit — "the God of the present."

[65]Herbert Butterfield, *Christianity and History* (London: Collins Fontana Books, 1957), p. 168.

[66]See chapter 1.

[67]Danto, *op. cit.*, p. 12.

[68]"Der Sinn der Welt muss ausserhalb ihrer liegen" (Wittgenstein, *Tractatus Logico-Philosophicus*, 6.41).

then? Not by constructing philosophical towers of Babel that inevitably produce confusion because they attempt the impossible, but by recognizing that "no man hath ascended up to heaven, but he that came down from heaven, even the Son of man" (John 3:13). Lacking the eternal perspective necessary to discover history's meaning, we must forever remain in darkness concerning it unless a shaft of light from outside the world illumines the shadows of history.

Tillich, for all his ontological speculations and his overweening desire to escape from the historical, found himself compelled to locate the great *Kairos* in a minor province of the Roman empire during the reign of Caesar Augustus. Would that Tillich had given himself fully to that historical event, for there the Light of the world indeed shone forth. There a perspicuous revelation from outside of time clarified the meaning of history once for all.

7. GORDON CLARK'S HISTORICAL PHILOSOPHY

P HILOSOPHY OF HISTORY is neither fish nor fowl, or if you wish, it
is both fish and fowl. Partaking of some of the characteristics of history and philosophy, it lacks the transparency of
either. Thus relatively few philosophers or theologians — even
those who have made great contributions to historiographical
thinking, such as Augustine, Kant, Marx, or Reinhold Niebuhr —
have been philosophers of history *per se*. Indeed, to the extent that
a philosopher or theologian is drawn away from the flux of human
experience by his general world-view (e.g., transcendental idealism), his methodological commitments (e.g., preference for mathe-
matico-deductive models), or his temperament (e.g., Kant's intro-
verted parochialism), the more difficult it will be for him to involve
himself first and foremost in the problems of philosophy of history.

But involve himself the philosopher will, whether he likes it
or not, for — as Giambattista Vico so persuasively argued — no
realm is closer to the heart of human experience than history, since
it is a child for whom we ourselves have suffered the birthpangs.[1]
No philosopher who intends to provide a synoptic understanding
of reality can avoid the questions that human history poses. And

---

[1]Cf. John Warwick Montgomery, *The Shape of the Past: An Introduction to Philosophical Historiography* ("History in Christian Perspective,"
Vol. I; Ann Arbor, Michigan: Edwards Brothers, 1963), pp. 68-70, 187-
216.

for the philosopher who is also a Christian, even less chance exists to by-pass problems of historical meaning. Any tendencies toward historical indifferentism will suffer from the apostolic declaration that "when the fullness of the time was come, God sent forth His Son." Herbert Butterfield (whose declarations of historical objectivism, typical of the practicing Christian historian, are nonetheless anathema to Professor Clark) makes the already quoted point in a manner fully compatible with Professor Clark's own views: "It would be a dangerous error to imagine that the characteristics of an historical religion would be maintained if the Christ of the theologians were divorced from the Jesus of history."[2]

Gordon Haddon Clark, though impelled to philosophy of history neither by his philosophical orientation (axiomatic-deductive presuppositionalism, which disallows the building of a world-view by inductive examination of experience in general, much less historical experience), nor by his confessional commitment (Calvinism,[3] with its starting-point the sovereign decrees of God in eternity, prior to all historical experience), has been inexorably drawn into historiographical problems both through his need to demonstrate the comprehensive applicability of his *Weltanschauung* to all major spheres of human thought and through the historical character of the biblical faith to which he is committed. Thus his *Christian View of Men and Things*,[4] the prolegomena volume from which his more detailed examinations of religio-philosophical problems have proceeded, included a chapter on philosophy of history. His individual articles in encyclopedias and scholarly

---

[2]Herbert Butterfield, *Christianity and History* (London: Collins Fontana Books, 1957), p. 168.

[3]No attempt will be made in this essay to settle the moot question as to whether Professor Clark is a faithful representative of Calvinism. Obviously the issue turns on one's definition of Calvinism (Calvin's view? the views of particular Calvinist confessions? the views of the theologians of 17th century Calvinist orthodoxy?), and on the exegesis of Calvin's *Institutes* and his other writings. Since this is not my area of specialty or my confessional commitment, I leave the field of battle to others — frankly hoping, however, that Calvinists such as J. Oliver Buswell, Jr., can sustain their argument that Calvin was less presuppositional, less sovereignty-orientated, and less double-predestinarian than he appears to be in the eyes of Cornelius Van Til and Professor Clark. (Cf. note 28 below.)

[4]*A Christian View of Men and Things* (Grand Rapids, Mich.: Wm. B. Eerdmans, 1952).

journals have touched on vital historiographical topics such as determinism and the nature of Time. His critiques of contemporary theologians have pointed up their failures in the realm of historical *a priori*. And now he is in process of writing a full-scale treatment of historiographical issues which will expand the positions set forth in his earlier publications.

Clark's approach to history is therefore worth study in its own right, though it requires a piecing together of arguments and insights found in a number of his writings. While moving in a generally chronological fashion in the presentation of his views (chronological order seems wholly appropriate where history is the subject of interest!), we shall focus on the two chief aspects of his (or any) philosophy of history: what Danto has called the *analytical* and the *substantive*.[5] By "analytical" is meant the rigorous critical treatment of philosophies and theologies of history other than one's own. This is the Socratic, "gadfly" function of the philosopher, and, as we shall see, Clark especially excels in it. "Substantive" philosophy of history is the positive, constructive work of establishing one's own historiographical foundation. If a zoological symbol is required for it, we would suggest the "owl."

The conviction of this writer, which will be supported *in extenso* particularly in the later sections of this essay, is that Gordon Clark makes a better gadfly than an owl — perhaps because "the owl of Minerva flies best at twilight," while Clark's Calvinistic presuppositionalism, as a species of what Luther called the Theology of Glory, remains always flooded in noonday brightness. But even though on the issue of philosophical and theological starting-point (presuppositional Calvinism) I cannot agree with Professor Clark, and would even go so far as to say that his philosophical methodology is perilous in the extreme for an evangelical thinker, I believe that the present essay can be justified, and for two good reasons.

First, it will be obvious that on the most basic level of the formal and material principles of Protestant theology (a totally reliable Scripture, whose salvatory message is justification by grace alone through faith alone in Christ alone), and on the most funda-

---

[5]Arthur C. Danto, *Analytical Philosophy of History* (Cambridge, England: Cambridge University Press, 1965), chapter 1 and *passim*.

mental existential level of personal commitment to the saving Christ, Professor Clark and I are at one. Secondly, Professor Clark has shown on numerous public occasions — noteworthy was the Wheaton Philosophy Conference where his philosophical position was the focus of discussion — that he can take criticism magnificently. Indeed, as a thoroughgoing presuppositionalist he knows that, in the final analysis, even when the chips appear to be down, and a philosophical ophthalmologist seems to have shown that the owl of Minerva has been blinded by the sun, the presuppositional sanctuary still remains undefiled.

PHILOSOPHY OF HISTORY IN
A Christian View of Men and Things

As Carl Henry has properly observed, *A Christian View of Men and Things* is the *point de départ* for understanding Professor Clark's thinking on major philosophical issues; his subsequent writings are largely elaborations of the basic positions affirmed in that book — positions which "Clark has not altered." One is readily reminded of the contemporary philosophical endeavors of Paul Weiss, whose presuppositionalistic interlocking of epistemology and metaphysics, in the tradition of the 19th century, has surprising parallels with Professor Clark's thought. Each volume from his pen deductively expands one phase of a general philosophy whose clear outlines had been initially set forth with such clarity that one could virtually predict the content of subsequent elaborations. Properly, then, we shall receive our introduction to Clark's philosophy of history from Chapter Two of *A Christian View of Men and Things*, where this topic is specifically treated.

Modern Secular Philosophers of History
under Clark's Critical Guns

In line with Professor Clark's great strength as a critic of other positions, the major portion of his chapter on "The Philosophy of History" is devoted to an analysis of leading secular attempts to find meaning in history in modern times. Karl Marx, the advocates of inevitable Progress in history (such as Spencer), and Spengler and Toynbee all come in for deserved criticism. While the presentation is not without technical faults (Is it possible to understand or adequately criticize Marx without treating Hegel? Ought not Marxism to be viewed in itself as a most perfect example of the "philosophy of Progress"? Can one do justice to Spengler or Toynbee without a thorough sifting of the extensive and significant critical literature on these thinkers?), nonetheless, Clark's negative evaluations strike home. Marx's economic determinism is seen as "an oversimplification of the problem" of historical meaning, since "to grant that economic motives have a widespread effect on the form of development of civilization is far from granting that everything can be so explained." Attempts to ground a philosophy of historical Progress by scientific knowledge, political or social planning, or biological evolution are weighed in the balance and found wanting. And the Progress concept as a fundamental category is shown to be self-contradictory — to contain the seeds of its own destruction:

> If progress is the law of history, if our moral and intellectual baggage is superior to that of antiquity; and if our society and our ideas are to grow into something better and vastly different; if our imagination is to evolve to a degree not now imaginable; if all the old concepts which served their time well are to be replaced by new and better concepts, does it not follow that the theory of progress will be discarded as an 18th and 19th century notion, which no doubt served its age well, but which will then be antiquated and untrue?
>
> Could it be that the best contemporary evidence of progress is a growing disbelief in "progress"?

In comparing Spengler and Toynbee, Professor Clark finds that in spite of their radically different judgments on the future of Western civilization, they make the same basic historiographical errors. Each selects his own facts to support his contentions: "Toynbee accumulates a mass of sober facts and claims to discover the laws in the facts themselves. The facts, however, are not the facts that Spengler uses. While a few may be found in both authors, it is surprising that works of such ample proportions overlap so little." Neither Spengler in his pessimism concerning the future of the West nor Toynbee in his qualified optimism about our future is able to justify his choice of chronological limits for civilizations, his preference for societal or individual explanations of historical action, or his basic definition of what in fact a society is.

The net result of the discussion so far may seem somewhat discouraging. Determinism has not been refuted, nor has it been established. Spengler has made plausible and stimulating remarks and Toynbee has contradicted him in a most impressive and persuasive manner. Neither of the two seems to have proved anything. Analogies cannot be trusted and empirical evidence is not decisive.

Clark makes plain that in the conflict between pessimistic and optimistic views of the state of our society, he classes himself with the pessimists. A full section of his chapter on the philosophy of history is devoted to a catalog of evidences pointing to social breakdown today. War, brutality, "socialistic coercion" in the United States (Clark's rightest political views come out loud and clear in remarks such as "taxation is becoming legalized theft"), and immorality (sexual misconduct, crime, suicide, and the repudiation of solemn promises and commitments by governments) are regarded as clear examples — "proceeding from the more specific to the more general, from the more obvious to the less obvious, and from the more derivative to the more original" — of the social collapse American civilization is undergoing. (One might well ask, however, if civilizations of sinners have not always displayed these same characteristics. Ecclesiastes noted that among sinners there is nothing new under the sun. As an inheritor of the Puritan dream of making America a theocratic utopia, is Professor Clark not perhaps overreacting to the inevitable collapse of such an expectation?)

Professor Clark is well aware that his criticism of contemporary American life involves value judgments as to what is ethically desirable and what is not. Suppose one heralds as signs of positive societal transformation the very factors that Clark regards the most negatively?

A decision on these two interpretations cannot be settled by an appeal to facts. There is involved a moral and normative judgment; and before a philosophy of history can be satisfactorily established, it will be necessary to erect some system of morality as its foundation. No theory of history rests on an empirical basis; no theory of history can dispense with the underlying phases of philosophy.

This fundamental theme in Clark's historiography — that empirical investigation of facts is inadequate for grounding a philosophy of history, and that problems of philosophy of history have to be solved outside of history, in a more basic realm of aprioristic philosophical commitment—recurs again and again in his writings, and will be subject to close examination later in this essay.

The Christian Corrective: St. Augustine

Everyone has his heroes, and it is by no means strange that Professor Clark, at once a specialist in classical philosophy and a Calvinist, should find his historiographical ideal in Augustine of Hippo.[6] The final section of the chapter titled, "A Christian Philosophy of History," in *A Christian View of Men and Things*, is largely devoted to a summary of Augustine's thinking on the meaning of historical experience. Five years after the publication of that volume, Clark again made reference to his conviction that the biblical and Augustinian historiographies need to be juxtaposed: "The idea of a philosophy of history is originally a peculiarly biblical concept, and St. Augustine exploited the material in his great *City of God*."[7] In 1964, it was Professor Clark who appropriately wrote the "Augustine" article for *The Encyclopedia of Christianity*, Vol. I, and there a lucid section is devoted to that great Western church father's views of history.

Augustine receives high marks in Professor Clark's book be-

---

[6]Nash says of Clark, Henry, and Carnell: "These men are, in a sense, 'Neo-Augustinians'" (Ronald H. Nash, *The New Evangelicalism* [Grand Rapids, Michigan: Zondervan, 1963], p. 117). The point of comparison is Augustine's famous (though ambiguous) epistemological principle, *Credo ut intellegam*.

[7]Clark, "Apologetics," in *Contemporary Evangelical Thought*, ed. Carl F. H. Henry (Great Neck, New York: Channel Press, 1957), p. 143. On this same page Clark gives a brief summary of the "Philosophy of History" chapter in his *A Christian View of Men and Things*.

cause, according to Clark, he deduced his philosophy of history from uniquely Christian presuppositions.

> The first of these presuppositions, in fact the first of all Christian principles, is the Being and Nature of God. A philosophy that is based on the existence of God will differ throughout from a philosophy that has no place for God; and similarly two systems that do not agree as to what sort of Being God is, will also differ in all their details. Augustine therefore had to distinguish the Christian conception of God from the popular Roman polytheism and from the philosophic One of Neoplatonism.[8]

What is the distinctive historiographical view which Augustine developed on the basis of his Christian doctrine of God?

> First of all, Christianity teaches that God created the universe by a voluntary fiat. This excludes Neoplatonic emanationism. Second, Christianity is a system of redemption that takes place, not through the Neoplatonic discipline that is consummated in a mystic trance, but through the course of historical events culminating in the death of Christ. Both of these factors, the creation and the crucifixion, are instances of something that happened once for all; hence Christianity attaches an importance to history that Neoplatonism never could.[9]

With his high view of history, stemming from his Christian convictions, Augustine produced a spirited apologetic for the importance of unique events (as distinguished from the universal principles so dear to Greek thought), and analyzed the total human drama in terms of its "two cities." Instead of a single human society (which existed in blessedness before the Fall and would have existed in misery after it if God had not provided for man's redemption), actual history is for Augustine "the struggle between two antagonistic societies — the City of God and the worldly city. The earthly city is motivated by the love of self to the contempt of God; the heavenly City is motivated by the love of God to the

---

[8]Clark, *A Christian View of Men and Things, op. cit.,* p. 85.

[9]Clark, "Augustine of Hippo," *The Encyclopedia of Christianity,* I, ed. Edwin H. Palmer (Wilmington, Delaware: National Foundation for Christian Education, 1964), 491.

contempt of self. Their origins, their policies, and their destinies are different."[10]

Professor Clark agrees with Augustine's analysis, and steps behind it to the scriptural teaching which served as Augustine's source. From this perspective Clark presents three general principles of Christian historiography: God controls history; God will bring history to its culmination; and God Himself acts in history.[11] To Joad's objection ("Why am I expected to believe that what happened in Palestine is of such unique importance?"), Clark delivers the *coup de grâce*: "By what process of reasoning can one come to the conclusion that the location of an Englishman's residence is the cause of the importance of . . . events?" A nice point; doubtless Augustine himself would have made it had Joad the misfortune to encounter him.

The positive presentation of an Augustinian philosophy of history over against secular views necessarily poses the question: Which view of history (if any) is correct? Three extended quotations from *A Christian View of Men and Things* will make Clark's answer, grounded in his basic epistemology, crystal clear. We shall not pause here to discuss the argument, but it will offer fruitful ground for criticism shortly.

> Empirical history is inherently impossible. If a person with a completely unbiased mind should try to study history, the thousand and one events that happen every minute the world over would foredoom him to speedy failure. To make any progress at all, he would have to select some of these events and pay no attention to others. In doing so, however, he would have to use a principle of selection not found in the events themselves. Unconsciously, and in spite of himself, by an unrecognized psychological law, and by the nature of history and the world, Toynbee or any other student of history must select his facts and in the selection begin to impose his interpretation upon them.[12]
>
> In conclusion one may ask, what has all this discussion proved? The answer is, the discussion has *proved* nothing. The philosophy of history, however interesting or even important it may be, is only a derivative aspect of philosophy, and before a

---

[10]*Ibid.*, p. 492.
[11]*A Christian View of Men and Things*, pp. 89-92.
[12]*Ibid.*, pp. 56-57.

view of history can be established, either by strict demonstration or even by persuasive argument, there are underlying problems that must be settled. These problems have not been faced in the preceding discussion. Therefore neither the secular nor the Christian view has been "proved."

The two views, however, have been sketched as two pictures in outline. If the secular standpoint is chosen, history has no significance; human hopes and fears are to be swallowed up in oblivion; and all men, good, evil, and indifferent, come to the same end. Anyone who chooses this view must base his life on unyielding despair. If however, he chooses the Christian view, then he can assign significance to history; human hopes and fears in this life contribute to the quality of a life after death, when two types of men will receive their separate destinies. Anyone who chooses this view can look at the calamities of western civilization and say, "We know that all things work together for good to them that love God." There has been no proof, but there is a choice.[13]

The volume as a whole has . . . tried to show that Christian theism is self-consistent and that several other philosophies are inconsistent, skeptical, and therefore erroneous. With the presuppositions of Marx, Russell, or Spengler, history becomes meaningless; a humanistic utilitarianism and the Kantian autonomy of the will are equally incapable of justifying moral distinctions; and some forms of religious philosophy are inconsistent mixtures of naturalistic and theistic elements. As a contrast to these views it has been argued that Christianity is self-consistent, that it gives meaning to life and morality, and that it supports the existence of truth and the possibility of knowledge. Thus theism and atheism have been examined in considerable detail. It remains for each person to make his choice.[14]

CLARK AS CRITIC OF CONTEMPORARY THEOLOGY OF HISTORY

In his role as gadfly, Professor Clark has bitten both philosophers and theologians, but nowhere have the wounds been as deep or as surgical as in the theological area. Doubtless this is in part due to the blithe muddleheadedness of so much of modern theology — reveling as it does in irrationality and the kind of illogical sloppiness that would cause a freshman logic student to be cash-

---

[13]*Ibid.*, pp. 92-93.
[14]*Ibid.*, pp. 324-25.

iered. (One is reminded of Professor Clark's *bon mot*: A paradox is a charley-horse between the ears.) But the effectiveness of Clark's criticisms of contemporary theologians rests essentially with his precise and rigorous philosophical training, and illustrates well Paul Tillich's principle (which Tillich himself could have followed with more exactitude): No theologian should be taken seriously unless he takes philosophy seriously.

Clark vis-à-vis Barth

Historiographical issues do not loom large in Clark's magisterial volume, *Karl Barth's Theological Method*, but the centrality of revelation-through-historical-event in Barth's thought affords Clark the opportunity to point up serious weaknesses in Barth's theology of history. True, one misses an analysis of the exceedingly unfortunate consequences attendant on Barth's use of Martin Kähler's distinction between ordinary, verifiable historical events (*Historie*) and the "significant" and "historic" — but unverifiable — events of biblical revelation (*Heilsgeschichte*).[15] However, Clark touches on this problem (at root, the question of the genuine objectivity of biblical history) from another angle: Barth's tendency to blend the historical events of scriptural revelation with our contemporary experience of them, and to depreciate the interpretations of these events that historical revelation presents. Writes Clark:

> Barth had been talking of an event in which the words of the Bible become the words of God for us, and therefore of an event or series of events continually repeated. But the incarnation of Christ happened once for all. Now, this substitution of one event for another leads to confusion. The historical existence or event of Jesus Christ is indeed different from any narrative of it. Jesus Christ is the singular Word, spoken by God directly at a date in history. But it is hardly true that the Bible consists of human attempts to repeat the Incarnation, especially in the time when Israel's political position between Egypt and Babylon was a matter of importance. But if we are interested not simply in the mere physical existence of Jesus as an historical surd, if we are mainly interested in what he said and in the

---

[15]Clark will undoubtedly deal with this subject in his forthcoming work on historiography. See also above, chapter 5.

intelligible explanation of his actions, *Paulus dixit* and *Deus dixit* are not two different things. They are not materially different, if the sentences are identical; nor are they even formally different, if God speaks through Paul. The Bible is neither merely nor mainly a narrative, which of course must be formally different from the events narrated. Historical events are essential to the Bible, but only as interpreted and explained. The bare existence of a man Jesus means nothing. Rational religion requires attention to what he said and must find an explanation of what he did. If he remains dumb and no one explains his actions, gazing upon him will be of no value. And if the explanation is incorrect and his words false, the value can only be negative.[16]

This difficulty in Barth's historiographical understanding comes out with particular force in his views of the contemporaneity of biblical events. Clark notes that Barth rightly rejected Lessing's answer to the "ditch" Lessing dug between history (regarded as an inadequate ground of truth) and present experience (the only valid test of "the necessary truths of reason"). Lessing made the great error, which gained widespread influence through Protestant liberalism, of "asserting an immanent power in human nature by which is discerned the coincidence of revelation and history."[17] Barth endeavors to avoid such humanistic anthropocentrism and yet to cross Lessing's ditch by asserting that the Word of God (preached, written, and presented through revelational events) is in fact a contemporaneous act. But, asks Clark, "if the time of Christ is made contemporary with the time of the apostles, and with our time also, what does 'contemporary' mean?"[18] An excellent question; and Barth's inability to answer it leads Clark to his final query:

> Can we agree with Barth that this solves the problem? It is easy to begin with levels of authority and to suppose that a preacher today repeats the exact words of Paul who received these exact words by divine inspiration. But if we do not begin

---

[16]Clark, *Karl Barth's Theological Method* (Philadelphia: Presbyterian and Reformed Publishing Co., 1963), pp. 169-70.

[17]*Ibid.*, p. 23.

[18]*Ibid.*, p. 183. We shall see shortly how strong an interest Professor Clark has in the philosophical and theological problem of the nature of time.

with levels of authority and wish to justify the superior position
of the apostles over us today, the idea of contemporaneity is not
only insufficient, but impossible. Nothing is clearer than that
two times separated by centuries — other differences are im-
material — are not contemporaneous.

In conclusion therefore, and in spite of Barth's immense
erudition and his stimulating discussions, of which a student will
always remain deeply appreciative, it must be maintained that
he has not succeeded in solving his problem. In all these de-
tails, so carefully and perhaps so tediously examined, not only
'contemporaneity' but also 'revelation' fails of intelligible definition. This leaves the unity of Barth's three forms unclear and
obscures the identity of the Word of God. These difficulties
could easily be met, or, better, they would not arise, if the Word
of God is identified with the Biblical text, rendered accurate
by God's control of the wording. But this would be to revert to
the theology of the Protestant Reformation, and that is what
Barth does not care to do.[19]

Clark contra Bultmann

Professor Clark's short but weighty contribution to Carl F. H.
Henry's *Jesus of Nazareth: Saviour and Lord*[20] is titled, "Bultmann's Historiography." Here the Marburg Heideggerian and
demythologizing exegete is taken over the philosophical coals for
existentializing biblical history. Clark analyzes Bultmann's position on the historical Jesus by way of the Introduction to *Jesus
and the Word*. There Bultmann expresses his basic views: that
the "hermeneutical circle" binds us as observers to the historical
events observed, thus preventing an objective account of the past;
that the life of Jesus cannot therefore be reconstructed; that the
problems of isolating the oldest layer in the Gospel records are so
complex that we can never be sure that we have found Jesus' own
words; and, finally, that this makes no difference, since Jesus'
personality is a matter of indifference to the theologian, who must
find the Christ in personal, existential encounter with history.

Clark finds such an historiography "unintelligible." "Why,"
he asks, "should we not seek the encounter in Herodotus or Henry

---

[19]*Karl Barth's Theological Method*, pp. 183-84.
[20]*Jesus of Nazareth: Saviour and Lord* (Grand Rapids, Mich.: Wm. B.
Eerdmans, 1966).

Thomas Buckle? The texts of any such authors can be encountered, existentialized, and allegorically interpreted. Any of them
can be used for a continuous dialogue with history. Why select
one epoch of history rather than any other?" These questions
are unanswerable for Bultmann because of the fallacies in his methodological commitments. "His New Testament criticism is as
arbitrary as that of Strauss, and his demythologizing is on a level
with the allegorical method of the early patristics; . . . and he stirs
together the objectivism of the nineteenth-century historians with
the subjectivism of twentieth-century existentialism." Further:

> I know what it means to learn political lessons from history and
> to evaluate on non-historical moral grounds the crimes or the
> virtues of great men, but I haven't the slightest idea of what
> Bultmann means by encounter or achieving being. Such empty
> phrases will never furnish a defensible view of historical investi-
> gation.

An especially interesting section of Professor Clark's chapter
(and one pregnant with significance as a barometer to his own
historiographical approach) takes up Bultmann's argument that
"there cannot be impersonal observation of history in the same
sense that there can be impersonal observation of nature." One
would expect the orthodox Christian critic of Bultmann to argue
against such a dichotomy on the ground that both scientific and
historical data are able to be objectively identified: the data of
nature because God has given them objective existence through
His creative acts, and the data of history because history is the
sphere of His objective work of judgment and redemption.

Clark does indeed point up the unity of scientific and historical
study — but in terms of the impossibility of arriving at the data
of either field in an objective manner. "Pure, objective impersonal
observation of nature is not well accepted today as a description or
as a goal of science," for the advent of operationalism in the
philosophy of science has caused many to "insist on the personal
involvement of the scientist in his problem" and to hold that "the
formulations of science depend in part on the aesthetic preferences
of the formulator." A strange counter to a subjective existentialist
— the yielding of more territory to "personal involvement"
and "aesthetic preference"!

The reason for Clark's approach, however, is not hard to find;

indeed, we have touched on it already. He insists on maintaining that "empirical history is inherently impossible," even as he holds that a purely empirical scientific method is by definition impossible (the thesis of his work, *The Philosophy of Science and Belief in God*). Why does not Professor Clark take the more obvious and seemingly more advantageous approach of smoking out the non-empirical, illegitimate presuppositions that Bultmann endeavors to pass off as scientific method in his New Testament studies? Why give the impression that no one, scientist or historian, Bultmannian or non-Bultmannian, can arrive at objective truth through direct investigation of data? For Professor Clark, one *must* accept this conclusion, troublesome though it may be in dealing with a Bultmann, for only the prior acceptance of the "axiom of revelation" will yield factual truth in any sphere of knowledge. Here again, the influence of Clark's epistemology on his philosophy of history poses disturbing questions — questions which will more and more insistently demand critical answers as this essay proceeds.

THE DEEPER ISSUES

Professor Clark's analysis of philosophical and theological views of history presented by leading thinkers has given, by implication at least, the outlines of his own philosophy of history. We shall now endeavor to obtain a clearer picture of Clark's historiography by observing his approach to three issues basic to any view of historical meaning: the problem of Time, the conflict between determinism and free will, and the question as to how philosophies of history are to be verified. In terms of evaluation, these issues will be ranged according to the degree of success Clark manifests in treating them. In the judgment of this writer, Clark stands most closely on the side of the angels in dealing with the Time problem, less so in handling free will, and in severe difficulty where the verification of Christian philosophy of history is involved. This descending order of success is in itself significant, as we shall quickly discover.

The Problem of Time

The inadequacies of Barth's approach to contemporaneity stood plainly revealed in Clark's examination of his theological method. Professor Clark has been much concerned with a proper understanding of the nature of Time, and in this connection has subjected various views to analysis and criticism.

Along the lines of his dissatisfaction with Barth's treatment of the temporal factor in revelation, Clark is intending to devote substantial attention in his forthcoming work on historiography to Oscar Cullmann's influential book, *Christ and Time*. Cullmann holds that the events at the beginning and end of the revelational time-line (creation and last judgment) cannot be regarded as historical in any ordinary sense. Although he is unwilling to employ a *Historie-Geschichte* device to remove the biblical events along the time-line from the sphere of full historicity, he finds it impossible to place the scriptural accounts of the world's origin and final disposition in the same category.[21] Clark has already shown how he will treat this approach, for he has published a short article taking Dutch philosopher Herman Dooyeweerd to task for his conception of "cosmic time," which has unpleasant parallels with Cullmann's views. In *A New Critique of Theoretical Thought*, Dooyeweerd speaks of eschatological happenings "beyond the limits of cosmic time" and outside of the sphere of history — happenings that can be apprehended only in the realm of faith; and he illustrates with the creative days of Genesis. Asks Clark: "If that which occurs is not historical, what can history be?" For Clark, such a view is extremely dangerous. His own belief is that the totality of factual events comprising biblical history must be regarded as exactly that — historical instances of God's activity.

Now, in view of the neo-orthodox antithesis between time and eternity, in view of paradox and supra-temporal contemporaneity, and in view of the reduction of the Biblical events to symbols and myths, Dooyeweerd's language is disturbing. Perhaps in the volumes yet to be published, he will strongly emphasize the verbal inerrancy of the Scriptures. Surely it is to be hoped that he will not neglect this subject. But until he stresses verbal inspiration, and possibly afterward too, one must

[21]The best analysis of Cullmann's thinking which has been published to date is Roman Catholic Jean Frisque's *Oscar Cullmann: Une théologie de l'histoire due salut* (Tournai, Belgique: Casterman, 1960). Hopefully, Clark's work on Cullmann will benefit from his insights. Cf. John Warwick Montgomery, "Lutheran Hermeneutics and Hermeneutics Today," in his *Crisis in Lutheran Theology* (2 vols.; Grand Rapids, Michigan: Baker Book House, 1967), I, 45-77.

ask what is really meant by denying that the first chapter of Genesis is historical. If any part of the Biblical events are beyond the limits of cosmic time — that is to say, in the light of the analysis in the first part of this paper, if some events did not occur in time — how does one decide which of the Biblical accounts are historical and which are not? If the six days of creation are not temporal, is the serpent's temptation of Eve historical? And is the crucifixion historical? What is the criterion by which one may distinguish an event that really occurred in time from some revelational, supra-temporal symbol?

Dooyeweerd, though he may not intend the same meaning, uses some of the language of the neo-orthodox. And one wonders whether it is possible on his construction to maintain the factual truth of Biblical history.

Thus, we may conclude that both theologically and philosophically Dooyeweerd's view of time in its present form is, at very least, inadequate.[22]

In another journal article,[23] Clark points up the two major difficulties into which secular philosophical views of Time have fallen. The Neo-Platonic philosopher Plotinus represents one extreme. He soundly maintained the unity of Time for all of nature and all mankind, but was able to relate this to individual and separate minds only by affirming a single Soul which is present everywhere in nature and which actually constitutes the souls of all individuals. Time thus becomes the life of this universal Soul. Kant, on the other hand, displays the opposite extreme. He correctly avoided a blending of individual minds, but, owing to his rejection of "any preformation system that would unite all minds and all nature under the plan of the Creator" (in opposing Leibniz, he eliminated both theism and pantheism from his philosophy), Kant was "left with a pluralistic universe in which each person has his own space, time, and categories."

> Thus Kant began with time in the individual mind and failed to achieve unity. Plotinus, on the contrary, begins with the unity of time as the life of the Soul and faces the problem of getting it into each individual mind.

---

[22]Clark, "Cosmic Time: A Critique of the Concept in Herman Dooyeweerd," *The Gordon Review*, II (September, 1956), 98-99.

[23]Clark, "The Theory of Time in Plotinus," *Philosophical Review*, LIII (July, 1944), 337-58.

Does a way out of this impasse exist? Clark suggests it at the end of his article. St. Augustine has often been regarded as heavily dependent on Neo-Platonism, even after his conversion to Christianity. Clark, however, stresses that Augustine did not follow Plotinus' erroneous tack of unifying Time through a world Soul. Augustine "brings us back to earth again and locates time in created minds." The unification of past, present, and future can occur in the individual mind because it has been harmonized with all other minds by their common Creator, the God of Christian revelation.[24] Thus Augustine — and Clark with him — would preserve the one and the many in respect to the nature of Time, and would sustain both the unity and the uniqueness of man's historical experiences.

The Lord of History: God and Determinism

As a Calvinist, Professor Clark centers his theologizing on the creative activity of the sovereign God. Not unnaturally, then, we have found his approach to the nature of Time, intimately related as it is to God's creative work, both stimulating and valuable.[25] Another area in which the strengths — but also the weaknesses — of such a theological orientation manifest themselves is that of determinism-freewill in history. Here our attention will be directed to Clark's early article on "Determinism and Responsibility,"[26] which, as Carl Henry has pointed out, played a crucial role in Clark's career by separating him as a strict Calvinist from those evangelicals who insist that predestination is set forth as an incomprehensible mystery in the Bible.

On the positive side, Clark, like his theological mentor Calvin, holds high the God of revelation as the supreme and unqualified Lord of history.[27] "Calvin has rejected that view of the universe

[24]Cf. Clark's brief discussion of Augustine's conception of Time in The Encyclopedia of Christianity, I, 492.

[25]Though, again as an archetypal Calvinist, Clark does not penetrate very deeply into the relations between Time and redemption. For the possibilities that exist in this realm, cf. Anglican lay theologian and littérateur Charles Williams' concept of "coinherence" (see my Shape of the Past, pp. 150-51).

[26]Clark, "Determinism and Responsibility," Evangelical Quarterly, IV (January, 1932), 13-23.

[27]On Calvin in this regard, see Shape of the Past, p. 52.

which makes a law, whether of justice or of evolution, instead of the law-giver supreme. Such a view is the Platonic dualism which posits a World of Ideas superior to the Artificer." To judge the God of history by the historical process or by value systems that have arisen within it was one of the root errors of Protestant modernism: "The modernists object to a vicarious sacrifice because they do not think God is that sort of a person. Theirs is not the God of the early Christians."

Further, Clark makes the exceedingly important point that when God moves actively in history or in one's personal life, deliberate volition on man's part is by no means excluded. Over against the views of Georgia Harkness, Clark writes:

> First of all, she claims moral action requires choice and choice requires the ability to have done otherwise. This is the first thing to be denied. Choice is that mental act, that deliberate volition — I do not intend a comprehensive definition — which initiates a human action. The ability to have chosen otherwise is an irrelevant consideration and has no place in the definition. It is still a deliberate volition even if it could not have been different. True we are not always conscious of our limitation. Those who appeal to the consciousness of freedom and consider that such appeal closes the issue rely on cherry or apple pie as illustrations. If illustrations be necessary we can refer to Luther's sentiments: "Here I stand, so help me God, I can do no other." The more important the decision, the less power of contrary choice we feel. And I venture to suppose that Luther's is a fairly common experience with serious, responsible persons.

On the negative side of the ledger, one notes in Clark's article a summary handling of the grave question, "Does the view here proposed make God the Author of sin?" Clark's answer is simply that "Author of sin" is a bad metaphor ("Why the learned divines who formulated the various creeds so uniformly permitted such a metaphorical expression to becloud the issue is a puzzle"), and that the non-paradoxical double-predestinarian view "most certainly makes God the first and Ultimate Cause of everything."

But the reason why so many learned divines and Christian creeds employed the expression that troubles Clark is that the gravity of sin struck them more forcefully in relation to the predestination question than it strikes Clark. For them, it seemed inconceivable to make a non-mysterious connection between the Father of our Lord Jesus Christ and the panorama of man's sinful acts through history. To do so would turn Christ's weeping over Jerusalem into a charade, and His very death for the sins of the world into a theatrical performance. Clark, consistent with hyper-Calvinism,[28] approaches the propitiatory Atonement and the Incarnation from the standpoint of God's eternal decrees, instead of the other way around (indeed, at the end of his article, he even classes the former as "specific doctrines" as compared with the fundamental doctrine of God's sovereignty). But many sensitive souls through Christian history have felt that God's sovereignty ought to be approached by way of the Incarnation and the Cross.

Luther, for example, was at pains to emphasize that double predestination ceases to be an option when you stand at the foot of the Cross. As you look into the face of the dying Saviour, you do indeed find a "single" predestination — a predestination of the elect, for as a saved person you realize that you can contribute nothing to the saving work of Christ for you, and that even your faith is God's gift. But at the same time you find that the possibility of tying man's sin and unbelief non-paradoxically to the Christ totally disappears. Thus Scripture holds the believer to the sharp edge of a genuine paradox (John 1:12-13; Philippians 2: 12-13), which will not be resolved as long as we remain under the Cross in a sinful historical situation.

Christian interpretation of history (thank God) does not have to choose between determinism and free will. Both apply, but always in such a way that the evil of history is man's work and the good of history, God's. Man is free to choose his own poison, and continues to do so; he is not free to save himself or his world. Only God can do that, and the Cross is the best evidence of how seriously God has acted to remedy man's self-destructiveness.

Parenthetically: Is this matter of starting point perhaps a reason

---

[28]Did Calvin himself hold to double predestination, or was this teaching introduced by subsequent Calvinist orthodoxy? Dr. Buswell is convinced that Calvin did not maintain double predestination, and I would like to think that he is right; however, passages in Calvin's *Institutes* seem difficult to reconcile with anything but a double-predestinarian view (see especially the *Institutes*, trans. Henry Beveridge, II [Grand Rapids, Michigan: Eerdmans, 1947], 206).

why — even though Professor Clark does include all the salvatory doctrines in his presentation of Christian faith — he is so widely regarded as a "cold rationalist"? Similar criticisms of Calvin readily come to mind. Does the starting point of God's sovereign decrees prior to and outside of human history, rather than the commencement of theology at the heart of history, the Cross, succeed in turning even an endomorphic personality (Clark) into an ectomorphic personality (Calvin)?

The Choice between Philosophies of History

Carl Henry has properly noted that Professor Clark's most basic philosophical concerns lie in the area of epistemology: his "interests even in history of philosophy are mainly epistemological." For "even in history of philosophy" we can substitute "especially in philosophy of history," for lying behind Clark's treatment of historiographical problems is almost invariably an endeavor to illuminate the truth-question. This epistemological thrust is clearly manifest in Clark's projected book of historiography, for which some 250 typewritten pages have been completed to date and kindly put at the disposal of this essayist by the author. Immediately prior to the section on "Statistical Law" in the manuscript, Clark sets forth the conviction that informs the entire work:

> Historiography is more intricate than some historians believe. Admittedly, general philosophy takes us away from the details and narrative of ordinary history; and in a later chapter some attention will be given to Professor Mandelbaum's contention that questions of epistemology should not be discussed. It will be argued that this contention is unsound. True enough, methodology or historiography must do justice to the narrative of events, and the attempt must be made to satisfy the historical researcher.
>
> At the same time, however, questions concerning the significance of the great movements of peoples and nations, concerning the purpose of social and political life, concerning natural teleology or divine providence, cannot be brushed aside as mere philosophy or irrelevant epistemology. Those who try to do so not only fail in the attempt, they also fail, of necessity, in their account of historical narrative. In this volume these profounder problems will not be omitted.

Professor Clark begins his book with an introductory division provisionally titled, "What Is History?" Here a dichotomy is made between those eras and thinkers who have "disliked" history (the Greeks, Descartes, Voltaire, Hume, Spinoza) and those who have "esteemed" it (the 19th and 20th centuries). Contemporary historiographers, whose confidence in history arose in the progressivistic (Hegel), evolutionary (Darwin), positivistic (Comte) 19th century, now generally dispute only the specific locus of historical worth: Is history valuable for its own sake? Is its worth to be found in its contributions to the present? Is it valuable for the sake of philosophy? Clark does not explicitly answer these questions here (the entire volume will constitute his answer), but the direction of his thinking is made entirely plain. He looks with a jaundiced eye at contemporary confidence in history, regarding this as essentially misplaced. He summarily (and, if we may say so, superficially) dismisses the contention of Collingwood, Butterfield, and Harry Elmer Barnes that history has *sui generis* value; and he suggests that "the utility and justification of history may then be found in the position it holds as a part of an all embracing philosophy."

In moving to a treatment of how history is to be defined, Clark endeavors to reinforce this subordination of history to philosophy: he ranges nine definitions of history to show cumulatively that even one's definition of historical activity is a special case of one's general philosophy of life. (Least indicative of this is J. H. Hexter's definition; most indicative — quite significantly, I would judge — is Rudolf Bultmann's; the present writer's definition, predictably, is placed on Hexter's side of the ledger.)

Here we have *in extenso* the unhappy reiteration of the principle Clark enunciated in *A Christian View of Men and Things*: "Empirical history is inherently impossible." To make this point, Clark virtually embraces historical skepticism:

> Let this be clear: the love of information for its own sake and the watching of change and complication simply for the sake of change provide no guide for choosing what change to watch or what information to acquire. Everything is reduced to a level of equal importance, and that level is the level of equal non-importance.

For Clark, historical facts are so incapable of conveying significance in themselves that apart from a general *Weltanschauung* the historian cannot say why he does not concentrate on such facts as "how many miles Pfc. Smith walked on Fridays, and the average length of sergeants' shoestrings after basic training." Such an extreme position is, of course, totally impossible to sustain, and even Professor Clark himself does not maintain it in practice. In arguing against a statistical approach to historiography later in his book, he writes:

> Figures on suicide or murder or misaddressed letters might possibly contribute something to a science of sociology; but just as life insurance statistics contribute nothing to medicine, so such figures can contribute nothing to history. No doubt murders occur with some regularity, and there may be some value in listing the number of murders committed every year. But not all murders are of historical importance. There may have been a thousand murders committed in 1914, but there was just one, the murder of Archduke Ferdinand, that affected the course of history. Doubtless also, many children were killed in the Middle Ages; but the murder of just two princes in the Tower is a matter of history. And with respect to these unique, dated events, statistics offers no understanding.
>
> If the reply be made that other murders also may have historical consequences, let the point be granted; but such lists of figures do not explain Napoleon or the World Wars of the twentieth century. The singular dated event of Napoleon's decision to march on Moscow, which because of his loss of a great army is supposed to have made his final defeat at Waterloo inevitable, is a matter of legitimate interest. By tradition this is the historian's sphere, and here sociology has no explanations to offer.

Quite so; but this simply illustrates that historical events do not in themselves display a "level of equal non-importance." It is the statistician's mistake to think that they can be computertized on the same level, and Clark instinctively (if inconsistently) recognizes that to refute this notion he must appeal to an inherent variation in significance-level where historical facts are concerned.

Indubitably, in our contingent world there are an infinite number of *possible* interpretations and value judgments for any single historical fact (Hitler *may* have incinerated Jews because, out of misguided love, he wanted them to have their eternal reward more quickly; Jesus *may* have been a Martian, so cleverly disguised in a

Jesus suit that no one could tell the difference). But, just as obviously, not all explanations are equally plausible, and diverse interpretations and value judgments can and must be examined against the facts.themselves. In the process, less satisfactory judgments will go by the board, and one will arrive at an interpretation as to meaning and significance that best fits the facts under analysis (Hitler eliminated Jews because he hated them; Jesus was God incarnate).

The conviction that historical facts do carry their interpretations (i.e., that the facts in themselves provide adequate criteria for choosing among variant interpretations of them) is essential both to Christian and to general historiography. The Apostles proclaimed the fact of Christ's resurrection and their interpretation of it as objective, ascertainable truth (I Corinthians 15, and the sermons in Acts), and they did so even to those (such as Athenian philosophers) whose world-views did not make them hospitable to such facts or such interpretations.[29] The apostolic community was convinced that Christ's resurrection and the interpretation they (and He) placed on it could be fully sustained by the facts, and they invited their contemporaries to check the matter out for themselves. If Christians today take any other approach to historical meaning (even from laudable motives), they are rendered incapable of presenting the Gospel history as necessarily having any more inherent significance than (to vary Clark's illustration slightly) the average length of Pilate's shoe-latchet.

Moreover, such a position lands the general historical investigator directly in the arms of Bultmann, who locates the meaning of historical events in the "responsible decisions" of present interpreters.[30] Here, with secular existential historiographer Raymond Aron, the relativity of history can only be overcome by "the absolute of decision,[31] and no single view of historical experience

---

[29]I have developed this point in my articles contra presuppositionalist and fideist apologetics: "The Place of Reason," *His* (Inter-Varsity Christian Fellowship), XXVI (February, 1966), 8-12; (March, 1966), 13-16, 21.

[30]Rudolf Bultmann, *The Presence of Eternity: History and Eschatology; the Gifford Lectures 1955* (New York: Harper & Row, 1957), p. 155. Cf. *The Shape of the Past*, pp. 120-22.

[31]Raymond Aron, *Introduction to the Philosophy of History*, trans. George J. Irwin (London: Weidenfeld and Nicolson, 1961), p. 334. Cf. *Shape of the Past*, pp. 94-95.

genuinely or demonstrably has any greater value than any other
— an absurd conclusion. Ironically, while (as we have seen) Clark
most decidedly rejects Bultmann's works and ways, his historical
approach has disquieting similarities to Bultmann's. For both, history *per se* is powerless to decide between philosophies of history.
One's world-view (for Bultmann, Heideggerian existentialism; for
Clark, Calvinistic orthodoxy) determines historical meaning, and
thus the ultimate issue in finding the significance of the past is not
historical facts but *choice*. As Clark says repeatedly: "There has
been no proof, but there is a choice."[32]

What drives Professor Clark in this unfortunate direction is
plain, though *tout comprendre* is not *tout pardonner*. In the major
section of his projected volume devoted to "Secular Theories of
History," he correctly observes that no secular philosophy has succeeded in adequately explaining man's total historical experience.
This is the case whether the interpretations have been of a "non-
historical, reductionist" character (geographical explanations of
the human drama, exemplified by Herder and Montesquieu;
physical explanations, such as Kant's; statistical explanations, as
typified by Buckle and Durckheim),[33] or whether they have been
genuinely "historical" explanations in that they have endeavored
to take human volition into account (Beard's economic determinism and Marx's historical materialism). Clark's criticisms of
these views are both trenchant and entertaining (Buckle, for example, is taken over the coals — in withering detail — for his "intense prejudice" against Scottish Presbyterianism; it is evident that
Buckle made the worst possible move to deal negatively with a
country and a confession so dear to Clark's heart!).

Most assuredly these philosophers and historians did not discover the meaning of the past. But, Clark notwithstanding, the
reason for their failure does not have to be located (and must not
be located) in the inability of historical facts to speak clearly apart
from philosophical commitments. The difficulty is rather, as I have
noted elsewhere, that "such a welter of historical data exists that

---

[32]See above, the quotations corresponding to note numbers 13 and 14.

[33]At this point in his presentation, Clark inserts as an Appendix the section on Progress from his *Christian View of Men and Things*; "partly
reconstructed and partly quoted verbatim," it well illustrates the close ties
between the two books.

we do not know how to relate all the facts to each other. Our lifetime is too short and our perspective is too limited."[34] Putting it otherwise, the trouble with secular philosophy of history is not that it has looked into history instead of to aprioristic first principles in endeavoring to understand the past; it is that the secularists have been deflected by their extra-historical commitments from looking at history objectively — and particularly from looking at the Christ of history objectively.[35] When the historical facts of Christ's life, death, and resurrection are allowed to speak for themselves, they lead to belief in His deity and to acceptance of His account of the total historical process.

"Confidence in history" is indeed worthy of disapprobation if by the expression is meant man's ability to arrive at a valid comprehensive account of the entire human drama apart from the Christ of history. Contemporary analytical philosophy of history has in fact demonstrated the impossibility in principle of such a program.[36] But "confidence in history" is laudable if it means that, over against existential and solipsistic skepticism, one confidently endeavors to find the meaning of historical events by objective study of the events themselves. Only in this way can one avoid imposing a philosophy, as a Procrustean bed, on the past. If the Christian philosophy of history is truly valid, it must arise from within history itself. And it does: for it derives from the historical Christ. The Christian philosopher or historian will therefore do the cause of Christ no good by deemphasizing historical objectivity. If one is incapable of discovering the meaning of historical events from the events, then one is incapable of finding the divine Christ in history, and history will most certainly reduce to "a tale told by an idiot, signifying nothing."

Yet Professor Clark, in his projected work on historiography, is quite willing to concede the field to the historical relativists.

---

[34]John Warwick Montgomery, "Frontier Issues in Contemporary Theology: Church History," *Evangelical Theological Society Bulletin,* IX (Spring 1966), 77; reprinted in the present volume as the Afterword.

[35]A laboratory illustration of this is provided by the historiography of the University of Chicago's historical generalist W. H. McNeill. See above, chapter 4.

[36]See Danto's *Analytical Philosophy of History, passim* (cited above in note 5).

The last major section completed to date treats the arguments marshalled by objectivists and relativists. On the side of "fixed truth in history" Hexter, Butterfield, and Barzun are weighed in Clark's scales and rejected. Carl Becker's historical relativism is considered much more persuasive than the objectivist arguments. The issue of causation is examined, and Clark (consistent with his position in *The Philosophy of Science and Belief in God*) remains unsatisfied with attempts to establish the meaning of causation, and regards this difficulty as a damning criticism of objective history. Finally, Mandelbaum's and Nagel's defenses of historical objectivity are presented as heroic but inadequate measures to stave off relativism. Though Clark expressly postpones the question of normative judgments in history to a later (as yet uncompleted) chapter, his general viewpoint on the objectivity issue is patent. Listen to his conclusions:

> A review of the chapter makes it clear that fixed, absolute, objective, unalterable truth is not attainable by historical research. No one of Von Ranke's school has been able to refute Descartes' criticism that fragmentary accounts cannot be trusted. Further research may at any time result in a complete rewriting of previous history books.
>
> The best defenders of fixed truth in history have made such damaging concessions that their main thesis is overturned. Hexter admitted that order and coherence can be introduced into history only by the use of tentative frameworks.
>
> Rickert's courageous attempt to list the criteria of objectivity results in a vicious circle. In particular, the concept of causality, which is the mainstay of objectivity, is theoretically incoherent and practically inapplicable.
>
> Carr delights us by picturing the historian as rummaging in a rag-bag, selecting pieces, and sewing together the rational quilt of "knowledge."
>
> Mandelbaum (among other things, for not everything should be repeated) defends objectivity by trying to divorce historical research from epistemological problems. This is utterly impossible, as, for example, the discussion of causality showed.
>
> Finally, Nagel's attempt to save objectivity in the social sciences emptied them of everything but statistics.
>
> Since none of these authors was able to overthrow the arguments of the relativists, we may conclude that the latter had the best of it.

But Clark's chapter is woefully unconvincing. First, his dismissal of "the best defenders of fixed truth in history" on the ground of their "damaging concessions" is unwarranted. The "concessions" simply involve the admission that historical truth is synthetic and not analytic, i.e., that it is arrived at by the empirical examination of documents and therefore never attains the level of one hundred percent certainty. Thus Clark on Barzun (*The Modern Researcher*):

> When a set of events is public, he says, and is attested by dozens of independent witnesses, we *know* (italics his; p. 140). When the skeptic complains that the witnesses may be mistaken, Barzun replies that the objection depends on the postulation of some perfect record with which the extant accounts can be compared. Since there are none, Barzun seems to say, the extant accounts must be true.[37]

Exactly! Barzun is simply pointing out that historical research, like investigation of the present, is based on observation, and that "objectivity" in both cases is arrived at when independent witnesses agree as to what actually happens. Clark, however, is unwilling to allow that historical research can arrive at "objective truth" unless it can produce "absolute," "unalterable" results — in other words, the kind of results characteristic of a deductive, axiomatic system (always Clark's model for truth, and he permits no compromise with it).

Absolute truth in this sense, however, is possible only in formal logic (or in pure mathematics, which Whitehead and Russell in their *Principia Mathematica* showed to be a special case of deductive logic). And these formal systems are absolute only because they are *so defined* and insofar as they stand independent of empirical experience. The moment the realm of experience is introduced, "absolute," "unalterable" results become impossible. But to argue that objectivity disappears at the same time is to ignore all the ordinary operations of life (in which decisions are made by weighing concrete evidence), and in effect to embrace solipsism. The choice is very clear: formal perfection without empirical

---

[37]Note, parenthetically, the direct relevance of Barzun's argument to apologetic problems such as the reliability of the New Testament accounts of Jesus' life, including His miraculous acts.

content, or the acceptance of empirical objectivity without putting impossible demands upon it. And since the Christian faith centers on a revelation *in* historical experience, there is no question as to what path the Christian must take.

Secondly, Clark implies that historical explanations are like metaphysical systems: they are inevitably imposed on history from without and determine the data instead of being judged by the data. This argument exactly parallels Clark's operationalistic view of scientific activity (*The Philosophy of Science and Belief in God*) and accords with the conception of science presented by such philosophers as Thomas S. Kuhn (*The Structure of Scientific Revolutions*). But this position is misinformed whether it is offered as an account of scientific or of historical activity. "Crucial experiments" (the results of which depend squarely on the nature of factual reality) shift the evidential weight for or against rival scientific explanations and are the causes of "scientific revolutions"; and the weight of factual evidence is likewise the only proper determining factor in the choice between competing historical explanations.[38] It is manifestly unjust for Professor Clark to attribute to scientists and to historians a besetting sin of metaphysicians: the sin which Hegel was supposed to have committed when a student had the temerity to object, "But, Herr Professor, the facts do not agree with you"; Hegel is said to have replied: "Then the facts be hanged." This is exactly what the historian cannot legitimately do: hang the facts; it is *they* which will hang *him* if his constructs do violence to them.

Thirdly, in conjunction with the preceding points, Clark misconceives the causation issue. True enough, as Max Black has shown even more decisively than the thinkers Clark cites, "any attempt to state a 'universal law of causation' must prove futile."[39] But instead of seeing this as a superlative advantage for the objective, empirical presentation of the historical Christ (vs. anti-

---

[38]On the nature of empirical theorizing and its relation to theological method, see my paper, "The Theologian's Craft: A Discussion of Theory Formation and Theory Testing in Theology," *Journal of the American Scientific Affiliation*, XVIII (September, 1966), 65-77, 92-95.

[39]Max Black, *Models and Metaphors* (Ithaca, New York: Cornell University Press, 1962), p. 169.

miraculous arguments based on an unalterable "law of nature"),[40] Clark considers a universal causal law to be "the mainstay of objectivity" and the impossibility of the one to establish the impossibility of the other. Here again, Clark demands absolute (analytic) justification for causality or nothing. He does not see that causation, like the historical or scientific explanations that incorporate causal thinking, is no more than an empirical, synthetic construct which is employed *ad hoc* to deal with historical facts. Causal explanations are grounded in, and tested against, the facts for which they endeavor to account. Where normal causal explanations are wanting (e.g., in regard to the nature of light in physics or the nature of Christ's resurrection in history), no one properly rejects the objectivity of the phenomena. Light is still there, and so is the resurrection! The Christian historian Butterfield is by no means "evading" the issue (*pace* Clark) when he maintains that the objectivity of historical truth is not dependent on an unalterable law of historical causation.

Lastly, Clark buys the general position and arguments of historical relativist Carl Becker, without apparently being aware that his approach to historiography has been demolished by analytically trained philosophers of history who have dealt with it in recent years. After surveying the latest work done on this problem, particularly in reference to the anti-objectivism of such writers as

---

[40]See above, chapters 2 and 3. In fairness to Professor Clark it should be noted that over a quarter of a century ago, before he consistently expanded his epistemological approach to embrace scientific operationalism and the arguments of the historical relativists, he himself saw that basic to an effective Christian apologetic for biblical miracles is the firm maintenance of historical objectivity. "The religious thinker either in choosing a particular law of physics, or even more so in choosing a fundamental world view, should first consult history, and after deciding by historical evidence what has happened, should then choose his laws within the limits of historical actuality. The non-Christian thinker, intent on repudiating miracles, proceeds by a reverse method. He chooses his law without regard to historical limits, and then tries to rewrite history to fit his law. But surely this method is not only the reverse of the Christian method, it is clearly the reverse of rational procedure as well" (Clark, "Miracles, History, Natural Law," *Evangelical Quarterly*, XII [January, 1940], 34). What a pity that Professor Clark did not follow through on this superlative insight, which would surely have led him to an objective-empirical historiography!

Becker and W. H. Walsh, J. W. N. Watkins perceptively concluded:

> My own belief is that, while it is no doubt desirable that the historian should be as aware as possible of the sources of potential bias within himself, what really matters, in connection with the problem of historical objectivity, is not so much the historian's mentality as the logical structure of what he writes. The regulative moral and metaphysical convictions, the passion and controversy, which Walsh regards as the causes and symbols of subjectivity in history, have their counterparts in the natural sciences, which Walsh regards as paradigms of objectivity. The objective character of a scientific theory is not a function of its author's temperament and mentality, but of its *criticisability*. Thus for me, the question "How objective can history be?" boils down to the question, "To what extent is a systematic historical reconstruction exposed to criticism?" . . . The informal, common-sense answer is plain enough. There are plenty of excellent historical works in which a previous descriptive interpretation is cogently challenged with the help of fresh evidence or of old evidence presented in a fresh light. It has been done, therefore it can be done.[41]

It will be noted that here Watkins turns the argument around that the "rewriting of previous history books" militates against historical objectivity: quite the contrary, says he; rewriting on the basis of new evidence or evidence presented in the light of previously unnoticed facts is a most powerful proof that historical activity is soundly objective. The very fact that the divine picture of Christ in the New Testament documents has stood so effectively the critical (as opposed to rationalistic) scrutiny of the historical evidence is our best reason for holding to its objective veracity.

J. A. Passmore, author of the monumental work, *A Hundred Years of Philosophy*, has reinforced Watkins' arguments in an exceedingly important paper on "The Objectivity of History."[42] There Passmore maintains that "the historian proceeds scientifically

---

[41]J. W. N. Watkins, "Philosophy of History: Publications in English," in *La Philosophie au milieu du vingtième siècle*, ed. Raymond Klibansky (4 vols., 2d ed.; Firenze, 1961-1962), III, 174.

[42]First published in *Philosophy*, XXXIII (1958), 97-111, and reprinted in *Philosophical Analysis and History*, ed. William H. Dray (New York: Harper & Row, 1966), pp. 75-94.

— in the sense that he puts forward hypotheses, or constructs narratives, which are subject to the constraint of facts."

How exactly is the historian to choose amongst his material? The determining factor, I have suggested, must be the nature of the problem from which he sets out, just as it is in the case of the physical scientist. There is, however, an important difference in the character of his problems; historical problems are more like a certain type of problem in applied science than they are like problems in pure science. This is a consequence of the fact that the historian is interested in what happens in a particular situation on a particular occasion; just as an engineer may have to ask himself: "why did *that* aeroplane collapse?" so the historian asks: "why did *that* monarchy collapse?" Furthermore, again like the engineer, he may, usually does, solve his problem by constructing a model.

But why, then, do the "models" presented by historians to explain the same events sometimes differ so notably from one another? Does this not destroy an objective understanding of the historical task? Hardly, Passmore argues with cogency:

What ought to surprise and gratify us is the extent to which the spirit of objectivity has won its triumphs. Roman Catholic and Protestant accounts of the Reformation, considered as a story about social institutions, come more and more into conformity. If the test of objectivity is that there are regular ways of settling issues, by the use of which men of whatever party can be brought to see what actually happened, then I do not see how one can doubt the objectivity of history. But if we are satisfied with nothing less than the production of histories which all men the least rational will accept as final, then that would be a greater victory for the scientific spirit than we have any reason to expect. Such unanimity, however, is not to be found in any branch of human inquiry. Once again, if we press the criterion of objectivity too hard, it applies to no form of inquiry; slacken it slightly and history edges its way in with the rest.

Professor Clark, however, insists on pressing the criterion of objectivity very hard — indeed, strangling it to death. To be sure, his reason for doing this is very different from that of the historical relativist; the latter generally operates from humanistic motives (a desire to establish or preserve man's freedom of action, existential self-authentication, etc.), while Clark is motivated by theistic considerations (the desire to establish objectivity, as well as everything else, solely through the axiomatically veracious revelation of the sovereign God). Historical facts, then, cannot be ultimately determinative when diverse and contradictory philosophies of history vie for acceptance. The issue in such cases is one's fundamental philosophical commitment — one's choice of axiomatic starting-point. As Clark wrote in 1946 in *A Christian Philosophy of Education* and reiterated a decade later in his contribution to Henry's *Contemporary Evangelical Thought*:[43] "Instead of beginning with the facts and later discovering God, unless a thinker begins with God, he can never end with God, or get the facts either." Here we have the root problem with Clark's philosophy of history: Can one "begin with God" (the Christian God) *without* benefit of objectively discoverable historical facts? I say No, and the reasons why must now be set forth, together with an alternative proposal capable of avoiding the difficulties presented by Professor Clark's historiographical approach.

THE PRESUPPOSITIONALIST DILEMMA AND CHRISTIAN PHILOSOPHY OF HISTORY REORIENTED

The Surd Problem in Clark's Historiographical Presuppositionalism

In analyzing major objections "against our being able, with *any* set of techniques, to make true statements about the past,[44] Arthur C. Danto discusses an argument dear to Professor Clark's heart — the argument which runs as follows:

> (3) Historical statements are made by historians, and historians have motives for making historical statements about one past thing rather than another. Not merely that, but historians have certain feelings about the past things they are concerned to describe. . . . Such attitudes induce historians to make emphases, to overlook certain things, indeed to distort. Because of the baggage of attitudes they bring with them, they themselves are not always able to detect the distortions they make. But those who pretend to detect distortions have themselves a special set of attitudes, and hence their own manner of emphasizing, overlooking and distorting. Not to have attitudes is

---

[43]*Op. cit.* (in note 7 above), p. 152.
[44]Danto, *op. cit.*, chapter 3, pp. 27-33.

not to be a human being, but historians are human beings, and cannot, accordingly, make perfectly objective statements about the past. Every historical statement, as a consequence of un-expungeable personal factors, is a distortion, and hence not quite true. So we cannot succeed in making statements about the past which *are* quite true.

Danto then comments:

> This argument would seem, on the face of it, open to an easy charge of meaninglessness. What, for instance, would it mean to say that every object in the world were crooked? We can only determine crooked things in comparison and contrast with straight things, and if there are no straight things, we cannot significantly apply the expression "crooked." It is a term which logically requires its polar opposite. But so with distortions. If we have no idea of what an undistorted statement about the past is like, what sense can we give to the expression "distorted statement"? And if we *do* have such an idea, then we can in principle produce instances of undistorted statements, and the argument is wrong. So, this objection concludes, either the argument is meaningless or wrong.
>
> But in fact this objection is not especially compelling, and the proponents of (3) can, and commonly do get around it easily. For they are not saying, in effect, something like "Everything is crooked' but only that a certain class of things are crooked. Then there might be a class of straight things which would make this statement intelligible. So again, they are not saying that every statement is a distortion, but only that *historical* statements are. The class of historical statements is then contrasted as a whole with another class of statements, presumably undistorted, namely, the class of scientific statements.

The standard attempt to depreciate history by way of pure science is therefore not meaningless (though, as Passmore, Watkins, and many others have shown, it is invalid, since scientific and historical methods are in principle the same empirical technique). Now Clark recognizes the unity of scientific and historical activity, but for him this unity signifies an absence of genuine objectivity in *both* areas. Not only this: Clark is convinced, as we have seen, that one cannot consistently arrive at objective facts in *any* sphere until one accepts the axiom of revelation. This is true, then, not merely of science and history, but of ethics, politics, education, and even family life (Clark suggests, in "The Axiom of Revelation," that apart from a priori commitment to the God of Scripture one cannot be sure who one's wife is!). But, if this is the case, the charge of meaninglessness discussed by Danto comes down with full force on Clark, for there is no class of undistorted statements by which to judge historical statements: every object in the world is crooked, and the word "crooked" thus loses all significance.

But, Clark replies, there is *one* undistorted object: Holy Scripture; *its* statements are not crooked, and so I judge all observational statements by the revelational axiom. Unfortunately, however, where Christian revelation is involved, such a recourse is absolutely impossible. As Mavrodes has sagely argued: "Whenever the Bible forms a link in an epistemological chain, then sensory contact with the Bible must form the very next link." Why? because the Bible is a sensory object, and can only be met in the world of sensory, synthetic experience. And what is even more important for our purposes: the Bible is an *historical* object, and can only be met if we take objective history seriously. How, for example, do we know what constitutes the Bible? Only by examining the historical evidences for the genuine canonicity of the biblical books. If these evidences are *ex hypothesi* "crooked" — if we cannot trust historical method in determining them — then, perforce, we cannot be sure we have a revelation at all. Christian revelation is irreducibly historical, and its fortunes are thus (for good or for ill) bound up with the fortunes of history. Ironically, therefore, any attempts to reduce historical objectivity in the interests of revelational truth always and by logical necessity boomerang: they eliminate the possibility of all significant talk about revelation itself. For Professor Clark, who has cut himself off from all empirical avenues to truth, the result is even more disastrous. With the collapse of meaningful talk about the axiom of revelation, only solipsism remains.

An Unsuccessful Rehabilitation

In his book, *The New Evangelicalism*, Ronald H. Nash argues that negative critics of Professor Clark such as J. Oliver Buswell, Jr., have misunderstood Clark's position and consequently have not appreciated its epistemological and apologetic soundness.[45] Since the foregoing presentation does not differ materially from Dr. Buswell's interpretation of Clark, something needs to be said concerning Nash's argument.

Nash offers a most attractive picture of Professor Clark's pre-suppositionalism: the axiom of revelation, we are told, is not an untouchable *a priori* which must simply be accepted or rejected apart from any common evidential ground between believer and unbeliever. Rather, it is comparable to a scientific hypothesis or theory, which can be tested in terms of its "coherence." Since two equally coherent, but mutually contradictory world-systems do not exist simultaneously, the higher coherence level of the Christian world-view offers a sound and rational ground for affirming the axiom of revelation.

But this rehabilitation of Professor Clark's epistemology just will not do — for a number of reasons, most of them supplied by Clark himself. First, one cannot parallel the axiom of revelation with the "hypotheses" of scientific method. The latter can be dislodged by contrary factual evidence (indeed, this is what is meant by theory-testing in science or history), but Professor Clark has expressly said: "The English word 'fact' has too many con-notations to be useful in a carefully formulated theory"; and "Un-less a thinker begins with God, he can never end with God, *or get the facts either*."[46] In other words, even if one can speak clearly about "facts" (which is doubtful), they cannot judge the axiom of revelation; for, in reality, facts only enter the picture *after* one has accepted the revelational axiom. Moreover, Clark's *Philosophy of Science and Belief in God* totally destroys the possibility of paralleling his revelational starting-point with scientific hypotheses. Clark specifically reduces scientific truth to operationalism and sets his axiom of revelation — the only source of unalterable, ob-jective truth — in contrast to the merely tentative, revisable con-clusions of scientific investigation.

It follows, then, in the second place, that the "coherence" test of the truth of a presupposition can only mean its "internal con-sistency," not any external fitting-of-facts. That this is definitely

---

[45]Nash, *op. cit.*, (in note 6 above), chapters 8-9, pp. 111-43.

[46]*Contemporary Evangelical Thought* (cited in note 7 above), pp. 145, 152 (italics ours).

Clark's thrust can be seen in his approach to the philosophical criticism of other systems, e.g., Plotinus'[47] and Barth's.[48] But it should be painfully clear that to blast other systems for internal inconsistencies does not necessarily destroy them, since in a real sense life *is* bigger than logic. The paradoxical wave-particle character of light does not destroy the empirically established evidence of light's characteristics or the physics that investigates it — and the paradoxical character of the Trinity surely doesn't destroy the biblical evidence for God's trinitarian nature or the validity of Christian faith in the Triune God! Further, after one has destroyed x-number of non-Christian systems, one has by no means established the truth of the Christian system, since (a) there can always be, in a contingent universe, system x + 1 to contend with, (b) it is sheer whistling in the philosophical dark to assume that two coherent (internally consistent) but mutually contradictory systems can't exist simultaneously in the universe, and (c) even if one were to eliminate all possible alternatives to the Christian world-view, its internal consistency would not assure its truth, for it could still be false — *consistently* false — consistently out of whack with the universal state of affairs.

Thirdly, what Nash refers to as "common ground" between believer and unbeliever in Clark's epistemology is actually not "common" ground at all. Clark does indeed distinguish his position from Van Til's in that he (Clark) holds to a *personal* "common ground" between Christian and non-Christian. But this "common ground" exists only by virtue of the unbeliever's *inconsistency*

---

[47]Clark, "The Theory of Time in Plotinus" (*op. cit.* in note 23 above), p. 349: "As one would expect, Plotinus' positive theory of time is a consequence of his basic worldview. Whatever adverse criticisms may be made against Plotinus, no one can deny that to a high degree of philosophic consistency he succeeded in solving detailed problems by relating them definitely to his first principles. So true is this that it might seem unfair to criticize his theory of time, or of any subsidiary point, by arguments drawn directly from phenomena; one ought, so it would seem, to test the rigor by which consequences are derived from first principles, and, if satisfactory, either approve those consequences or argue against the principles on high metaphysical grounds. This method of procedure, *always a valid one* [italics ours], seems particularly applicable in the case of Plotinus. . . ."

[48]Clark, *Karl Barth's Theological Method,* especially chapter 4, pp. 76-108.

in accepting some aspects of the Christian world-view. Only in this sense (the unbeliever's inconsistent tromping on the *Christian's* ground) does "common ground" come about; in reality, it is the Christian's territory, and no one else's. Thus, "it should be obvious that there cannot be any common ground, any common proposition, shared by two systems."[49] Facts are still in principle incapable of proving Christian truth to the unbeliever, for facts belong solely to the Christian. Indeed, even formal logic, by which consistency is established, is justifiable exclusively by the Christian's axiom of revelation.

Lastly (and inevitably, in light of what has preceded), the only assured proof of Christian revelation for Clark is supplied by "the inward work of the Holy Spirit."[50] As with all genuinely presuppositional theologies, Clark's grandiose, seemingly "rationalistic" system reduces to fideism and to what the theologians of the German Reformation called *Schwärmerei*. The Spirit serves as a *deus ex machina* to resist the overwhelming pull toward solipsism.[51] But Scripture cautions us to "test the spirits." How? Not by internal consistency (the devil is an exceedingly coherent logician, as are all great liars), but by empirical comparison of doctrine with the objective, historically given Scriptures. Thus we are brought back again to the absolute necessity of an objective historiography, for without it we can establish no scriptural testing-stone.

A Proposed Refocusing of Christian Philosophy of History

To avoid the insoluble dilemmas attendant on a presuppositionalist theology of history, a fresh start must be made. I have set forth and defended an alternative approach elsewhere,[52] and only its general outlines can be sketched here. First, though Kant was quite right that all arguments begin with a prioris, it does not

---

[49]Clark, in *Contemporary Evangelical Thought*, p. 156. Cf. also chapter 4 of *Karl Barth's Theological Method*.

[50]Clark, "Holy Scripture," *Evangelical Theological Society Bulletin*, VI (Winter, 1963), 4.

[51]Is this the invariable function of the *testimonium internum Spiritus sancti* in presuppositional Calvinism? One is led to ask this disquieting question in reading such works as Bernard Ramm's *Witness of the Spirit*.

[52]In my *Shape of the Past*, especially pp. 138-45. See also chapter 1 of the present book.

follow that one presupposition is as good as another. Properly, we should start not with substantive, "content" presuppositions about the world (e.g., the axiom of revelation), which gratuitously prejudge the nature of what is, but with heuristic, methodological presuppositions that permit us to discover what the world is like — and (equally important) what it is not like. Such are the a prioris of empirical method, which are not only heuristic but *unavoidably necessary* in all of our endeavors to distinguish synthetic truth from falsity.[53] Proceeding on the basis of empirical method as applied to history, one can inductively validate the Christian revelation-claim and the biblical view of total history. Here is the argument in outline, as set out in *The Shape of the Past*:

1. On the basis of accepted principles of textual and historical analysis, the Gospel records are found to be trustworthy historical documents — primary source evidence for the life of Christ.

2. In these records, Jesus exercises divine prerogatives and claims to be God in human flesh; and He rests His claims on His forthcoming resurrection (John 2:18-22; Mt. 12:38-41).

3. In all four Gospels, Christ's bodily resurrection is described in minute detail; Christ's resurrection evidences His deity.

4. The fact of the resurrection cannot be discounted on *a priori*, philosophical grounds; miracles are impossible only if one so defines them — but such definition rules out proper historical investigation.

5. If Christ is God, then He speaks the truth concerning the absolute divine authority of the Old Testament (Mt. 5:17-19; John 10:34-35) and of the soon-to-be-written New Testament (John 14:26-27; 16:12-15; cf. Acts 1:21-26; I Cor. 14:37; II Pet. 3:15); concerning His death for the sins of the world; and concerning the nature of man and of history.

6. It follows from the preceding that all biblical assertions bearing on philosophy of history are to be regarded as revealed truth, and that all human attempts at historical interpretation are to be judged for truth-value on the basis of harmony with scriptural revelation.

---

[53]A point definitively argued by Georg Henrik Von Wright in his epochal work, *The Logical Problem of Induction* (2d ed.; Oxford: Blackwell, 1957).

But does not such an approach leave us in the throes of uncertainty? Does it not force us into the camp of Dr. Mavrodes, who holds that the lack of certainty in the empirical establishing of revelation necessitates the abandonment of all claims to a higher level of knowledge in the Bible?[54] Accordingly he blends the Scriptures with "history, tradition, science, scholarship, sense experience, mystical experience, logic and deduction, joy, pain, crisis, and perhaps many other" avenues to knowledge (thus obliterating any qualitative distinction between special and general revelation, and eliminating the possibility of biblical judgment upon these other areas). He also makes the Bible only man's "translation" of God's event-language into human language.[55] Faced with such appalling consequences, one's first reaction is to leap back into Professor Clark's arms!

But Mavrodes fails to see that the epistemological route by which one arrives at biblical truth does not determine the value of what one arrives at — any more than the use of a less than perfect map requires one to reach a city having corresponding inadequacies. As Harvard logician Willard van Orman Quine has soundly pointed out, one doesn't need to put supports under every inch

---

[54]George I. Mavrodes, "Revelation and Epistemology," in *The Philosophy of Gordon Clark: A Festschrift*, ed. Ronald H. Nash (Philadelphia: Presbyterian and Reformed Publishing Co., 1968), pp. 227-56.

[55]The latter argument is the substance of Mavrode's paper, "The Language of Revelation," *Journal of the American Scientific Affiliation*, XVIII (December, 1966), 103-107. It is incredible that Mavrodes did not acquaint himself with the publications of Old Testament scholar James Barr, whose work has decisively refuted the contention that biblical revelation can be understood in terms of the Neo-Orthodox, "biblical theology movement" dichotomy between "divine event" and "human word." See Barr's book, *The Semantics of Biblical Language* (London: Oxford University Press, 1961), *passim;* and his Princeton inaugural address, "Revelation through History in the Old Testament and in Modern Theology," *Interpretation*, XVII (April, 1963), especially 201-202, where he pulls no punches: "God can speak specific verbal messages, when he wills, to the men of his choice. But for this, if we follow the way in which the Old Testament represents the incidents, there would have been no call of Abraham, no Exodus, no prophecy. Direct communication from God to man has fully as much claim to be called the core of the tradition as has revelation through events in history. If we persist in saying that this direct, specific communication must be subsumed under revelation through events in history and taken as subsidiary interpretation of the latter, I shall say that we are abandoning the Bible's own representation of the matter."

of a roof in order to hold it fully and completely up. The empirical, historical evidences in behalf of Christian revelation are not absolute (no synthetic proof can be), but they are sufficiently powerful to bring us to the feet of a divine Christ who affirms without qualification that biblical revelation is trustworthy.[56] We have already quoted Ian Ramsay on this point at the end of the previous chapter. Probability is the guide of life, in that moral response (Butler's term) or "real assent" (Newman's phrase) are necessarily based on empirical probabilities. "So our Christian convictions based on historical uncertainties are in principle reasonable as being one with the rest of life."[57]

Thus can one preserve an empirical historiography — which we have found to be essential to Christian epistemology — together with a qualitatively unique, inerrantly truthful revelation — belief in which (one cannot emphasize too strongly) constitutes the great strength of Gordon Clark's scholarly contributions to Christian thought in the 20th century.

---

[56]Thus is Mavrodes' canonicity problem solved. True, II Timothy 3:16 does not give us a list of biblical books or establish Paul's authority for making such a statement. True also that Revelation 22:18-19 does not necessarily say anything for other biblical writings. True again that few biblical books specifically establish the authority of other biblical books or demonstrate their own authority. But all of this is a straw man and beside the point. The Hebrew Scriptures Christ used (and we can readily determine their composition) He consistently treated as, and expressly declared to be, God's holy Word, far above all other words; and He gave the gift of total recall to His apostles (John 14:26), under whose aegis the New Testament documents were subsequently written (and Acts — produced by one of the accepted Gospel writers — confirms Paul's reception as a genuine apostle by the original apostolic band). Circular reasoning, because the historical evidence for Jesus' deity is itself contained in the Bible? Hardly, for the initial establishing of Jesus' divine authority is accomplished by analyzing the New Testament documents, with their primary accounts of His resurrection, as nothing more than historical records. (See chapters 2 and 3 above.) *Having* done this (note the logical priority), we discover that one of the chief implications of finding a divine Christ in these documents is that the documents themselves, together with the Old Testament Scriptures, are declared to be the very Word of God. (On this subject, see my articles, "Inductive Inerrancy," *Christianity Today*, March 3, 1967, and "Inspiration and Inerrancy: A New Departure," in *Crisis in Lutheran Theology* [cited above in note 21], pp. 15-44.)

[57]Ian T. Ramsay, *Christian Discourse: Some Logical Explorations* (London: Oxford University Press, 1965), pp. 23-24. See chapter 6 above.

8. TOWARD A CHRISTIAN PHILOSOPHY OF HISTORY

In 1950, the English philosopher W H. Walsh began his *Introduction to Philosophy of History* with these words: "A writer on philosophy of history, in Great Britain at least, must begin by justifying the very existence of his subject."[1] It is doubtful whether today any such justification is required. The last decade and a half has witnessed a tremendous revival of interest in philosophy of history, as is evidenced, among other things, by the 1958 Cerisy-la-Salle colloquium on "L'histoire et ses interprétations," which brought together the great thinkers in the field;[2] by a demand for Toynbee's *A Study of History* which has resulted in the publishing of the entire unabridged work in a series of paperbound volumes; by the appearance of the journal *History and Theory*; and by the extensive recent monographic and periodical literature in the field.[3]

---

[1] This book is published in the United States under the title, *Philosophy of History: An Introduction* (rev. ed.; New York: Harper & Row, 1960).

[2] The proceedings have recently been issued; see Raymond Aron (ed.), *L'histoire et ses interprétations; Entretiens autour de Arnold Toynbee* ("Ecole Pratique des Hautes Etudes-Sorbonne. VIe Section: Sciences économiques et sociales. Congrès et colloques," No. 3; Paris & The Hague, 1961).

[3] A total of 794 books and journal articles published from 1951 through 1957 are listed in John C. Rule, *Bibliography of Works in the Philosophy of History, 1945-1957* ("History and Theory Beihefte," No. 1; The Hague, 1961). Items which Rule missed are included as an appendix to M. No-

But to conclude from the great interest and activity in philosophy of history that its perennial problems are being rapidly solved would be a gratuitous assumption. More effort seems to be expended in pointing up the fallacies of existing comprehensive historical syntheses than in offering new solutions.[4] The reason for this is suggested by a trenchant remark of the French existentialistic historian Aron: "The meaning of 'total' history is the meaning which we attach to human existence and to the succession of forms that it takes through time."[5] Philosophy of history, in other words, derives from one's general *Weltanschauung;* and the absence of decisive solutions to the great issues of philosophy of history reflects the incapacity of contemporary intellectual life to arrive at a meaningful world-view.

It is not really so strange that the central problem of history's meaning should remain murky in an age which, to use the expression of Hans Sedlmayer in his metaphysics of art, has "lost its center."[6] Both our philosophies of history and our general philosophies of life have been given classic expression in Camus' *The Plague,* in the diseased city of Oran, which one critic has described thus: "To step . . . into the landscape of Camus' novel is like listening to Bach's *Christmas Oratorio* when your small son has fumblingly turned the knob slightly and allowed the jazz

wicki's *Bibliography of Works in the Philosophy of History, 1958-1961* ("History and Theory Beihefte," No. 3; The Hague, 1964); from 1958 through 1961 an average of 35 books and 45 journal articles on philosophy of history were published annually in the Western languages. These figures, high as they are, do not include writings on "certain major historians, like Toynbee, for whom special bibliographies are projected." Of the latter, the Toynbee bibliography (covering 366 treatments of him published 1946-1960) has just appeared in *History and Theory,* IV (1965), 212-33.

[4]Note, for example, the high proportion of journal articles *contra* Toynbee listed in each issue of the quarterly *Historical Abstracts (H. A.) Bulletin.*

[5]Raymond Aron, "Evidence and Inference in History," in Daniel Lerner (ed.), *Evidence and Inference; the Hayden Colloquium on Scientific Concept and Method* (Glencoe, Ill.: Free Press, 1959), p. 46. Cf. my book, *The Shape of the Past: An Introduction to Philosophical Historiography* ("History in Christian Perspective," Vol. I; Ann Arbor, Mich.: Edwards Brothers, 1963), *passim.*

[6]See Sedlmayer's *Verlust der Mitte* (Salzburg, 1948).

rhythm of a jam session to come yowling into the world of angels and shining skies."[7] The recent republication of Spengler's *Decline of the West*[8] is a commentary both on our current interest in philosophy of history and on Nietzsche's accurate depiction in *Die froeliche Wissenschaft* of the intellectual climate of our epoch: "The ice that bears weight today has already grown extremely thin; the thawing wind is blowing. We ourselves, we homeless ones, are things that break through ice and other realities which are all too thin."

In such a dispossessed era one might suppose that Christian theologians and historians would stand forth as beacon lights pointing the way to solid historiographical ground. Did not the great Scottish philosopher Robert Flint effectively argue, even before the turn of the present century, that "if history has meaning, this meaning is not historical, but theological; what is called *Philosophy of history* is nothing else than a *Theology of history*, more or less disguised"[9]? Yet one looks in vain for twentieth-century Augustines. The cry, "Wanted: Christian Interpretation of History,"[10] is heard in all quarters, but response is either non-existent or disappointing. If the need is so great and the Christian responsibility to meet it so clearcut, why has contemporary theology produced no *Civitas Dei?* In philosophy of history as in medicine, effective treatment of disease requires effective diagnosis; it is therefore to this diagnostic problem that we address ourselves.

---

[7]Helmut Thielicke, *Nihilism*, trans. John W. Doberstein (New York: Harper & Row, 1961, 1962), pp. 96-97.

[8]Edited and abridged by Helmut Werner.

[9]Robert Flint, *History of the Philosophy of History* (Edinburgh: 1893), p. 62. Flint, whose fame as a theologian rests chiefly on his Baird Lectures of 1876-1877 (*Theism* and *Anti-Theistic Theories*), evidenced his profound grasp of philosophy of history by the work here cited, by his detailed *Philosophy of History in Europe*, and by his analysis of the thought of Giambattista Vico contributed to Blackwood's series of "Philosophical Classics" (see my essay "Vico and the Christian Faith," in *The Shape of the Past*, pp. 187-216).

[10]The title of a recent article by Peter DeJong in *Christianity Today*, IX (March 12, 1965), 13-16. For a valuable orientation to the present state of Christian philosophy of history, see Georges Florovsky's essay, "The Predicament of the Christian Historian," in *Religion and Culture: Essays in Honor of Paul Tillich*, ed. Walter Leibrecht (New York: Harper & Row, 1959), pp. 140-66 (with extensive literature cited on pp. 359-62).

CONCEPTUAL PERPLEXITY

On one major point virtually all theologians of history — past and present — are in agreement: the meaning of general human history is to be found in Jesus Christ. This conviction is common to such radically different positions as Rudolf Bultmann's neo-Protestant existentialism[11] and Hans Urs von Balthasar's sophisticated Catholicism.[12] Reinhold Niebuhr expresses the Christocentricity of theology of history with particular effectiveness: "The Christian faith finds the final clue to the meaning of life and history in the Christ whose goodness is at once the virtue which man ought, but does not, achieve in history, and the revelation of a divine mercy which understands and resolves the perpetual contradictions in which history is involved, even on the highest reaches of human achievements.[13] For the theologian, the answers to the questions posed by the history of mankind are, in the most profound sense, bound up with Jesus Christ — who was Himself an historical person.

But precisely here the crux problem arises for contemporary theology: the problem of the historicity of Jesus the Christ. Vagueness as to what is meant by Christ's historicity must necessarily result in vague and indecisive theologies of history. This atmosphere of confusion and perplexity is well illustrated in the essays contained in the recent composite work, *The Historical Jesus and the Kerygmatic Christ*, and its editors accurately describe the

---

[11]See Rudolf Bultmann, *The Presence of Eternity: History and Eschatology; the Gifford Lectures 1955* (New York: Harper & Row, 1957), *passim.* Cf. Gordon H. Clark's essay, "Bultmann's Historiography," in *Jesus of Nazareth: Saviour and Lord*, ed. Carl F. H. Henry (Grand Rapids, Mich.: Wm. B. Eerdmans, 1966).

[12]The final sections of Balthasar's *Theologie der Geschichte* (2d ed.; Einsiedeln, 1959) are appropriately titled, "Christ the Norm of History," and "History under the Norm of Christ." Karl Barth, in his book, *The Humanity of God*, has acknowledged the Jesuit Balthasar as the most penetrating of his critics.

[13]Reinhold Niebuhr, *The Children of Light and the Children of Darkness; a Vindication of Democracy and a Critique of Its Traditional Defence* (New York: Charles Scribner's Sons, 1944), p. 188. On Christ as the center of history, see Adolf Köberle's essay treating this theme (chapter 5 of *Jesus of Nazareth: Saviour and Lord*).

theological situation reflected in their book as the "winter of our discontent."[14]

Whence arises this "discontent"? Evidently not from the character of the historical evidence for Jesus' life, since the documentary testimonies relating to Him are not qualitatively different from the evidence upon which portraits of other historical figures are built.[15] The issue cuts to the deeper level of the *meaning* of historicity in relation to the Christ; it is thus, to use Enrico Castelli's expression, a question of the presuppositions involved in one's theology of history.[16] Perplexity in contemporary Christian philosophy of history exists chiefly because of presuppositional ambiguities about the concept of history itself.

In an article entitled "Five Meanings of the Word 'Historical' " in the winter 1964 issue of *The Christian Scholar*, Will Herberg endeavors to schematize the major uses of the term "historical" in present-day theological discussion. Herberg isolates five fundamental conceptions: (1) History as "past facticity"; this is the "ordinary usage" of the term, and "in this sense the historical is opposed to the fictitious, the fabulous, the mythical, the legendary, and the like." (2) History as temporal enactment, as contrasted with "the timeless and the eternal." Theologians frequently speak of the radical difference between the eternal truths and abstract concepts of the Eastern religions on the one hand, and the concrete historical revelation in Judaism or Christianity on the other. (3) History as *Geschichte* (in contrast with *Historie*). Here theologians such as Martin Kähler[17] have attempted to "go beyond, or even ignore, the element of facticity" by making the historical refer to what we

---

[14]Carl E. Braaten and Roy A. Harrisville, (eds.), *The Historical Jesus and the Kerygmatic Christ; Essays on the New Quest of the Historical Jesus* (New York: Abingdon Press, 1964), p. 11.

[15]Cf. F. F. Bruce, *The New Testament Documents; Are They Reliable?* (5th rev. ed.; London: Inter-Varsity Fellowship, 1960).

[16]Enrico Castelli, *Presupposti di una Teologia della Storia* (Milano, 1952); translated into French under the title, *Les Présupposés d'une théologie de l'histoire* (Paris, 1954). Castelli, who holds a professorship at the University of Rome, here provides a stimulating, though excessively existentialistic, orientation to the fundamental issues of Christian philosophy of history in our time.

[17]Martin Kähler, *Der sogennante historische Jesus und der geschichtliche, biblische Christus*, hrsg. von E. Wolf (2d ed.; München, 1956).

"deem to be especially influential on the future course of events." In reference to the historicity of Jesus Christ, this approach argues that "the Christ who is effective in history is he who is proclaimed by the apostles as the crucified and resurrected one, and not an 'historical' Jesus who must first be painfully discovered anew behind the documents by our scientific technique."[18] (4) History as the essence of man's being. Theologians such as Reinhold Niebuhr insist that neither individual man nor man in community is to be understood in terms of fixed structures of being; rather, man is what he is because of his historical involvement. (5) History as existential decision in the face of future possibilities. Here man's "nature" is "forever being made and remade by choice, decision, and action, which is what constitutes man's historicity." Rudolf Bultmann provides the best theological illustration of this approach to history; for him, the meaning of history is to be found in "responsibility over against the future."[19]

Herberg notes that these five interpretations of the meaning of "historical" run a gamut from history as *past facticity* to history as *future possibility*. What he does not observe is the even more important consideration that a radical difference exists between the first two usages and the last three. Usages (1) and (2) assume the subject-object distinction (the distinction between the observer of the past and the past itself) and attempt to subordinate the former to the latter; while usages (3), (4), and (5) increasingly disregard the subject-object distinction and place emphasis not on the objectivity of the past but on the interpretive position of the present-day student of it — whose personal "historicity" is held to be the only key to the meaning of the past. These five approaches to history are thus not as "closely connected" as Herberg claims. In reality, they point to the fundamental cleavage between *Weltanschauungen* that focus on the objectivity of the external world and those that derive from the subjective stance of the interpreter. In terms of this exceedingly basic presuppositional distinction, where is the present-day post-Bultmannian theology to be located, and what degree of validity is to be attached to its historical a prioris?

---

[18]Thus Wolf restates Kähler's thesis (*ibid.*, p. 8).
[19]Bultmann, *op. cit.* p. 143.

THEOLOGY OF HISTORY IN THE "NEW HERMENEUTIC"

Tillich has pointed out that one of the chief thrusts in the development of modern existentialism has been the effort to "cut under the subject-object distinction."[20] Thus Bultmann, who is indebted to existentialism for this philosophical orientation, claims that "for historical understanding, the schema of subject and object that has validity for natural science is invalid."[21] In place of the subject-object distinction, Bultmann substitutes his "circularity" principle: historical exegesis requires an existential "life-relation" between the past (e.g., biblical subject matter) and the interpreter.[22] In such an approach, the interpreter necessarily assumes first place; thus Bultmann concludes his Gifford Lectures with the reiterated assertion: "Always in your present lies the meaning in history, and you cannot see it as a spectator, but only in your responsible decisions."[23]

As is well known, the current "post-Bultmannian" phase in theology grew out of dissatisfaction with Bultmann's relative indifference to the historical Jesus. Bultmann's disciples found great difficulty in their master's unwillingness to pursue the historical question beyond the perspective of the church's interpretation of Jesus.[24] Thus, parallel with Barth's introduction of objectifying elements into his theology, Bultmann's students and former disciples have endeavored in various ways to conjoin more meaningfully the Jesus of history with the Christ confessed by the early Church. Does this mean that the post-Bultmannian "New Hermeneutic" has shifted from an existentialistic concept of historical investigation to a presuppositionally objective approach?

---

[20] Paul Tillich, "Existential Philosophy: Its Historical Meaning," in his *Theology of Culture*, ed. Robert C. Kimball (New York: Oxford University Press, 1959), p. 92. Tillich's essay first appeared in the *Journal of the History of Ideas* in January, 1944.

[21] Bultmann, "Ist voraussetzungslose Exegese möglich?", *Theologische Zeitschrift*, XIII (1957), 409-417.

[22] On Bultmann's circularity principle, see Armin Henry Limper, "Hermeneutics and Eschatology: Rudolf Bultmann's Interpretation of John, Chapters 13-17" (unpublished Ph.D. dissertation, University of Chicago, 1960).

[23] Bultmann, *The Presence of Eternity*, p. 155.

[24] See Ralph P. Martin's essay, "Historical Survey of the 'New Quest' Debate," in *Jesus of Nazareth: Saviour and Lord*.

The answer to this exceedingly important question is a very definite "No." Wherever one turns in the "New Quest" debates, one finds — even when criticism of Bultmann is most severe — unshakeable and uncritical adherence to his principle of the "hermeneutical circle" and to the existential "transcending of the subject-object distinction." Indeed, an attitude of superiority and scorn not infrequently characterizes post-Bultmannian theological judgments of "objectivistic" thinking. Listen to Heinrich Ott, Karl Barth's successor at Basel, as he dispenses with "the so-called 'subject-object schema' and the view that all thinking and language to a very great extent necessarily have an objectifying character":

> According to this view faith and theology's thinking and speaking are to be basically distinguished, that is, one cannot at all speak of a believing thinking, since in this view all theological talking and thinking always take place from an objectifying distance. I shall refrain from going further into these misunderstandings. The thinking of Martin Heidegger performs the inestimable service of teaching us to see in a more primal way the nature of thinking, of language, and thus of understanding. If we listen to him and follow him even only a bit on his way, perhaps the day will dawn upon us when those obscuring premises will fall like scales from our eyes.[25]

On this side of the Atlantic, Roy A. Harrisville's essay, "Representative American Lives of Jesus," offered as a contribution to the "New Quest" discussions, purports to show that "apart from an abandonment of the subject-object polarity in the interpretation of history, Jesus 'returns to his own time' as much an enigma as before, and that little more is to be gained from his biography than a portrait of his biographer."[26] To Ott, Harrisville, and the New Hermeneutic in general, the Dilthey-Kähler rejection of objective history is self-evident and axiomatic; and even the Dilthey critic Hans-Georg Gadamer, who is endeavoring to give an

---

[25]Heinrich Ott, "What Is Systematic Theology?", in James M. Robinson and John B. Cobb, Jr. (eds.), *The Later Heidegger and Theology* ("New Frontiers in Theology," Vol. I; New York: Harper & Row, 1963), p. 93. Ott's essay appeared originally in the *Zeitschrift für Theologie und Kirche*, Beiheft 2 (1961), pp. 19-46.

[26]This essay is included in Braaten and Harrisville, *op. cit.*; the sentence quoted appears on p. 196.

"ontological turn" to historical hermeneutic by concentrating on linguistic understanding rather than existential psychology, takes the "hermeneutical circle" for granted and asserts that "historic tradition can only be understood by recalling the basic continuing concretizing taking place in the continuation of things."[27]

What is the effect on Christian philosophy of history when the "obscuring premises" of the subject-object distinction have fallen "like scales from our eyes"? Unhappily, the result is not the promised panacea, but a relativistic, solipsistic chaos. The secular existentialistic interpreter of history, Raymond Aron, frankly admits that out of the marriage of the objective matter of history and the subjective stance of the historian a "plurality of systems of interpretation" comes forth — and his advice to the historian who would "overcome the relativity of history" is that he can do so only by "the absolute of decision," thereby affirming "the power of man, who creates himself by judging his environment, and by choosing himself."[28] Thus an interpretation of the past becomes "absolute" only to the interpreter who chooses it absolutely. As we have seen, this is also Bultmann's conclusion as to the meaning of history.

But whereas Aron and Bultmann at least admit to the existence of objectively verifiable historical facts (though they are quick to point out that concentration on them instead of on our existential "encounter with history" will cause us to "miss history's real nature"), post-Bultmannian Heinrich Ott endeavors to carry the rejection of the subject-object distinction to its logical conclusion. He argues the amazing propositions that "the objective mode of

---

[27]Hans-Georg Gadamer, *Wahrheit und Methode: Grundzüge einer philosophischen Hermeneutik* (Tübingen, 1960), p. 355. On Gadamer's place in the "New Quest" debates, see James M. Robinson's article, "Hermeneutic Since Barth," which introduces Robinson and Cobb (eds.), *The New Hermeneutic* ("New Frontiers in Theology," Vol. II; New York: Harper & Row, 1964), pp. 69-77. The best introduction in English to Dilthey's philosophy of history is H. P. Rickman's anthology, *Meaning in History: Wilhelm Dilthey's Thoughts on History and Society* (London: 1961).

[28]Raymond Aron, *Introduction to the Philosophy of History*, trans. George J. Irwin (London: Weidenfeld and Nicholson, 1961), pp. 86ff., 334. This translation from the second French edition of 1948 must continually be compared with the original, for the translator has frequently obscured the author's meaning.

knowledge is entirely inappropriate to historical reality because there are no such things as objectively verifiable facts and, secondly, that all true knowledge of history is finally knowledge by encounter and confrontation."[29] Ott introduces God's "seeing" of total history as a device to prevent his position from degenerating into total solipsism, but such a *deus ex machina* is far from successful, since apart from an objectively reliable revelation from God (which Ott's view eliminates *ex hypothesi*), man can never know if one human interpretation of the past is closer to ultimate reality than another.

Relativistic, solipsistic consequences are not accidental when one attempts to transcend the subject-object distinction; they are inevitable. This is the case because the finite, sinful human being is incapable of obliterating the distinction between the reality outside of himself and his own psyche without bending reality in his own direction. "Transcending the subject-object barrier" thus inevitably produces, not an experience with higher reality, but a falling back into subjectivism. The more perceptive existentialists have seen this and admitted it. Jean-Paul Sartre, for example, states that what Christian existentialists (such as Marcel) and atheistic existentialists (such as Heidegger and himself) "have in common is that they think that existence precedes essence, or, if you prefer, that subjectivity must be the starting point.[30] Gadamer's student, Heinz Kimmerle, has rendered theology a great service by showing that Dilthey, upon whom Heidegger and Bultmann based their existentialisms, derived his hermeneutic from the later Schleiermacher.[31] The chain is thus completed from the subjective

---

[29]Heinrich Ott, "The Historical Jesus and the Ontology of History," in Braaten and Harrisville, *op. cit.*, p. 148. Ott's essay appeared first in booklet form under the title, *Die Frage nach dem historischen Jesus und die Ontologie der Geschichte* (Zürich, 1960).

[30]Jean-Paul Sartre, *Existentialism and Human Emotions* (New York: Philosophical Library, 1957), p. 13 (section trans. by Bernard Frechtman).

[31]Cf. Robinson, *The New Hermeneutic*, pp. 70-71. Bultmann's dependence on Dilthey in opposing the subject-object distinction is evident from Bultmann's essay, "The Problem of Hermeneutics," which appeared first in the *Zeitschrift für Theologie und Kirche*, XLVII (1950), 47-69, and which has been published in English translation in Bultmann's *Essays, Philosophical and Theological*, trans. J. C. G. Greig (London: 1955), pp. 234-61.

psychologism of Schleiermacher (from which Ritschlian modernism grew) to the post-Bultmannian New Hermeneutic. The subjective soul of unreconstructed Protestant modernism (ironically rejected by all advocates of the post-Bultmannian era) has in fact transmigrated to the New Hermeneutic of the present decade — with all its deleterious consequences for Christian theology of history.

Will Herberg noted the "futuristic" orientation of existentialistic philosophies of history. This in itself should make us suspicious of them in relation to historical interpretation, for history, after all, has its *raison d'être* in past, not present or future, reality.[32] Since "future possibility" is the least knowable aspect of man's life, it is a singularly inappropriate basis for understanding his past; indeed, the "futurity" of existential-subjective approaches suggests the chief reason for rejecting them: their unverifiability. Heidegger's attempt, in his *Was Ist Metaphysik?* to assert the primacy of existence ("the Nothing") over essence ("the Negation and the Not") has been shown by Carnap to consist of analytically meaningless, unverifiable "pseudo-statements."[33] Likewise, claims such as Ott's that "all true knowledge of history is finally knowledge by encounter and confrontation" receive decimating criticism by philosophers of religion schooled in analytic and "ordinary language" philosophy; Frederick Ferré, for example, writes:

> If illusion is present sometimes or often in "encounter," what assures us that our experience is not *always* merely subjective emotion conjoined with personal interpretation? Even if the rapport between persons is sometimes veridical, as seems increasingly likely in the light of contemporary research into paranormal psychology, it is clear from the negative instances that

---

[32]Cf. J. W. N. Watkins on the inadequacy of pragmatic philosophies of history: "There is something to be said for pragmatism, but it so happens that history is the domain in which it works worst. History is backward-looking, pragmatism forward-looking" ("Philosophy of History: Publications in English," in *La Philosophie au milieu du vingtième siècle*, ed. Raymond Klibansky [4 vols., 2d ed.; Firenze, 1961-1962], III, 165).

[33]Rudolf Carnap, "The Elimination of Metaphysics through Logical Analysis of Language," in *Logical Positivism*, ed. A. J. Ayer (Glencoe, Ill.: Free Press, 1959), pp. 69-73. Carnap's paper originally appeared in German in Vol. II of *Erkenntnis* (1932).

this route to knowledge of other persons is far from trustworthy, and therefore hardly adequate to undergird the entire theological claim to the knowledge of God.[34]

Endeavors to deal with the issues of Christian philosophy of history by introducing a *geschichtliche* or "suprahistorical" level of understanding fare no better, for, like Heidegger's "Nothing" and Ott's "confrontation," *Geschichte* is subject to no verifiability tests.[35]

The only way out of the relativistic morass characteristic of the positions we have been considering is a frank acknowledgment of the subject-object distinction as the starting-point for all genuine understanding of the past. G. H. von Wright has shown, by a closely reasoned argument, that inductive method, presupposing the subject-object distinction, is the only entrée to verifiable knowledge of the external world: "its superiority is rooted in the fact that the inductive character of a policy is the very criterion by means of which we judge its goodness."[36] To disregard or try to circumvent inductive method in studying the past is to destroy all possibility of objective knowledge of man's history, and therefore to eliminate in principle a Christian philosophy of history. The theologian who thinks he is "transcending the subject-object barrier" becomes like Robert Benchley, who in his college biology course spent the term meticulously drawing the image of his own eyelash as it fell across the microscopic field. It is this sublime disregard of the self-imposition of subjective categories on biblical material that has vitiated so much of the Bultmannian and post-

---

[34]Frederick Ferré, *Language, Logic and God* (New York: Harper & Row, 1961), p. 103. Cf. C. B. Martin, "A Religious Way of Knowing," in *New Essays in Philosophical Theology*, edd. Antony Flew and Alasdair MacIntyre (London, 1955), pp. 76-95.

[35]See above, chapter 5 (my essay, "Karl Barth and Contemporary Theology of History").

[36]Georg Henrik von Wright, *The Logical Problem of Induction* (2d ed.; Oxford: The Clarendon Press, 1957), p. 175. I have related induction to deduction and Aristotelian retroduction in my paper, "The Theologian's Craft: A Discussion of Theory Formation and Theory Testing in Theology," presented at the 20th Annual Convention of the American Scientific Affiliation, August 24, 1965, (published both in the *Journal of the American Scientific Affiliation*, XVIII [September, 1966], and in the *Concordia Theological Monthly*, XXXVII [February, 1966]).

Bultmannian interpretation of Christian origins. In reality, *contra* Harrisville, the Jesus of history remains enigmatic to contemporary theology not "apart from an abandonment of the subject-object polarity," but precisely *because* of its abandonment.

THE PATH TO SOLID GROUND

The historiographical tradition from Dilthey to the post-Bultmannians has made the great error — so common in human life that the Hegelian dialectic formalizes it — of reacting too strongly to an erroneous position and thereby falling into an equally grievous error. In opposing nineteenth-century Positivistic Historicism, which mistakenly endeavored to structure man's history by way of categories derived from Newtonian science, the Dilthey tradition in philosophy and its Bultmannian counterpart in theology radically subjectivized the historical task. Instead of purging Historicism of its rationalistic, humanistic scientism, so as to free its sound empirical techniques from harmful metaphysical baggage, the Anti-Positivists threw out the most valuable insight that Historicism had to offer: inductive method.[37] In reacting against historicistic "life of Jesus" research, post-liberal theology never saw that the real trouble lay not with the heuristic employment of inductive technique based upon the subject-object distinction, but with the humanistic metaphysic of the liberal researchers.[38]

In contemporary philosophy of history there are faint glimmerings of light as analytically trained philosophers are turning from the bogs of existential subjectivism to a frank recognition of the necessity of inductive historiography. How unfortunate that contemporary theology is not yet prepared for the logic of such an analysis of the methodological problem as provided by J. W. N. Watkins, which we quoted in the preceding chapter. Watkins points out that "the objective character of a scientific theory is not

---

[37]Ironical to the highest degree is Bultmann's retention of the most reprehensible element in Historicism: its metaphysical assumption that "the whole historical process is a closed unity" and that "this closedness means that the continuum of historical happenings cannot be rent by the interference of supernatural, transcendent powers and that therefore there is no 'miracle' in this sense of the word" (Bultmann, "Ist voraussetzungslose Exegese mölich?", *loc. cit.*). Einsteinian relativity has made this worldview hopelessly obsolete.

[38]Harrisville's article, cited above at n. 26, is a concrete instance of such obliviousness in the interpretation of the "life of Jesus" era.

a function of its author's temperament and mentality, but of its *criticisability*. Thus for me, the question "How objective can history be?" boils down to the question, "To what extent is a systematic historical reconstruction exposed to criticism?"[39]

When the Christian philosopher of history is willing to approach the New Testament in this spirit, he finds that the seemingly insurmountable problem of the "historical Jesus" vs. the "kerygmatic Christ" well nigh vanishes away. Objective comparison of the problems in New Testament interpretation with parallel issues in extra-biblical historical and literary scholarship indicates that biblical theology has created its own difficulties through presuppositionalism. "Is it not true that our interpretation of Jesus comes only by way of the early Church?" Certainly, but this in no way forces the conclusion that the Church altered His portrait. We do not assume that such is the case with the other great men of history who have written nothing (e.g., Alexander the Great, Charlemagne) and who are seen by us through the eyes of their contemporaries. "Should we not presume redaction of Jesus' message by the Church that produced the New Testament documents?" To do so is to employ a technique (the Dibelius-Bultmann *formgeschichtliche Methode*) which proved debilitating in Homeric scholarship decades ago[40] and which has been rejected by students of the English ballad because of the lack of sufficient time periods for oral development — and "no Gospel section passed through such a long period of oral tradition as did any genuine ballad."[41]

Indeed, historians who stand outside of the existentialistically suffused atmosphere of New Testament study are frequently at a loss to know what is troubling the Christian historian. Thus A. N.

---

[39]Watkins, in *La Philosophie au milieu du vingtième siècle*, III, 174. Watkins makes the important point, vs. the Dilthey tradition, that recent analytical work by such philosophers as Ryle "dispels the old presumption, to which Hayek, Swabey and others are still inclined, that to understand Ghengis Khan the historian must be someone very like Ghengis Khan" (p. 159). The application to the New Hermeneutic, which makes historical understanding of the Christ of the New Testament dependent upon prior faith in him, should be obvious.

[40]See H. J. Rose, *Handbook of Greek Literature from Homer to the Age of Lucian* (London: Methuen, 1934), pp. 42-43.

[41]A. H. McNeile and C. S. C. Williams, *Introduction to the Study of the New Testament* (2d ed.; Oxford: Clarendon Press, 1955), p. 58.

Sherwin-White's Sarum Lectures on *Roman Society and Roman
Law in the New Testament* conclude with a section on "The
Historicity of the Gospels and Graeco-Roman Historiography"
in which we read:

> It is astonishing that while Graeco-Roman historians have been
> growing in confidence, the twentieth-century study of the Gos-
> pel narratives, starting from no less promising material, has taken
> so gloomy a turn in the development of form-criticism that the
> more advanced exponents of it apparently maintain — so far as
> an amateur can understand the matter — that the historical
> Christ is unknowable and the history of his mission cannot be
> written. This seems very curious when one compares the case for
> the best-known contemporary of Christ, who like Christ is a
> well-documented figure — Tiberius Caesar. The story of his reign
> is known from four sources, the *Annals* of Tacitus and the biog-
> raphy of Suetonius, written some eighty or ninety years later,
> the brief contemporary record of Velletus Paterculus, and the
> third-century history of Cassius Dio. These disagree amongst
> themselves in the wildest possible fashion, both in major mat-
> ters of political action or motive and in specific details of
> minor events. Everyone would admit that Tacitus is the best of
> all the sources, and yet no serious modern historian would ac-
> cept at face value the majority of the statements of Tacitus
> about the motives of Tiberius. But this does not prevent the
> belief that the material of Tacitus can be used to write a history
> of Tiberius.[42]

The Gospel records of our Lord's life, death, and resurrection do
not suffer from these historical difficulties, with regard either to
date, or to primary evidential value, or to internal consistency.
How unfortunate, then, that the contemporary Christ theologian
is hesitant to go to them and inductively discover there the true
grounds of theology of history.

And if one does so? One meets in the primary documents a
man who convinces both His friends and His enemies that He
regards Himself as no less than God Incarnate, come to earth to
die for the sins of the world. He places His stamp of divine approval on the Old Testament, as witnessing to Him, and promises
His Holy Spirit to the apostles in order that the Spirit may bring

---

[42]Sherwin-White's Sarum Lectures for 1960-1961 were published at
Oxford in 1963; the quoted passage appears on p. 187.

to their remembrance all things that He had said to them (John 14:26).[43] He rises from the dead — bodily — to manifest His *historisch* resurrection even to those such as Thomas who disbelieved. Here we see "historical Jesus" and "kerygmatic Christ" thoroughly united, providing an objective ground — the only objective ground — for an interpretation of total history that is not subject to the limitations of man's sinful situation.

In a moving symbolic novel, *Mount Analogue,* the late surrealist, Sanskrit scholar, philosopher, and poet René Daumal has one of his leading characters say:

> Experience has proved, I told myself, that a man cannot reach truth directly, nor all by himself. An intermediary has to be present, a force still human in certain respects, yet transcending humanity in others. Somewhere on our Earth this superior form of humanity must exist, and not utterly out of reach. In that case shouldn't all my efforts be directed toward discovering it? Even if, in spite of my certainty, I were the victim of a monstrous illusion, I should lose nothing in the attempt. For, apart from this hope, all life lacked meaning for me.
>
> But where was I to look? Where could I begin? I had already covered the world, poked my nose into everything, into all kinds of religious sects and mystic cults. But with all of them it came down to the same dilemma: maybe yes, maybe no. Why should I stake my life on this one rather than on that one? You see, I had no touchstone.[44]

For Christian theology of history (as for theology in general and life in general) the true and only Intermediary is Jesus Christ, and the true and only touchstone is Holy Scripture, which testifies of Him.[45]

---

[43]On the crucial significance of the apostolic "remembering" as the link between the "Jesus of history" and the "Christ of faith," see Oscar Cullmann's "The Resurrection: Event and Meaning," *Christianity Today,* IX (March 26, 1965), 8-9; this essay is from Cullmann's new book, *Heil als Geschichte.*

[44]René Daumal, *Mount Analogue,* trans. Roger Shattuck (New York: Pantheon Books, 1960), p. 59.

[45]See my essay, "Inspiration and Inerrancy: A New Departure," *Evangelical Theological Society Bulletin,* VIII, No. 2 (Spring, 1965). This essay has been reprinted with revisions in my *Crisis in Lutheran Theology* (2 vols.; Grand Rapids, Mich.: Baker Book House, 1967), I, 15-44.

Afterword:
CHURCH HISTORY TODAY*

In checking the October, 1965, number of *The Journal of Ecclesiastical History*, I encountered the following articles: "Unions and Confraternity with Cluny," "A View of Archbishop Lanfranc," "Piety and Charity in Late Medieval London," "Social and Economic Theories and Pastoral Concerns of a Victorian Archbishop," and "The Reactions of Church and Dissent towards the Crimean War." It would be possible for me to point out that as far as I know there has been no article published recently either by evangelical or non-evangelical dealing with piety and charity in late medieval Prague, or with the reactions of church and dissent towards the Boer War. Here we still have open subjects for investigation! But it seems to me that if we are concerned with the current issues in church history we've got to strike a good deal deeper than this. We've got to strike to the level of philosophical presuppositions that operate when one confronts the problems of church history. Specifically I want to discuss four such presuppositional questions.

*An invitational presentation at the 17th Annual Meeting of the Evangelical Theological Society, Nashville, Tennessee, December 27-29, 1965. These remarks were made in the course of a panel discussion of "Frontier Issues in Contemporary Theology," chaired by Dr. Carl F. H. Henry.

The first has to do with the nature of history. How do church historians today look at the nature of history? Do they consider historical events as having an objective existence apart from themselves? Do they hold that the events of history have meaning independent of themselves as interpreters? Secondly, I want to ask the question: How does the church historian's approach to the meaning of history in general influence his attitude when he deals with the events of sacred history? What is the bearing of the church historian's philosophical presuppositions on the treatment of the saving events upon which church history presumably centers? Thirdly (and this of course grows out of the first two questions): Is it possible for a Christian philosophy of history to be written? And lastly: What does the church historian have to say to the current confessional issues — particularly those relating to biblical authority — that are troubling many denominations in America today?

There is an article of considerable interest by Will Herberg in the Winter, 1964, issue of *The Christian Scholar*. It is titled, "Five Meanings of the Word 'Historical.'" Herberg points out that people operating in the area of church history today frequently do not analyze the way in which they are using the word "history." The word can be used in at least five different ways, and Herberg regards these as a continuum, extending from a subjective existential view of history all the way across to an objective view of history. On the one hand, we have those church historians who look at the past as basically a reflection of the existential stance of the church historian himself. On the other, we find church historians who look at history as having an existence independent of the historian and who are convinced that historical events give rise to interpretations not dependent upon their own stance.

Now it is important to note that in contemporary church history the vast majority of theoreticians opt for some kind of existential orientation. This is true not only of theologians who are evaluating what church historians do but of the church historians themselves. Among the theologians who have concentrated on this problem we have of course Rudolf Bultmann. Says Bultmann in his Gifford Lectures published under the title, *The Presence of Eternity*: "Always in your present lies the meaning in history, and you cannot see it as a spectator, but only in your responsible decisions." Observe: the meaning of history always lies in *your* present. For the church historian, the meaning of history lies in the existential commitment which he himself makes. This may seem pretty radical, but if we take a look at Heinrich Ott, Karl Barth's successor at Basel, and one of the primary figures in the current hermeneutic revival, we see that it is possible to go even farther in an existential direction. Indeed, Ott's position virtually reaches solipsism! Says Ott: "The objective mode of knowledge is entirely inappropriate to historical reality because there are no such things as objectively verifiable facts. . . . All true knowledge of history is finally knowledge by encounter and confrontation" (*Die Frage nach dem historischen Jesus und die Ontologie der Geschichte*).

We can see this approach applied to specific historical problems by such theologians of the "New Hermeneutic" as Gerhard Ebeling. Ebeling has spent most of his career interpreting Luther; for Ebeling, Luther supposedly held that we devote ourselves to the service of the "word-event." Luther is presented as an existentialist who dialectically unites the Scripture with the stance of the believer. The French Jesuit theologian Marlé expresses amazement that Ebeling has given Luther such *"une étonnante actualité"* — such a surprising contemporaneity. This is quite so. In fact, when one reads about Luther in Ebeling, Luther sounds just like Ebeling! The church historian Albert C. Outler well illustrates that the professional church historian today feels at home in this dialectic atmosphere. Outler became president of the American Society of Church History a year ago, and delivered his presidential address on the subject, "Theodosius' Horse: Reflections on the Predicament of the Church Historian." The horse threw Theodosius, whose death radically altered the course of Byzantine history and led to the establishment of Chalcedonian christology. In this essay Outler writes: "The frank acknowledgment of this inbuilt uncertainty in all historical knowledge might well be the beginning of historiographical wisdom" (*Church History*, September, 1965). The stress is placed on uncertainty, such as the horse throwing Theodosius.

Now the peculiar thing about this situation is that outside of the realm of church history as influenced especially by contemporary theology, people are seeing that existential historiography is not as attractive an option as it superficially appears to be. Strange to say, clarity has been achieved especially by those who are ap-

proaching historical problems from a secular standpoint. Consider
the interesting section at the end of Sherwin-White's 1960-1961
Sarum Lectures on *Roman Society and Roman Law in the New
Testament* (Oxford: Clarendon Press, 1963), where the writer
touches on the question of the historical objectivity of the biblical
accounts of Jesus' life and ministry: "It is astonishing that while
Graeco-Roman historians have been growing in confidence, the
20th century study of the Gospel narratives, starting from no
less promising material, has taken so gloomy a turn in the development of form-criticism that the more advanced exponents of it apparently maintain . . . that the historical Christ is unknowable
and the history of his mission cannot be written." Sherwin-White
thereupon compares the historical data in behalf of the Jesus of
New Testament with the historical data in behalf of Tiberius Caesar, "the best-known contemporary of Christ." He points out that
for Tiberius Caesar we have four basic documents that give us our
information, and that even though these documents are hopelessly
inconsistent at various points, no one doubts that these documents
provide an accurate picture of a historical person and that they
can be relied upon for the events of his life and for their interpretation. But in the case of Jesus, New Testament historians seem
overwhelmed by uncertainty — and this uncertainty is of course
connected with the fact that they have imported their existential
judgments into the historical process they are endeavoring to understand.

Recent work in analytical philosophy — for example, Danto's
Analytical Philosophy of History (Cambridge University Press,
1965) — has mercilessly exposed the existential presuppositions
that underly the commitment of many church historians today.
Danto points out that such existential presuppositions are utterly
unverifiable. What does it mean, for example, that history is finally "knowledge by encounter and confrontation"? Does it mean
that the historian bangs his head against the manuscript? This
makes me think of the problem that Robert Benchley had in his
college biology course. Benchley thought that he was drawing
what appeared on the microscope slide. As it turned out he was
drawing a reflection of his own eyelash as this was reflected by
the microscope. One also thinks of Schiaparelli's Martian canals
which may at least in part have been the product of incipient
cataracts in Schiaparelli's eyes reflected against the surface of

Mars. The existential involvement of the historian is frequently this sort of thing. J. W. N. Watkins in dealing with this question points out that the analytical work by such philosophers as Ryle "dispels the old presumption . . . that to understand Ghengis Khan the historian must be someone very like Ghengis Khan." This is a nice point.

And from the theological side one does begin to hear a voice or two raised against the irrationalities built into existential historiography. Pannenberg of Mainz, in his *Offenbarung als Geschichte*, argues that the distinction between *Geschichte* and *Historie* as made by the dialectical theologians must go, for it is impossible to take the New Testament at its face value (or, for that matter, the Old Testament if we attempt to separate the events of saving history from the *de facto* events of general history. And one can indeed discover what these events are; it's a matter of examining the documents, refusing to inject one's own existential stance into these documents, and permitting others to check one's investigations so that mutual criticism will uncover presuppositions inimical to objective historical analysis.[1] The significance of Pannenberg's position becomes evident when we see that for him (as for the biblical writers) the Resurrection has got to be dealt with as an objective event; it cannot be put into the realm of "suprahistory" or "metahistory." It's got to be considered just as the narratives obviously want it to be considered, as an event on the same historical level as the death of Christ, as the Sermon on the Mount, etc.

With Carl Michalson's recent death in an air crash, Schubert Ogden is probably the most prominent living theological exponent of a radical existential view in the U.S., and even he is trying to stiffen it with Whitehead's process philosophy. You will find an interesting article by Ogden in the January, 1963, *Journal of Religion*, entitled "What Sense Does it Make to Say, 'God Acts in History'?" Ogden has to engage in herculean labor to get it to make any sense, for if you hold with him that God is best understood as the universal process, what is the point of asserting that

---

[1]Incidentally, for Pannenberg one should look at the second edition of his work (1963), in which he adds an appendix criticizing his critics. His critics have been very nasty to him. Obviously they have over-reacted; why? Their own commitment to dialectic presuppositions has been so strong that Pannenberg makes them nervous.

God "acts" in a special way in history? Paul Van Buren, in his notorious but exceedingly valuable book, *The Secular Meaning of the Gospel*, nicely takes care of Ogden in a long section dealing with the analytical absurdity of the kinds of existential-process statements that Ogden is attempting to make. Neither existentialism nor process philosophy can make theological sense out of history.

What are the implications of this situation for the possibility of writing a Christian philosophy of history? It seems to me that a Christian philosophy of history has to begin with the assumption that there are objective events which do indeed carry their interpretation with them. This is true not only of the events of biblical history but of the events of history in general. If then we ask, "why do we need the Bible to help us to interpret history?" the answer is that such a welter of historical data exists that we do not know how to relate all the facts to each other. Our lifetime is too short and our perspective is too limited. By way of Scripture we are able to enter to the christological heart of the historical process and thereby understand the operation of other events. We can use the biblical narratives — particularly the narratives concerning our Lord — as a criterion of significance and also a means of comprehending human nature and ethical values, so that we can see meaning in the totality of human life as displayed in history.

Finally, what does church history say to the present confessional situation? Very briefly, I think that you can look at the church history discipline in your seminary or your college with a little more appreciation if you realize that by examining the confessional problem of the last half century one sees a paradigm of the very difficulties that we are encountering evangelically today. If the church historian at your seminary or Christian college were to provide a paper dealing with the history of liberalism in the Presbyterian Church U.S.A., for example, that discussion would have a remarkable correspondence to the kind of difficulties that are being faced by a number of other denominations (not excluding stalwart evangelical bodies!) at the present time. The church historian is able to look at the development of theology in the last fifty years and see there the logical interrelation and progress of heresy in the twentieth century. For example, the church historian sees the irony in Barth's horror when his former student Van

Buren sent him a précis of his *Secular Meaning of the Gospel;* said Barth in effect, "You have become a heretic"! Why did Van Buren, who took his doctorate under Barth at Basel, pass into death-of-God heresy? Robert Funk, who has posed this problem historically, gives the reason: "Neo-orthodoxy taught that God is never object but always subject, with the result that third generation neo-orthodox theologians have been forced to wrestle with the non-phenomenal character of God" (*Theology Today*, October, 1964). If God cannot be looked at objectively, then God can't be looked at — period. And when the analytical philosophers come along and rightly point out that there is then no verification whatever for Neo-orthodoxy's theological statements, the only possible conclusion is that God has died. His death, however, occurs not in reality but only in the Neo-orthodox dialectic process! He dies in the framework of presuppositions that entered the picture earlier in 20th-century theological development. The church historian can point out that if you jump on a theological train you may not be able to get off at the stop you would like to. The train keeps moving and though you may leap out the window your students will not necessarily do so. They will carry your ideas to their logical conclusion whether you like it or not. In the same connection it's very interesting that Tillich, just before his death, was much offended by the death-of-God people. He couldn't understand why this sort of thing was eclipsing his own theological approach. Yet it's not so difficult to understand. If one makes the kind of existential-dialectic commitment that has been characteristic of twentieth century Protestant theology, eventually one arrives at a point where God becomes non-phenomenal and disappears. Let us hope that the church historian can help us to reevaluate our own position and make sure that we hold fast to the faith once delivered to the saints — a faith clearly articulated in an inerrant Scripture and centering on the historical Lord Christ.

APPENDICES

APPENDIX A

Did Jesus Really Exist? by Avrum Stroll

Before beginning today's talk, I should like to discuss a matter with you which seems to me of great urgency and importance. And I should like to introduce what I have to say about this subject by reading the concluding paragraphs of a letter printed in the Letters to the Editor Column of the Vancouver Sun last Friday. This letter, signed with the name "Mrs. Ruth D. Golman," contains a lengthy and highly critical discussion of an address given before the Philosophy Club a week ago today by Professor Peter Remnant of the Philosophy Department. Its concluding paragraphs read as follows: (I quote):

> A man's religion is his own personal right and privilege, with which no other being has the right to interfere. Therefore, Dr. Remnant also has the right to his own personal views on the matter of God. But the University of British Columbia is, or should be, a purely educational institution. As a citizen of British Columbia, and a taxpayer, I therefore strongly protest his action in using the university and his affiliation therewith as the medium through which to express his personal ideas on religion by means of a lecture to over a thousand students. Not only are such views obnoxious to the time of the year, but to the time of world history. Never has mankind needed the consciousness of divine wisdom and strength as much as now.

There would be no point or purpose in reading this letter to you if it were simply an isolated expression of misinformation about the nature and function of a university in a democratic society. But unfortunately this is not the case. The views expressed by the writer echo a chorus of voices raised in condemnation of the university ever since the Cuban crisis. It is time that the character of this challenge be identified, be recognized for what it is, and that the sort of claims it makes be met head-on and resisted. If we fail to do so, we not only abandon one role of the teacher — to explain what he is about, and why his activities constitute important civic functions — but we also, by our inaction, open the door to further attacks on the democratic process itself.

For what we have here in Mrs. Golman's letter (and in the letters like it) is a direct challenge to the right of a professor or for that matter, anyone else, to speak his mind, before a group of university students. Mrs. Golman not only disagrees with Dr. Remnant's philosophical position — and we surely wish to defend, and even insist upon, her right to do so — but with his right to express it, using, as she puts it, the university facilities to do so. This is a clear and unmistakable challenge to academic freedom.

But the challenge does not end here: and it is this further threat to freedom of inquiry in the university which I wish to stress at this gathering. Dr. Remnant addressed this club at the invitation of its executive; the professors who spoke to a student group about the Cuban situation did so at the invitation of the executive of that group. What is being challenged here, in effect, is the right of student groups in a free university in a democratic society to invite speakers of their choice to address them.

What I wish to insist on today is that it is the defining function of a university in a democratic society to provide a forum where free debate and free inquiry can take place. It is not only the right, but indeed the duty, of faculty members and students to consider, examine, judge and make appraisals of the issues which concern them and this right can only be exercised in those circumstances where there are no barriers to free inquiry. The university is, in this respect, a model or smaller image of the wider democratic community itself. The university student exposes himself to a wide variety of opinions, views, and doctrines on the assumption that the techniques and procedures he develops in the process of making such judgments will be carried on into his daily activities as a citizen of the community when he leaves the university. It is a condition of being a good citizen in a democratic community that one treat the issues which come before him in this way; and it is important to stress that it is the university which provides part of the training ground for his becoming a good citizen in this sense.

The voices which speak with Mrs. Golman are in effect threatening us with censorship; with some restriction upon the right of faculty members and students to inquire into the subjects of their interests in an effort to develop mature, responsible and informed views of the world. This threat must not go unanswered. I urge you here today to protect against this challenge to your right to freedom of inquiry and investigation. How you go about doing this, I leave to you. But speak out. As the long history of tyranny only too well teaches us: if we do not speak out under such conditions, we may ultimately lose the right to speak out at all.

As a philosopher speaking (by invitation I might add) to the members of this philosophical association, may I use this opportunity for purposes of instruction? Let us not forget the best argument which has been proposed against the imposition of censorship. Roughly speaking, it is this: One of the paradoxes involved in the notion of censorship itself is that it cannot be applied to *all* members of a society. Even Plato, history's most celebrated defender of the need for censorship, wished only to apply it to the masses of his ideal society, but not to the ruling classes. And why? Because he correctly saw that those who are required to make wise and judicious laws for society must expose themselves to all the facts, to full and open debate about them, to all the pros and cons of a question which untrammeled investigation could produce. He saw clearly that without a free inquiry of this sort all the facts could not come under the surveillance of those responsible for making just laws; and so he argued, correctly I believe, that they should be exempted from censorship. In a democratic society, which is a self-governing institution, it is the citizen who participates in the governing process and who is, in the end, responsible for the laws which bind the members of the body politic. By the reasons I have just advanced, it follows that there can be no censorship in a democratic society: that all of its citizens must be in a position through free and unhampered inquiry to assess the merits of a question by having access to all the facts and opinions concerning it. As a training ground for the discovery and appraisal of facts the university is thus at the core of the democratic, decision-making process itself.

Let us now turn, if I may employ a Gilbertian phrase, from matters political to matters theological. And here I wish to discuss the question: Did Jesus of Nazareth really exist? This question, did Jesus exist, is to be distinguished from the question Did Christ exist? I will illustrate why later on. I might also point out that in distinguishing these questions from one another, I do not mean to revive any variant of the Monophysite heresy, a heresy which turned on the question whether Jesus was fully human or fully divine, or to what degree he was both.

What I want to do, instead, may be summarized as follows. In contemporary philosophical theology one of the most widely debated questions concerns the relation between the historical Jesus, a man supposedly living in Palestine sometime between 9 B.C. and A.D. 32, and the Jesus described in the Gospel writings. The form this discussion takes is reminiscent of the discussion which historians of ancient philosophy have engaged in concerning the existence of Socrates. Did Socrates really exist. Some scholars, Winspear for example, have argued "No." Most historians of the period have rejected this view, and have argued that he did. But the evidence for his existence is fragmentary. It mainly consists of a report by Xenophon of the trial of Socrates, allusions to a certain Socrates in two of the plays of Aristophanes, and the writings of Plato which purport to contain an eye witness account of the life and activities of Socrates. But even if it is granted that there was such a person, it is difficult to separate the views of the real Socrates from those of Plato: and all sorts of conjectures about the relation between the views of Socrates and those of Plato have been put forth in recent years. A typical and characteristic response of many philosophers who are not historians is to raise the question: What difference does it make whether there was a real Socrates or not? The figure who appears in the Platonic dialogues, even if only a literary invention, represents a certain philosophical position on all sorts of important matters: on the nature of knowledge, or the relation between knowledge and virtue, and so forth

— and it is these positions which are, and ought to be, of interest to the contemporary philosopher.

I find it of some interest that a comparable issue should exist in contemporary theology about the nature of the historical Jesus and his relation to the figure portrayed in the gospels. This issue is the main theme which runs through Albert Schweitzer's book, *The Quest of the Historical Jesus,* first published in 1910. In concluding this work, Schweitzer says: "There is nothing more negative than the result of the critical study of the Life of Jesus. The Jesus of Nazareth who came forward publicly as the Messiah, who preached the ethic of the Kingdom of God, who founded the Kingdom of Heaven upon earth, and died to give His work its final consecration, never had any existence. He is a figure designed by rationalism, endowed with life by liberalism, and clothed by Modern theology in an historical garb." (p. 398). And again, in developing this theme, he remarks: "Jesus means something to our world because a mighty spiritual force streams forth from Him and flows through our time also. This fact can neither be shaken nor confirmed by any historical discovery. It is the solid foundation of Christianity. The mistake was to suppose that Jesus could come to mean more to our time by entering into it as a man like ourselves. That is not possible. First because such a Jesus never existed." (p. 399).

One of the most important Christian theologians of the postwar period is Rudolf Bultmann whose work evidences a remarkable lack of concern with the historical Jesus. Expressing what has been described as "a mixture of radical historical skepticism and existentialist disinterest in objective history," (Schubert M. Ogden), Bultmann from the time of his 1926 monograph on Jesus to his lecture given before the Heidelberg Academy of the Sciences in 1959, takes the view that there is a difference in principle between the historical Jesus and the message of the church that sets an impassible limit to any attempt to establish their identity. Insofar as the old quest for the historical Jesus sought and seeks to reconstruct a picture of the life and personality of the historical Jesus and in that way to provide historical justification for the existential decision of faith, Bultmann completely rejects the question. In his view, such an effort is historically impossible and theologically illegitimate. The knowledge available to us, he argues, through responsible critical analysis of the Synoptic Gospels simply is insufficient for the reconstruction of a picture of Jesus' character and inner development.

This view has, of course, had its critics among New Testament Scholars, among them James Robinson in his "A New Quest of the Historical Jesus," published in 1959, Gunter Bornkamm (a pupil of Bultmann's), in his *Jesus of Nazareth*, Shubert M. Ogden (see his article, "Bultmann and the New Quest," in the July 1962 issue of the *Journal of Bible and Religion*). Now I do not wish to take part in this controversy; not only am I not a theologian and hence not competent to form judgments on this matter, but the issues which turn on detailed considerations, are simply too complex to be discussed in such a meeting as this one.

What I should like to do, though, is to raise the question: What evidence is there for the existence of the historical Jesus? without in any way attempting to relate this evidence to the figure presented in the gospels.

I should begin by pointing out that the number of modern, or even relatively modern, scholars who explicitly deny the existence of Jesus is few indeed. The orthodox position, which is one of caution, is expressed by Bornkamm who says, writing in 1956, that (and I quote) "admittedly the difficulties in the way of arriving at a reasonably assured historical knowledge in the field of tradition about Jesus have increased. That is inherent in the nature of the sources . . . their investigation has, in point of fact, greatly enriched our understanding, but at the same time has made our knowledge of the historical Jesus ever more uncertain. It has also driven the ship of enquiry so far in another direction that the map of the actual history of Jesus, once so clearly marked, must in the opinion of many today be in all honesty left blank." But there do exist even stronger views than these, although they are expressed by a minority of scholars. Bruno Bauer's work, especially his *Criticism of the Gospel History of the Synoptics*, written in 1841, contains an explicit denial of the existence of Jesus; Toynbee notes that the suggestion by Frazer that the Jesus legend may have risen from annual rites celebrating the death of a mock king, cannot be entirely discounted; while Robertson and P. L. Couchoud are both modern proponents of the purely legendary origin of Jesus. But the weight of scholarly opinion is against these writers, and in his *From the Stone Age to Christianity*, first published in 1946, William Foxwell Albright, biblical archeologist at Johns

Hopkins, dismisses Couchoud's work as containing "historical extravagances."

One may, I think not unfairly, summarize the scholarly opinion on this question as follows: the existence of Jesus is beyond question; but the information we have about Him is a composite of fact and legend which cannot reliably be untangled.

Given that this is the situation, what I should like to do here today, then, is to examine the evidence which is often adduced in favor of the view that Jesus did exist. It seems to me that a review of the available evidence will be of some interest to you. I find it tenuous; more tenuous, indeed than do the scholars I have quoted, but nonetheless, for reasons which I shall advance in connection with recent findings involving the Dead Sea Scrolls, I also find it persuasive that there was an historical Jesus. This is a matter I shall turn to after considering the evidence in detail.

The first question which strikes anyone who approaches the question of the existence of Jesus is whether there is any first hand evidence for his existence; for example, documents written by eye witnesses to his ministry.

Our possible sources of such direct evidence fall into three classes: the writings of Roman Historians of the first Century A.D.; the writings of Jewish historians such as Philo and Josephus Flavius; and the writings from Christian sources.

The works of Seneca, Petronius, Pliny the Elder, Juvenal, Martial, Quintilian, Epictetus, Plutarch, Appian and Philo, written in the first century, make no reference to Jesus or even to the existence of Christianity: a fact which has weighed heavily with some scholars when they discuss the question of possible interpolations by later writers into the works of Josephus, the Jewish Historian. Gibbon, for example, in his *History of the Decline and Fall of the Roman Empire* (written during the late eighteenth century) ironically comments on this fact as follows:

> During the age of Christ, of his apostles and of their first disciples, the doctrine which they preached was confirmed by innumerable prodigies. The lame walked, the blind saw, the sick were healed, the dead were raised, demons were expelled, and the laws of Nature were frequently suspended for the benefit of the church. But the sages of Greece and Rome turned aside from the awful spectacle, and pursuing the ordinary oc-

cupations of life and study, appeared unconscious of any alteration in the moral or physical government of the world.

The case of Pliny is of particular interest in this connection. According to Christian tradition, the whole earth, or at least Palestine, was covered with darkness for three hours after the death of Jesus. This took place within the life of the elder Pliny, who has a special chapter in his Natural History on the subject of eclipses; but he says nothing of this eclipse (see Gibbon, Chapter XV, Vol. ii, pp. 69-70).

The first mention of Jesus by a Roman historian occurs in Tacitus' *Annals* written in A.D. 117, or about 85 years after the death of Jesus. Tacitus says (Fifteenth Book, Chapter 44); speaking about the burning of Rome under Nero in A.D. 64: I quote:

> In order to counteract the report which laid the blame for this conflagration on Nero he accused persons who were called Christians (by the people) and who were hated for their misdeeds of the guilt, and visited the most excruciating penalties upon them. He from whom they had taken their name, Christ, had been executed in the reign of Tiberius by the Procurator Pontius Pilate; but though this superstition was thus for a moment put down, it arose again not only in Judea, the original home of this plague, but even in Rome itself, in which city every outrage and every shame finds a home and wide dissemination. First a few were seized who confessed, and then on their denunciation a great number of others, who were not, however, accused of the crime of incendiarism, but of that of hating humanity. Their execution was made a public amusement; they were covered with the skins of wild beasts and then torn by dogs or crucified or prepared for the pyre, and then burned as soon as night came, to illuminate the city. For this spectacle Nero lent his gardens and he even arranged circus games in which he mingled with the people in the costume of a charioteer, or mounted a racing chariot. Although these men were criminals deserving of the severest punishment, there was some public sympathy for them, as it seemed they were being sacrificed not to the general weal, but to the cruelty of a single man.

Scholars have disagreed about the weight to be attached to this passage. The contemporary Roman historians do not mention the

Christians in connection with the burning of Rome, and Dio
Cassius writing a century after Tacitus does not mention them
either. It is worth noting that the name "Jesus" is not mentioned;
and as I shall point out later, the fact that these people are called
Christians is also not regarded as particularly significant. The
words "*ho christos*" are simply the Greek equivalents of the Hebrew term, Mashiah, or Messiah: and in a period of Messianic
fervor it is quite likely that many individuals were declaring themselves to be the Messiah, come to fulfill the prophetic claims advanced in the Old Testament. Homer Smith in *Man and His Gods*
(p. 179) commenting on this passage says: "Some historians have
debated whether this passage is wholly authentic, or contains
Christian interpolations; but the answer is relatively unimportant
since at this late date Tacitus could have obtained the all-important
name of Pontius Pilate from Christian tradition."

The earliest mention of Jesus by a non-Christian is to be found
in Josephus Flavius's *Antiquities*, a work written in A.D. 94-95 or
some 15 years after his *History of the Jewish Wars*. In Chapter
3 of the eighteenth book of this work, Josephus says:

> About this time there lived Jesus, a wise man, if he may be
> named a man, for he achieved miracles and was a teacher of
> men, who gladly accepted his truth, and found many ad-
> herents among Jews and Hellenes. This man was the Christ.
> Although Pilate then had him crucified on the accusation of the
> most excellent men of our people, those who had first loved him
> remained faithful to him nevertheless. For on the third day he
> appeared to them again, arisen to a new life, as God's prophets
> had prophesied this and thousands of other miraculous things
> of him. From him the Christians take their name; their sect
> has since then not ceased.

In the 20th book, ninth chapter, Josephus again speaks of Jesus,
saying that the High Priest Ananus, under the rule of the Governor
Albinus (in the time of Nero) had succeeded in having "James,
the brother of Jesus, the so-called Christ, haled to court, together
with a number of others, indicted as transgressors of the law and
stoned."

Josephus, who was born approximately in 37, could not have
been an eye-witness to the events reported; and, in view of the
fact that he was an Orthodox Jew, a Pharisee who had no par-

ticular reason to color the facts in favor of the Christians, these passages have long been suspect as interpolations into his works by later Christian writers. Shurer, in his *History of the Jewish people during the Time of Jesus Christ*, published in 1901, argues that the first passage I have cited was added in the Third Century by a Christian copyist who was evidently offended by the failure of Josephus to produce any information concerning the person of Jesus while he repeats the most childish gossip from Palestine; and Karl Kautsky adds in 1907, that it is certain that the passage is a forgery and not written by Josephus at all. Origen who lived from A.D. 185-254 mentions in his commentary on Matthew that it is peculiar that Josephus did not believe in Jesus as the Christ, given that he refers to James as Christ's brother. Scholarly examination of the evidence surrounding this matter indicates that the second passage is also, in all probability, an interpolation by a Christian writer sometime in the second century; the problem raised by this passage, however, is too detailed for examination here.

These passages from Josephus, and the passage from Tacitus, contain the only information we have about the existence of Christ from non-Christian sources in the first Century. It is clear that neither writer could have been an eye witness to the events he describes; and that considered as indirect evidence for the existence of Jesus, none of the three passages will bear much weight.

The remaining evidence we possess which might possibly contain first hand information about the existence of Jesus comes from Christian sources: this evidence itself falls into two classes: the Gospels according to Matthew, Mark, Luke and John forming one of the categories, the writings of St. Paul forming the other main category. Let us turn to the Gospels first.

The Gospels, of course, purport to contain descriptions of the life and activities of Christ, from the time of his nativity, through his baptism, crucifixion and resurrection. Until the attention of historical scholarship was directed to these documents early in the nineteenth Century, it was commonly assumed that they contained eye witness reports of the events described. This assumption was questioned later in the century by D. F. Strauss in his *Leben Jesu* (1835), by Reimarus, Bauer and others. The issue which was debated by these scholars turned upon the dating of the documents

in question, members of the Tubingen School for example dating
the Gospel according to St. John as late as A.D. 140. This led to a
distinction between the Gospels — a distinction first noted by
Origen. It was pointed out that the Gospels of Mark, Matthew
and Luke formed a unit: that similar phrases, a similar arrangement
of the narrative, takes place within them. Placing these Gospels
side by side, one can correlate passage with passage for large sections of the discourse they contain. Hence they were called the
Synoptic Gospels in contradistinction to the Johannine Gospel.
K. Lachmann in 1835 also suggested that the Gospel according to
St. Mark was the oldest of these documents, and that many of the
common features exhibited by the Gospels of Luke and Matthew
were derived from the Marcion gospel. This general result is still
accepted, although the dispute about the dating of the Gospels
still continues. C. H. Roberts in 1935 published a fragment of the
Gospel according to John which dates from the early part of the
2nd century, and which showed that the Gospel in question cannot have been written much later than A.D. 100; but even accepting this date, it is unlikely that the author of John could have
been an eye witness to the events he describes. Even this is disputed by C. C. Torrey who argues that all the Gospels are trans-
lations into Greek of works originally composed in Aramaic and
that none of the Gospels dates from the period later than A.D. 70;
but in general, New Testament Scholars have been hesitant to accept this result and contend instead that Mark was written about
the time of the Fall of Jerusalem in A.D. 70, and that Matthew and
Luke were probably composed between A.D. 70 and 90, with the
Gospel according to John being composed shortly thereafter.

The issues involving the dating of the Gospels are extremely
complex. According to many New Testament scholars even the
document we now have called The Gospel According to St. Mark
is antedated by an older document originally written by Matthew, one of the twelve disciples, and commonly called the "Q"
document. The existence of this document is inferred primarily
from the fact that the Gospels of Luke and Matthew contain in
common large sections of the teaching of Jesus not borrowed from
Mark or from one another, and therefore presumably derived
from some other common source. This document called "Q," it
is argued, for example by C. J. Cadoux, was originally written in
Aramaic, and was subsequently translated into Greek. If it does

contain the testimony of a personal disciple of Jesus its date may be very early and its reliability may be very great; unfortunately, there is no direct evidence for the existence of this document, the only evidence being an inference from the large amounts of common material found in Luke and in Matthew.

In recent years, though, the question whether the documents we have in the Gospels were actually composed by eye witnesses to the activities of Christ has been relegated to a position of secondary importance. For interval reasons it is extremely unlikely that the writers of the documents we possess would have been eye witnesses to the activities of Jesus. C. J. Cadoux, late professor of Church History at Mansfield College in Oxford, describes the situation in the following words: (because of time I shall read his comments only about the Gospel of Matthew pp. 14-15).

> The Gospel which bears the name of "Matthew" probably owes its designation to the fact that it incorporates Q (which it seems the real Matthew did write), but that, unlike the Gospel of Luke, the name of its final compiler had been forgotten. The compiler produced it in Greek, probably at or near Antioch in Syria in the eighties. He took Mark's Gospel as his framework. Into this he sandwiched large sections of Q, rearranging them in topical order, and also numerous passages from yet another supposed collection of material (usually called "M") which was strongly Jewish and even anti-Pauline in tone. It has been plausibly suggested, though there is no means of proving it, that the compiler desired to bridge the gulf between the Judaistic Jacob of Jerusalem and Paul the Apostle of the Gentiles, not only by utilizing these various sources, but by placing *Peter* in the position of the chief of the Apostles. Where "Matthew" (so I propose to designate this anonymous evangelist) is quoting Q or — as in the parables of the Treasure and the Pearl — drawing on some, other obviously-trust-worthy source, his authority stands high. But a close examination of the treatment he gives to his borrowings from Mark show that he allowed himself great freedom in editing and embroidering his material in the interest of what he regarded as the rightful honouring of the great Master. The same tendencies are often visible elsewhere when he is reproducing Q or providing matter peculiar to himself. Anything, therefore, strictly peculiar to "Matthew" can be accepted as historical only with great caution.

But independently of these difficulties, even if there were reason to believe some of the material to express eye witness accounts of Jesus life, the accretion of legend, the description of miracles performed by Jesus, which exist in these writings make it difficult, if not impossible, to extract from them any reliable historical testimony about the events described; and it is this fact which has led to the views of Dibelius, Schweitzer and Bultmann to the effect that the questions of the historical reliability of the picture of Christ given us in the gospels ought not to be the basis for the Christian tradition which stems from the gospels.

The last source which I wish to consider is St. Paul. We have thirteen epistles which are attributed to St. Paul, and all of them have at one time or other been challenged as genuine. But even independently of challenges of this sort, it is agreed that Paul never met Jesus, although he does claim personally in A.D. 68 to have met one of Jesus' contemporaries — his brother Jacob, also known as James. Paul also speaks of having persecuted "Christians" before his conversion experience — his seeing of Christ in a vision while on the road to Damascus.

In the foregoing account, then, I believe that I have summarized all the available evidence from writers of the first century A.D. — evidence which seems to me, in the light of this account, to be tenuous indeed.

In view of this is it then likely that the Jesus of the Gospels did not exist at all? I do not think that this conjecture is a likely one, and I shall now proceed to explain why:

This explanation will turn upon the history of Judaism after the Destruction of the Temple in 586 B.C. From this period on, the Jews of Palestine lived in a power vacuum between the great powers of Egypt on the one side, and between Babylon, Persia on the other. The lives of Jewish citizens from this time until the beginning of the Christian period were insecure indeed. After the eclipse of Persia as a power, the Mediterranean world was conquered by the Greeks under Alexander, who regarded the Jews as barbarians and who insisted upon Hellenizing them. With the fall of Alexander, the Jews came under the domination of the Persian Seleucids, and then the Romans, both of whom initiated legislation inimical to the religious traditions of the Jews. The history of this period, as revealed by recent studies, exhibits a picture of a people living under the domination of foreign rulers, but unable to throw them off. Under such conditions, when revolution fails and all other alternatives are exhausted, the appeal of consolative religion, especially of another worldly sort, becomes very compelling. These frustrations produced documents such as the Book of Daniel of the O.T. and hundreds of apocryphal works written in the 1st and 2nd centuries B.C., documents of a species called "eschatological" and "apocalyptic" by Biblical Scholars. They stress the coming of a Messiah or Redeemer who will throw off the hated conquerors, restore the law, bring about an era of peace. These documents clearly reveal the character of the post-exilic, pre-Christian era. It is difficult for us today — except in contemplating the consequences of Nuclear War — to imagine what the temper of the time must have been like. With Judgment Day at Hand, with the Kingdom of God momentarily expected, with the Messiah awaited, the intellectual ferment and the psychological instability produced by such expectations must have been tremendous. These expectations were reinforced by the writing of apocryphal works containing predictions of just these events to come. Not all the Jews accepted such apocalyptic teachings: the Sadducees for example rejected some of them, and they were in other respects inconsistent with the main teachings of Orthodox Judasim. Splinter groups formed, breaking away from these main areas of traditional Judaism, to go off into the wilderness there to await the coming of the Messiah, the Anointed One, the Christ. It is clear that the Essenes formed one such group: indeed, it is believed that John the Baptist emerges from an Essene Community preaching his doctrine that the Kingdom of God is at hand. It is also clear that recent investigations into the history of the period, aided by findings based on the Dead Sea Scrolls, indicate that the Essenes formed a much larger group within the Jewish community than had previously been believed. The belief in a coming apocalypse must thus have been part of the everyday views of a large segment of the Jews of the period.

Recent findings also reveal that persons whose lives and careers are strikingly parallel to that of the Christ as He is portrayed in the gospels — persons who practiced baptism, who defied the laws of the Pharisees, who were crucified and who even advanced a redemptive doctrine of salvation — were identified with the Messiah, or with the so called King of the Jews, by the Essenes (see Matthew Black's *The Scrolls and Christian Origins*, 1961). There can be no doubt that this messianic fever was characteristic of the age, not only in the sense that the Messiah was awaited or expected momentarily, but more than that, there can be no doubt that some of the Jews contended, as early as the 2nd Century B.C. that the Messiah had in fact arrived. Many contemporary scholars now believe that the origins of Christianity are to be located in the activities of these splinter, eschatologically dominated groups — and that the Pauline teaching that Jesus is the arrived Christ exhibits the influence of this group upon St. Paul. Paul's own reference to his previous persecution of Christians (i.e., of followers of the Messiah) bears this out, as does the gospel warning in Matthew that we must be aware of false christs, of false messiahs.

Given these facts, it seems to me likely that during this period a prophet arose, belonging to one of the apocalyptically minded Jewish sects, such as the Essenes, and that he did preach the doctrine that the Kingdom of God was at hand, that he did preach the soteriological doctrine that through his coming death mankind would be saved (it is in this sense that I believe one can justify or support the claim that the historical Jesus lived); but an accretion of legends grew up about this figure, was incorporated into the Gospels by various devotees of the movement, was rapidly spread throughout the Mediterranean world by the ministry of St. Paul; and that because this is so, it is impossible to separate these legendary elements in the purported descriptions of Jesus from those which in fact were true of him.

APPENDIX B
Letter from C. S. Lewis

After delivering my "Jesus Christ and History" lectures (chapters 2 and 3 of the present volume) at the University of British Columbia on January 29 and 30, 1963, I was approached by the Lutheran Student Movement — U.B.C. Chapter to invite C. S. Lewis — with whom I had been in correspondence since I had published an article on his Narnia Chronicles in *Religious Education*, (September-October, 1959) — to follow up my lectures with apologetic presentations of his own on that campus. I therefore sent copies of my lectures to him with the request that he come to Canada under L.S.M. sponsorship. The following was his reply. It was one of the last letters he wrote before his death less than three months later (November 22, 1963). The letter does not appear in Lewis' posthumously edited correspondence: it is published here for the first time.

— John Warwick Montgomery

29 August 63

Oxford

Dear Mr. Montgomery,

I am afraid the days of my lecturing and traveling are over. Last July my death was hourly expected, and tho' I didn't get through the gate I have had to resign all my posts and settle down (not unhappily) to the life of an invalid.

Your two lectures did me good and I shall constantly find them useful. Congratulations. The only criticism I'd venture is that you have possibly a little bit over-called the blow about *kyrios*. Admittedly, like Lat. *dominus* and English *Lord*, it may represent JHVH: but like them it can also mean a human superior. The vocative *kyrie* often needs to be translated "Sir" rather than "Lord." Otherwise I don't think it could be bettered.

Yours sincerely,

C. S. Lewis

APPENDIX C
Letter from Edwin M. Yamauchi

Sir:

I would like to express my appreciation for your article, "History and Christianity." I am in agreement with his basic arguments, but would like to offer some comments.

The citation of Kenyon stressing the "textual advantage of the New Testament documents over *all other ancient manuscripts*" (italics mine) needs qualification. The writer is stressing the shortness of the interval between the composition of the N.T. books and our earliest extant manuscripts. This is, however, not unique. From ancient Mesopotamia we have the original autographs of a number of texts inscribed in stone or clay, e.g. the Harran inscriptions of Nabonidus. In N.T. times we have possibly the autographs, or at any rate early copies, of writings from the Qumran community. We have many originals or duplicates of letters from all periods, such as the Lachish letters, the Amarna letters, etc. The Qur'an of Muhammad was collated within a generation of the Prophet's death with relatively few variants.

The writer may have been thinking of Greek and Latin literary texts, most of which have come to us from medieval copies. Even here we have papyri representing half of the text of the Odyssey dating from as early as the 3rd century B.C.; the composition of the Odyssey is generally placed in the 8th century B.C.

With these qualifications, we must admit that the quantity and the antiquity of the manuscript evidence for the N.T. are impressive. Kurt Aland from the Institut für Textforschung in Münster, speaking in New York last month, pointed out that we now have 5000 Greek manuscripts of the N.T. and N.T. portions. The writer cited Robertson, who in 1925 spoke of 4000 Greek manuscripts. Westcott and Hort who provided a definitive edition of the Greek N.T. before the turn of the century had only 1500 Greek texts available to them. Very significant has been the increase of papyri from the 4th, 3rd, and even 2nd centuries A.D. Before 1900 only 5 papyri had been published; we now know of 78 papyri.

I would agree with your stricture of Bultmann. Bultmann has attempted to demythologize the N.T. on the basis of a pre-Christian Gnostic myth, which he has constructed from late sources. On the one hand, the Coptic Gnostic codices from Nag-Hammadi in Egypt (1946) call for a radical revision of Bultmann's Gnostic construct. On the other hand, the Dead Sea Scrolls from Qumran (1947) corroborate the 1st-century, Palestinian origin of the Gospel of John. Bultmann's attempt to criticize the 1st-century N.T. documents on the basis of much later sources is methodologically unreasonable.

Yours truly,

Edwin M. Yamauchi
Assistant Professor of History
Rutgers — the State University
New Brunswick, New Jersey

APPENDIX D

Faith, History and the Resurrection

*On the occasion of Carl F. H. Henry's lecture series early in
1965 at Trinity Evangelical Divinity School in Deerfield, Illinois,
several Chicago-area theologians shared in a vigorous panel discussion on problems of faith and history. Participants were Dr.
William Hordern, then professor of systematic theology at Gar-
rett Biblical Institute, Evanston; Dr. Jules L. Moreau, professor of
church history at Seabury-Western Theological Seminary, Evanston; and Father Sergius Wroblewski, professor of New Testament
and church history at Christ the King Seminary (Franciscan),
West Chicago. Joining them were Dean Kenneth Kantzer and
Professor Montgomery of Trinity, and Dr. Henry. This is the
edited transcription of the discussion as it originally appeared in*
Christianity Today, *March 26, 1965.*

DEAN KANTZER: The focus of our interest is on the nature of
history, and the relationship which Jesus Christ bears to history in
our Christian faith. Perhaps Dr. Henry will state the issues briefly
for us, and then we will be asking one another some questions.

DR. HENRY: Frontier issues in the dialogue on the Continent
at the moment include the relationship of revelation and history
and the relationship of revelation and truth. At this breakpoint
over faith and history the cleavage occurs between Barthian dialectical theology and Bultmannian existential theology, and then also
between many post-Bultmannians and Bultmann himself, and finally also between the *Heilsgeschichte* scholars and the post-Bultmannians. The further question is raised over the connection between revelation and truth, which is a subject of debate among
the dialectical theologians and which recalls Barth's modifications
of his own point of view, and the consequent assault on Barth's
views by both evangelical scholars and the Pannenberg school.

DEAN KANTZER: If I remember correctly, you hold that the
lack of objectivity in Barth's view of the relationship between
Jesus and history represented a fatal weakness in the Barthian
position, which led to a more easy victory of Bultmann in his
distinction between the Christ of faith and the Jesus of history.
Would you care to say just a further word about that?

DR. HENRY: Confessedly Barth's introduction of objectifying elements into his theology places a wide distance between Barth and the existential theologians, whether Bultmannian or post-Bultmannian. Yet the objectifying elements Barth introduced into his system are not really objects of historical research. And for all the objectifying factors with which he buttressed his doctrine of the knowledge of God, he agreed in spirit with Bultmann that God is not an object of rational knowledge. Both scholars reject the objectivity of God as an object of rational knowledge. Barth and Bultmann shared the fundamental dialectical premise that divine revelation is never objectively given — neither in historical events nor in concepts or words — and in agreement with this underlying premise Bultmann dispensed entirely with the objectifying elements that Barth sought to preserve with a surer instinct for biblical theology.

DEAN KANTZER: Now, Dr. Hordern, we would be interested to know whether you agree that this was a flaw in Barth that made Bultmann's victory more easily accomplished.

PROF. HORDERN: It seems to me that there is a great deal more objectivity in Barth than you imply. His revolt from existentialism was not quite so belated; he made it when he started writing his *Church Dogmatics.* He tore up the original version because it had too much existentialism in it. I am aware of the fact that Bonhoeffer spoke of Barth's revelational positivism, and I think that is a more apt criticism in some ways than to say that Barth does not have sufficient objectivity. He very definitely believed — quite apart from man's knowledge of it — that God was in Christ, that the Bible *is* (as he puts it in *Church Dogmatics* I/2) *the* Word of God, and that this is true whether or not man recognizes it. The real problem, when you raise the question of the objectivity of history, is, What does one mean by *history?* And maybe also, What does one mean by *objectivity?*

If by history you simply mean investigation of what has happened in the past, it is very obvious that Barth's whole system was built upon the historical nature of the revelation, that it was an event that happened — that Jesus Christ was born of a virgin and raised from the dead. These are events that happened. But if by history you mean what so many people mean today, that which can be verified by modern historical method (and when that in turn means that by definition any miracle cannot have been historical), then it seems to me that Barth is forced to say that historical criticism cannot help the Christian faith, or that it cannot produce anything other than a non-biblical Jesus. *By definition* it cannot, if this is what one means by historical method, and this is what is widely meant. That is why Barth, speaking of the resurrection, can say, Of course this is not historical if by history (I am not quoting him verbatim) you have the concept that miracles are not historical by definition. But, he says (and I can imagine the twinkle in his eye), that doesn't mean it didn't happen. In other words, Barth is arguing that more has happened objectively — whatever we mean by that — than what would be discovered by historical method. But it seems to me there is more objectivity here in Barth than you have given reason to suppose.

PROF. MONTGOMERY: I wonder what you would say — what Barth would say — if I claimed that in my backyard there is a large green elephant eating a raspberry ice cream cone, but that there is no way by empirical investigation to determine that he is there. Nonetheless, I maintain, as a matter of fact, that it is there in every objective and factual sense. Now I have a feeling that you would either regard this as a claim that the elephant is there and is subject to empirical investigation, or contend that it isn't there by the very fact that there is no way of determining the fact. I wonder if this doesn't point up the problem. To claim objectivity, but to remove any possibility of determining it, is by definition to destroy objectivity.

PROF. MOREAU: Would you be willing to use, instead of this green elephant monstrosity, the body of the late Herbert Hoover out in Iowa?

PROF. MONTGOMERY: The reason that I use my example is that I don't want an illustration which has merely natural repercussions. The problem here points to the question of the miraculous, and therefore I would like something bizarre in order to keep the aspect of miracle in view.

PROF. HORDERN: I'm not sure that the miraculous is bizarre. But to carry out the analogy Barth would have to say that one who knows (before he goes to your garden and looks) that there is no such thing as a green elephant — if he then "sees" it, he will obviously say, I have hallucinations. No evidence is going to prove the reality of a green elephant to this man. When you have a concept of history which has decided before it investigates any empirical facts that dead men stay dead, then if this is what you mean by history (as many people do), historical investigation proves nothing.

PROF. MONTGOMERY: Isn't this the very point: whether historical method necessitates the presupposition that the miraculous, whatever we mean by this, cannot take place? It seems to me that the confusion here is between historical method and what might be called historicism or historical prejudice. Historical investigation very definitely can take place on the empirical level without the positivistic presupposition that the nexus of natural causes cannot be broken. It seems to me that the question here is whether historical method, apart from that rationalistic presupposition, will or will not yield revelatory data concerning Jesus Christ. And if one says that it won't, then one strips away the meaning of the word "objectivity."

PRO. HORDERN: But this, I think, is Barth's point; he does not use this precise formulation, but what you call historical method without historicism, Barth definitely approves.

PROF. MONTGOMERY: Well, I get the impression that he would prefer not to speak of historical method at all in connection with the resurrection. He is willing to use it in connection with the death of Christ — with those events that are of a natural and normal type. But it appears to me that with regard to the resurrection, for example, there is a hesitancy that doesn't arise simply from Barth's refusal to take a rationalistic position on miracles. He seems unhappy with any use of historical method in relation to the resurrection.

PROF. MOREAU: What kind of historical method would you use in connection with the resurrection, when in the first place I'm not sure you know what you mean by the word "resurrection" — or at least *I* don't know what you mean by the word "resurrection." You have submitted a whole set of active verb sentences.

PROF. MONTGOMERY: The claim that somebody, as a matter of fact, rose from the dead following his death.

PROF. MOREAU: That I don't think is what the Bible says. The Bible says somebody "was raised," and I'm not altogether sure that *ek nekron* — "from dead" — can be taken to mean "raised from the dead" in that sense.

PROF. MONTGOMERY: Well, that's the sphere of death. I won't belabor the genitive.

PROF. MOREAU: Well, I will, because I think it is pretty important. I don't think there is any word "resurrection" as such. I don't think the Bible talks conceptually.

PROF. MONTGOMERY: Well, then, in concrete terms, take the question of a man rising from the dead. . . .

PROF. MOREAU: What kind of historical method would you use to investigate that?

PROF. MONTGOMERY: One has to determine empirically first of all whether this concrete man died, and secondly, whether after this event this concrete man engaged in normal human intercourse with other persons in a spatial-temporal situation.

PROF. MOREAU: You think that historical method is capable of doing this?

PROF. MONTGOMERY: Very definitely; but it's hardly capable of arriving at an *explanation*, of determining *how* it happened.

PROF. MOREAU: Now that historical method has done this, *what good* is that kind of information?

PROF. MONTGOMERY: Plenty, if you have a death problem — because you are obviously going to wonder why in thunderation this happened.

FATHER WROBLEWSKI: I would hold that you can accept the apostolic testimony as historical, and I think that in doing that you follow historical method. When I read historians who tell me that Napoleon carried on a war, I am unable to see it, but I go by the testimony of those who did so, and of those who have sifted the evidence. And so I feel that I can accept the testimony of the apostles for the same reason. They saw, they didn't merely imagine; and to me that is historical testimony. I will admit to a subjective element, however. The apostles who reacted to the human Christ (or rather to the suffering servant), and then to the risen Christ, appraised him differently. Each Gospel has a different method because each gospel author took a certain *view* of Christ. That was in a way subjective because it was peculiar to *him*. But even that was not achieved apart from the influence of the Holy Spirit.

DEAN KANTZER: I wonder if I could sharpen the issue by referring to the green elephant again. There is no question (so far as our discussion here is concerned) as to its facticity. There really was a green elephant there — unless perhaps it was Saturday night! The question, is, *How one can know that the green elephant was there?* And now, carrying this analogy over to the resurrection the question is, How we can discern this facticity which we are admitting? Then comes the question, Is this a matter of history? Some are saying it is, and some are saying it isn't. On the surface it might look as though it were simply a matter of definition, of the definition of history: whether history is a study in which you rule out the supernatural. But as we proceeded it became perfectly obvious that this wasn't the whole point, that the issue goes beyond whether or not you define history one way or another. The issue is whether in theory the idea of presuppositionless history is possible. Or whether one believes that history is a methodology which one must engage in with the presupposition that miracles do not happen. With that kind of presupposition one couldn't under any circumstances find any historical data about the kind of event that we call resurrection. There are those who, in other words, do not wish to make the distinction that Dr. Hordern was making (between a history that excludes supernatural events and a history that doesn't), and who prefer to say of Christ's resurrection, "*Incredible* — this is the kind of thing that nothing we have any right to call history (with any sort of presupposition) could touch!" Dr. Moreau, how do you feel about this latter position?

PROF. MOREAU: In part I think this is right. In one sense history is knowledge of the past. I think Father Wroblewski's statement about a Napoleonic war is very interesting. But that's perfectly accessible; you don't have to depend on someone's testimony for that — not really.

FATHER WROBLEWSKI: But you are surely dependent on the testimony of reliable witness, aren't you? You never saw Napoleon.

PROF. MOREAU: But then you have the problem of the differences in Scripture.

FATHER WROBLEWSKI: I think those differences in part at least are demonstrated by the fact that the Scriptures are written from a particular viewpoint. I don't think that the question is defining what is the object of history. I think that the difficulty lies in what you define as observable. If you decide from a philosophical point of view that miracles are impossible, necessarily as a historian you limit what you can observe. I think that this is the difficulty between the right and the left, in the interpretation of Scripture. Bultmann, for instance, would deny, from a philosophical point of view, that there is any miracle, and therefore he would exclude a witness's power to observe anything miraculous — I mean a man rising from the dead, or anything like that.

DEAN KANTZER: Do you think that the author of the Gospel of Luke thought that by inquiring from witnesses and by investigating sources you could come to the certainty of the events that are recorded in the Gospel of Luke?

PROF. MOREAU: I'm not sure, and I'm not sure that's relevant. In the light of other knowledge about the past it would be interesting.

FATHER WROBLEWSKI: Do you have more confidence in Napoleon's historians than in the gospel witnesses? Do you regard the fathers of the Church as "primitives" in science and in history?

PROF. HORDERN: One of the best things that I read on the current historical problem is something that CHRISTIANITY TODAY published not very long ago, which turned out to have been the inaugural address made by J. Gresham Machen in 1915. This shows you how theology goes around in circles. What is now the hottest issue was being discussed in a very interesting fashion there. I think Karl Barth would agree with that article, which is why I wonder about the debate over objectivity. But let's leave Karl Barth out of this; he is not here to defend himself. First of all, you have to recognize that there is a historical problem. For example, did Lee Oswald, unaided, without conspiracy, assassinate Kennedy? If this is a typical group of Americans, you divide 50-50 yes and no. Do you believe the Warren Commission's report? For the Gallup Poll, 50 per cent of us do and 50 per cent don't. It is a historical event that was investigated thoroughly, completely; probably no event in all history had such a thorough investigation of the facts so quickly.

PROF. MONTGOMERY: Are you suggesting a statistical test of a historical truth?

PROF. HORDERN: No, not at all! You could never hope to have an event investigated more thoroughly, more completely, than this assassination was investigated under the Warren Report. Yet it is not just "crackpots" that remain unpersuaded. It is not a matter of statistics. You cannot get absolute historical proof. And those who doubt the Warren Commission report say, Well, look; who did the investigating? Just one side there! Oswald didn't do the investigating; the American government did! What you've got here is what the American government wanted to find! And you can take the same attitude toward him who is talking about the resurrection of Jesus — the Christian. Always when you have a problem of history you have this kind of dubiousness.

DR. HENRY: Are you saying that, in principle, the question of the death of Napoleon is no different from the question of the death and resurrection of Christ — that both come under the same difficulties insofar as historical accessibility and research are concerned?

PROF. HORDERN: In principle, yes. This is the problem of history in general. It's one thing to empirically investigate this green elephant today, if we can rush outside and he is there now. It is another thing to decide whether we have historical evidence to persuade us that he was there last Saturday. Now we must ask if the witnesses are reliable. Perhaps Saturday night is the night they go out on the town.

DR. HENRY: But suppose one argues that it was really there, yet insists that facticity cannot be determined by historical research — that in point of fact this was a confrontation that took place on "the rim" of history?

PROF. HORDERN: You're going to make me defend Barth again; he's very capable of defending himself. But I would answer the question for myself. (Whether Barth would want me to say this or not, I'm not sure; perhaps it depends on where you draw your evidence from Barth. The historical question, What does Barth really think?, is also a problem.) What does Machen do — when he argues for the historicity of the resurrection? He points to those facts that cannot really be disputed because all you have to do is open your New Testament and there they are. Here's a man writing who says, *I* saw the risen Jesus! There a community was formed, and here *I* have it today — and we have something pretty empirical here. Here something comes through two thousand years, and here it is. And then Machen argues: Which is more likely: that these disciples got together when Jesus died and said, "Isn't this horrible; let's pretend he rose from the dead," and started a movement, and endured persecution for a lie — or that he arose? And now if this is what you mean by the historical argument, fine. The Gospel does depend upon historical argument. If this does not make any kind of sense, then we would be pretty silly to believe it. On the other hand, it will never persuade any of my skeptical friends who know that dead men stay dead.

PROF. MONTGOMERY: How do they know that?

DR. HENRY: They have a private pipeline to ultimate reality.

PROF. MONTGOMERY: Isn't it at that very point that the attack needs to be delivered — if I may succumb to military terminology. Isn't the area of difficulty not really the question of historicity but the question of presupposition with regard to the nature of the world? And it certainly can be shown that whoever enters an investigation with a presupposition such as Dr. Hordern describes feels that he has a kind of stranglehold on the universe — a stranglehold that simply can't be justified.

PROF. HORDERN: Don't argue with me. I don't hold that position.

PROF. MONTGOMERY: Granted: your presentation a moment ago was magnificent.

PROF. HORDERN: Machen's presentation, actually. There is still a further point, though, if we come back to the death problem. Machen makes the other point, that on the basis of historical evidence we may not be persuaded but that ultimately we believe because in the context of the Church we meet the risen Christ. And, therefore, what makes reasonably logical the historical account of the past is ultimately something at which you might shrug your shoulders and say, Well, isn't that interesting?

PROF. MOREAU: Too bad they didn't have a Society for Psychical Research there. They would have really gotten some good material. When we meet the risen Christ in our lives, then all this becomes significant and important to us.

PROF. MONTGOMERY: But make a distinction on the question of appropriation: appropriating the fact is not what makes it factual. This is the crucial consideration I think we tend to overlook; when, for example, Professor Hordern writes in his *Case for a New Reformation Theology* that religious objectivity can be arrived at only when we have faith in objectivity, he enters on a path that leads straight to solipsism. Apart from the distinction between the object (Christ historically resurrected, in the ordinary sense of "history" — *Historie*) and the subject (ourselves as believers in it) a clear distinction must be made.

PROF. MOREAU: Maybe God can make such a distinction — I can't!

FATHER WROBLEWSKI: What difference would it make whether

he rose or not? I would like to know, what difference, if you cannot establish that Christ rose from the dead? Paul said that we who are in Christ are united with the risen Christ. If he didn't rise from the dead, we are miserable. In fact, Paul said we then are of all men *most miserable.* But apparently Dr. Moreau wouldn't be very miserable. What would bother you about all this?

PROF. MOREAU: Come back to what the doctrine of the Holy Spirit is. What really makes the difference is whether or not there is some experience of the risen Christ at this moment in communal fellowship with him.

FATHER WROBLEWSKI: And this makes what difference for what?

PROF. MOREAU: Significance or non-significance.

PROF. MONTGOMERY: But then I think I would have to ask the question, if I were a non-Christian, Why should I involve myself in this kind of a community rather than in, let's say, another community? What criteria are men to employ in order to justify a choice or decision?

PROF. MOREAU: I simply refuse to become involved in dichotomies of that sort.

FATHER WROBLEWSKI: I would see no reality to the experience of the risen Christ if I had no proof of his resurrection.

[*At this point Dean Kantzer welcomed questions from the floor.*]

STUDENT: If Christ did not rise from the dead, how could I have any subjective benefits from the resurrection of Christ in my life today?

PROF. MOREAU: There are two points I would make in reference to that. First, I did not say he was not raised from the dead. What I am really concerned about is whether or not there is any historical verification. As far as I'm concerned the empty tomb story is a purely figurative account, an expanding of something which is quite real in the sense of an experience. And I think it is inaccessible for historical inquiry. I did not say that God did not raise him from the dead. I insist on keeping that physical language.

PROF. MONTGOMERY: But you would distinguish this from a "real" objectivity of the resurrection?

PROF. MOREAU: I don't like that language.

PROF. MONTGOMERY: But you distinguish between the resurrection and the empty tomb?

PROF MOREAU: I distinguish the statement that God raised Jesus from the dead from the statement that the empty tomb has anything to do with this in terms of inquiry or investigation or proof.

DR. HENRY: By what criteria do you distinguish this presence of the risen Christ from a mere immortality of influence?

PROF. MONTGOMERY: And how do you know (this is a terribly irreverent question) that your experience of Christ in the heart differs from heartburn?

PROF. MOREAU: I suppose ultimately I don't.

STUDENT: I would like to ask Dr. Hordern a question in view of his use of the example of the shooting of President Kennedy supposedly by Oswald. I hesitate to accept this analogy completely because, as far as I know, there is no record that Oswald claimed that he was going to do this. If the record of the New Testament writers is valid, I think there is a distinction here between the Christ event and the event of the shooting of John F. Kennedy, because of the claim here apparently that Christ was going to do his work. Maybe this accounts for the problem of so many people not believing the Warren Commission.

PROF. HORDERN: To me the parallel between the Kennedy assassination and the crucifixion and resurrection of Jesus is simply the parallel that both are history to us. And the very fact that a history so close to us, so thoroughly investigated, still cannot beat down all possible doubts indicates to me that when we have some history two thousand years old, with much less material, and without the intensive investigation — without the FBI to help out — how much less certainty we can have on this basis.

I've been trying to locate myself with Dr. Moreau here; we obviously have a number of things in common. I would warn him, however, as Barth has warned Bultmann, that if you too easily get rid of that empty tomb you're probably falling into Docetism. But to me the thing that you cannot argue has been raised here a couple of times: If Jesus Christ did not rise from the dead, how can it all be important to me? You have two questions here. One, Did Jesus Christ rise from the dead? — which you can settle somewhere, though I'm not quite sure where. And the other question is, What does it mean to me? Certainly my point is that before you even ask the question, Did Jesus Christ rise from the dead?, you ask it only because it concerns you in some way. One man is concerned because he wants all dead men to stay dead and therefore he wants as an answer: No, he didn't rise. Another man wants to answer it another way. My point is simply that we have to make the historical judgment on the basis of our own experience. It seems to me I've got Machen on my side here, because he says that if we didn't actually know the living Christ now, we could not believe the history of the past. And I'm arguing that you don't independently solve the one question, Did he rise from the dead?, and then ask, How do I appropriate this?, or, What does it mean to me?, but that these two are continually involved together. That doesn't mean, however, that you haven't any reason for this. You have a lot of reasons. There is a great difference between the guy who just shuts his eyes and believes and the fellow who doesn't — I know that Dr. Moreau has a lot of reasons for what he believes. But ultimately, if you really want to put it that way, none of us knows that we are even here, and a good philosopher could prove we aren't. We walk through this world as sojourners by faith and not by sight.

STUDENT: The question, though, is, By faith in what? Ultimately we've got to get back to the question of what the ground of faith is. Otherwise someone can come along and, maintaining that we walk by faith and not by sight, take a position exactly contrary to yours or mine, and there won't be anything that the Christian proclamation can say in relation to this at all.

STUDENT: I could push it back a little farther. You mentioned the rhythm of history, and that the character of the event was in question. It seems to me that one thing that distinguishes the data in connection with President Kennedy's assassination and the resurrection is the kind of material we have. Paul says this thing was not done in a corner. In the assassination we have an event which took place under the tightest security, deliberately obscured by the person who did it, and this is why the evidence is obscure. But in the case of Jesus, it was quite the opposite; it was right out in the open. I'd like to ask Dr. Henry if he believes that there is a distinction between the Napoleonic or Kennedy-assassination type of history and Jesus-event, and if the real question isn't about the supernatural rather than simply a question of events.

DR. HENRY: When you ask a historical question, you can answer only in terms of historical research and historical method.

The collective consciousness of the early Church, or my present psychological encounters of whatever nature, cannot give a decisive answer to the question of the historicity of an event some nineteen centuries ago. So I would agree with Professor Hordern that as history the New Testament saving events are subject to the same research as other historical events. There is, however, a broader frontier. Jesus Christ stepped into history from the outside; ultimately we do not explain him *in toto* from within history, but we explain history by him. And it is certainly true that there is more to the case for the resurrection of Jesus Christ than historical fact. The Christian does not argue the case for the risen Christ only in terms of the historical data. There is the relevance of Pentecost; I certainly would not want to drop the Book of Acts and the Epistles out of the case for the risen Christ. But when it comes to the question of a historical resurrection from the dead and the matter of the empty tomb, this can be answered only in terms of historical research and testimony. And I quite grant that one cannot get to absolute certainty in terms of historical method; absolute certainty is always something communicated by the Spirit of God. But the very heart of the apostolic preaching falls out if you lose the historical ingredient.

PROF. MONTGOMERY: Let me set up another analogy than Dr. Hordern's appeal to the Kennedy assassination. It is fairer to compare the resurrection to other events of classical times, because it's in the same general time area and therefore the amount of data is perhaps more comparable. I majored in classics in college, and to my amazement I never heard any questioning of the events of the classical period as to their *per se* historicity despite the fact that these are based on much less data than the resurrection of Christ. For example, the existence of Plato depends upon manuscript evidence dated over a thousand years later. If we must begin with sheer faith in order to arrive at the event-character of the resurrection, then we are going to drop out not simply the resurrection but a tremendous portion of world history, which I don't think we're prepared to do.

PROF. HORDERN: I couldn't care less whether Caesar crossed the Rubicon or not. It doesn't make any difference to me. I'm not going to lead my life any differently tomorrow either way; nothing stands or falls with it. Perhaps if I made my living out of history, and was battling with some other colleague, we might have ourselves a real battle among historians over precisely such questions. There is hardly anything that has happened in past history that doesn't get debated by historians at some time or other. Most of us couldn't care less, however; we have no real involvement with this. But here we have a story that comes to us from two thousand years ago, and if it is true, then my destiny not only here but hereafter depends upon this story — and you ask me to believe it on the basis only of the generally unreliable historical data?

PROF. MONTGOMERY: No, not quite. I say only that the historical probabilities are comparable to those of other events of classical times. Therefore there is an excellent objective ground to which to tie the religion that Jesus sets forth. Final validation of this can only come experientially. But it is desperately important not to put ourselves in such a position that the event-nature of the resurrection depends wholly upon "the faith." It's the other way around. The faith has its starting point in the event, the objective event, and only by the appropriation of this objective event do we discover the final validity of it. The appropriation is the subjective element, and this must not enter into the investigation of the event. If it does, the Christian faith is reduced to irrelevant circularity.

FATHER WROBLEWSKI: Dr. Hordern, as you realize, there is resistance today to the acceptance of miracles as proof. Why is it that Scripture itself urges miracles, the empty tomb, the charismatic gifts, the coming down of the Holy Spirit as proof? Would you resist those proofs, if the Scripture itself urges such proofs?

PROF. HORDERN: Show me where the Scripture urges these as proofs.

DR. HENRY: What of Paul's emphasis that Jesus was seen by more than 500 persons at once in proof of the resurrection?

PROF. MONTGOMERY: The Christian faith is built upon Gospel that is "good news," and there is no news, good or bad, of something that didn't happen. I personally am much disturbed by certain contemporary movements in theology which seem to imply that we can have the faith regardless of whether anything happened or not. I believe absolutely that the whole Christian faith is premised upon the fact that at a certain point of time under Pontius Pilate a certain Man died and was buried and three days later rose from the dead. If in some way you could demonstrate to me that Jesus never lived, died, or rose again, then I would have to say I have no right to my faith.

PROF. MOREAU: I couldn't do that, because you are beginning with the assumption that it did take place.

FATHER WROBLEWSKI: I hold that the apostolic witness to the miraculous in the life of Christ is equivalent to the kind of evidence history is based on. The apostles saw and heard these things happen in time and space, and I have no reason to disbelieve the soundness of their testimony. Rather I have more reason to trust their powers of observation because they signed their testimony in blood. Scholars who deny the miraculous do so on philosophical grounds in the face of Scripture's insistence on the miraculous as evidence. It is true that the evidence is not absolute if only because the "appointed witnesses" were few and their written record puzzling. But this is peculiar about biblical evidence: it leaves the intellect somewhat hesitant that the act of faith may arise more from the Holy Spirit's operation than intellectual proof.

PROF. MOREAU: The current preoccupation with the facticity of the circumstances surrounding the event called the resurrection reflects a concern for historical verification which is quite foreign to the attitude of the early Church. The "proof" that God had raised Jesus from among the dead was the experience of the living Lord in the community. The narrative of the empty tomb and the embroidery around it served an apologetic purpose rather than a verificational one. The involved argument advanced by St. Paul (I Cor. 15:35-58) seems only to underline this contention.

PROF. THORDERN: The life of Jesus is a historical event like other historical events and is known through the reports of those who witnessed it. It differs from other historical events because we have a unique opportunity to test the reliability of the witnesses. They tell us that Jesus did not stay dead and that we can know him as the risen Lord. As a result, our evaluation of the gospel records cannot be separated from our relationship to the risen Christ today.

APPENDIX E

GOD PLUS THREE: A Review of *History: Written and Lived*, by Paul Weiss (Southern Illinois University Press, 1962, 245 pp.).

The task of a philosopher of history is to bring man's past experiences out of what William James once described as the essence of babyhood: "blooming, buzzing confusion." Weiss, a professor of philosophy at Yale, believes that God must be posited in order for history to have meaning, for "only He is broad enough, persistent enough, powerful enough to endow the past with sufficient existence to enable it properly to be" (p. 222). However, the God of Weiss is by no means the God of Abraham, Isaac, and Jacob, or the Father of our Lord Jesus Christ; rather, taking his cue from Aristotle, Lucretius, Scheler, and Whitehead, Weiss uses the term "God" to refer to "a being superior to anything in this space-time world, but which is not absolutely perfect, not necessarily the creator of any substances, not necessarily concerned with man's salvation" (*ibid.*). Indeed as we learn from the author's other works, seven of which, together with the present volume, set out his general philosophy, Weiss's "God" is but one of four ultimate, irreducible, mutually related modes or dimensions of being (the other three are Actuality, Ideality or Possibility, and Existence).

As W. N. Clarke well noted in his comments on Weiss's *Modes of Being*, the Weissian system "leaves untouched the . . . fundamental and, for a metaphysician, unavoidable problem of the ultimate origin or source of existence and the ultimate principle of unity of this whole with its four irreducible modes" (*Yale Review*, Sept., 1958). Moreover, since Weiss regards systematic philosophy much as Barth, Tillich, and Bultmann regard systematic theology — as a circular enterprise in which epistemology grounds ontology and ontology grounds epistemology — his total system, to use Morris Weitz's expression, lacks "testability" (*Ethics*, October, 1961).

As I have tried to show in my *Shape of the Past*, the meaning of history (which is, after all, a special case of the meaning of life) can be discovered only if man has in fact received an objectively

[240]

reliable Revelation originating from outside the blooming, buzzing, confused human situation. Without the scriptural revelation of God in Jesus Christ, Professor Weiss is as much in the dark as to the meaning of the past as were his philosophical predecessors.

JOHN WARWICK MONTGOMERY

INDEX OF NAMES

INDEX OF NAMES

This index includes the names of all individual persons — ancient and modern, real and mythical — discussed or cited in the book.

[245]

Notes

Notes

Notes

Notes

Notes

Notes